DARREN LOCKYER

AUTOBIOGRAPHY

WITH DAN KOCH

EBURY
PRESS

An Ebury Press book
Published by Random House Australia Pty Ltd
Level 3, 100 Pacific Highway, North Sydney NSW 2060
www.randomhouse.com.au

First published by Ebury Press in 2011

This edition published in 2012

Addresses for companies within the Random House Group can be found at
www.randomhouse.com.au/offices

National Library of Australia
Cataloguing-in-Publication Entry

Lockyer, Darren.
Darren Lockyer autobiography/Darren Lockyer.

ISBN 978 1 74275 309 6 (pbk.)

Lockyer, Darren.
Rugby League football players – Australia – Biography.
Rugby League football – Australia – Biography.
Rugby League football – Australia – Anecdotes.

796.3338092

Cover photo by Grant Trouville © Action Photographics
Cover design by Luke Causby/Blue Cork
Internal design by Midland Typesetters, Australia
Typeset in Minion Pro 12.5/18.25pt by Midland Typesetters, Australia
Printed in Australia by Griffin Press, an accredited ISO AS/NZS 14001:2004
Environmental Management System printer

Random House Australia uses papers that are natural, renewable and recyclable
products and made from wood grown in sustainable forests. The logging and
manufacturing processes are expected to conform to the environmental regulations
of the country of origin.

For my parents, David and Sharon.
I know the privileged life I have lived and
the achievements I have made are only
possible because of the sacrifices you made
in order to provide for my brothers and me.

To Sunny and his future brothers or sisters,
and their future generations.
The following pages tell the story of my surreal
journey from my childhood to playing rugby
league to my retirement.
I hope the story contained is something you are proud to
acknowledge as part of your own history.

– Darren Lockyer

In loving memory of Kristopher Zealey,
R.I.P., 6 April 2011.
To Eli, you carry your uncle's name.
If you grow up to be half the man he was,
you'll have made your mum and dad proud.

– Dan Koch

Contents

'Locky's Last Goodbye' by Rupert McCall   vii

Foreword by Wayne Bennett   ix

Prologue   1

Chapter One: In the Beginning   12

Chapter Two: The Gold Miner – Cyril Connell   27

Chapter Three: The Early Years   36

Chapter Four: Racetrack to Real Estate   56

Chapter Five: The Pinnacle   70

Chapter Six: The Times They Are a-Changin'   95

Chapter Seven: Dreams Really Do Come True   116

Chapter Eight: Coach   144

Chapter Nine: Friends, Foes, Fun   169

Chapter Ten: The Deal That Changed the Game   185

Chapter Eleven: In Need of Direction   207

Chapter Twelve: Reforming the Family   228

Chapter Thirteen: Brave Sam   254

Chapter Fourteen: My Life   262

Chapter Fifteen: Rebuilding the Maroons Legend   283

Chapter Sixteen: What Tomorrow May Bring   302

Chapter Seventeen: What a Journey   318

Chapter Eighteen: The End   337

Chapter Nineteen: Rugby League Legend   372

Postscript: Bulla is Back   381

Acknowledgements   390

Statistics   394

Locky's Last Goodbye

by Rupert McCall

I went for many reasons when, at last, the moment came
More than just to say 'I witnessed Locky's final game'
More than just to honour his incredible career
And revel in the shiver of that curtain-closing cheer
The brilliance of his legacy alive in every stat
There was bound to be emotion, but I went for more than that
I went for more than fanfare . . . I went for more than praise
Beyond the recollection of his early Bronco days
The bandy blond-haired Roma boy who set the turf alight
As an undisputed golden-booted fullback in full flight
To the making of a genius packing all the magic tricks
When, again, he ruled the battlefield, but this time wearing 6
So many times responding to the pressure of the roar
His composure quite colossal, still, I went for something more
A loyal one-club team man and a journeyman untold
A stand-alone in proud maroon – a gun in green and gold
Every trophy-raising triumph – every title – every cup

A warrior of courage – knock him down, he gets back up
I went for more than knowing this and standing to applaud
A man of true humility collectively adored
In the gaze of those around me, I could feel the admiration
So many here to see him off – to own the inspiration
Every priceless memory unravelled in their eye
There was something in the gravel of his raspy last goodbye
Something that was welling in the hearts of grown men
It was hard to think we'd never see his pin-point pass again
Never laud his left foot roost, his balance and his speed
Never toast his poise and his ability to lead
Yet never, on the same hand, would the football world forget
Greatness shines forever in the names of some we've met . . .
Yes I went for many reasons when, at last, the moment came
But the most important reason why I went to see that game
When the full-time whistle echoed out and all was said and done
The truth defines a simple fact – I went to take my son
Because the day he put a Darren Lockyer poster on his wall
Was the day his father quietly smiled and stood so very tall

Foreword
by Wayne Bennett

I am on the record many times dismissing the assertion that footballers or other elite sportsmen and sportswomen are 'role models' for our youth, because I strongly believe that responsibility lies with parents and family.

But there is an exception to every rule, and Darren Lockyer is that exception.

The example he sets in every aspect of his life, on and off the sporting field, is one to which all young people could aspire if their desire is to live a rewarding life achieving their potential.

But Darren is an enigma. By nature he is shy, modest to a fault and happiest when he is sitting alone in a corner watching friends have a great time.

He does not need to be the centre of attention, the life of any party.

He is a perfectionist to the point of obsession, whether

it is combing his hair or passing a football, but he is strong-minded enough to not allow this trait to completely dominate his life.

Throw all that into the mix, and it is understandable for you to ask how it adds up to a brilliant athlete, a leader of men, and a fierce competitor in what is the toughest sport of all – rugby league.

I think it is because Darren has developed the intellectual capacity to balance his life. He can recognise when he needs a break, needs a night out, or just needs to get away from it all and spend quiet time with his family. People who compete at his level need that. Put bluntly, he knows himself well, knows his limitations, and is content with just 'being Darren'.

I am regularly asked to identify the qualities that made Darren the champion footballer also the great leader of his state's and nation's football teams for almost a decade. This has been one of his outstanding achievements, because he was not born with leadership qualities or aspirations. He just wanted to do the best he could and not be the centre of attention.

But he had the captaincy of the Broncos, Queensland and Australia thrust upon him, and typically he considered what was required to fulfil the position, took advice from those he trusted and accepted the challenge. The biggest change was to his own personality. A captain of an elite sporting team cannot expect to just lead by example. He has also to speak out, demand performance, inspire, be involved in game and personality analyses, and be the public face of the team, handling criticism in those times when things are not going well.

This was anathema to Darren, but he made himself change. He accepted the challenge, and history shows what a success he made of it.

What has most impressed me about Darren is his sportsmanship. He has never been sin-binned or sent off for foul play, never been penalised for arguing with a referee's decision, never been suspended and never thrown a punch on the field.

His sportsmanship has been unparalleled in my coaching career. Nobody ever tries to cheap-shot Darren Lockyer because these players have played with and against him many times, and they respect him too much to stoop to such conduct.

Youngsters – anybody for that matter who wants to better him or herself – should read this book and learn what makes Darren tick. The Darren Lockyer way is to do your best on and off the field, and that is all he has ever done – his best.

That is his legacy to sport, and to us all.

Prologue

'I was at a crossroads in my career. Where I am today in my life and so much of the career I have enjoyed can be traced back to that one specific play in one game.'

– Darren Lockyer

24 May 2006
State of Origin I
Telstra Stadium, Sydney

Walking from the field in Sydney that night, I knew what was coming. There would be calls for heads to roll and I knew mine would be at the top of many lists. I couldn't shake the feeling that this was the beginning of the end of my representative rugby league career. It ate at me for weeks.

Blues fans will remember halfback Brett Finch as the hero of the night. Called in just 24 hours before kick-off, Finchy slotted a 40-metre field goal in the 80th minute to seal New South Wales a 17–16 win in front of a big home crowd.

The final margin flattered us and I knew it.

The sound of the full-time siren hit me like a well-aimed body blow in the solar plexus from Lennox Lewis – I actually doubled over for a moment.

As a team, we had played really poorly, exacerbating the frustration and disappointment that losing any Origin match brings.

But, beyond that, I considered the team's below-par performance was a massive failure on my part. My play was poor, my captaincy was worse.

The game was Mal Meninga's first as head coach. He had taken on a role no one else wanted, given the dominance of the Blues in the preceding years. With Fittler, Buderus and/or Johns working behind a huge, mobile pack of forwards, New South Wales rolled to victory in 2003, 2004 and 2005. Some of the comments in the build-up to game one suggested both the Blues players and many within the southern media saw the 2006 series as a cakewalk into the history books – the first side to win four State of Origin series on the trot.

It was only at the behest of his fellow former Origin greats (FOGS) that Mal agreed to take the reins from Michael Hagan, who had stood down after two years in charge of the Maroons, citing the need to concentrate on his club commitments. Without the baggage of an NRL side to worry about, Big Mal threw himself into the role, travelling to all 16 clubs to meet with the Queenslanders at each. He employed a network of fellow former Origin stars or 'mentors' to liaise with the current players on a regular basis and report back to him.

Shortly after he'd accepted the job, Mal rang me. He wanted to meet for coffee at a café not far from Suncorp Stadium to discuss his plans and ideas for what he called the 're-education' of young Queensland rugby league players. Mal felt modern players had lost touch with what State of Origin football meant to people north of the Tweed. A history lesson was needed to re-ignite the flames of passion which had been so vital to Queensland's success in the 1980s.

Despite being in his mid-40s Mal's physical stature remained as imposing as ever. The sheer size of the man, coupled with his standing as a rugby league great – an Immortal in fact – gives him a unique presence wherever he goes. That ensured the passion with which he spoke about the Maroon jersey resonated with me, more so than it would have coming from almost anyone else. What probably surprised me and impressed me most, though, was the way in which Mal was able to integrate the emotions which were so central to the 'old-school' Origin camps with the professional, modern preparation he and assistant Neil Henry had devised. Mal had a vision about the sort of environment he wanted to create not just for the 17 Maroons, but also for those on the fringe. Early in the season, he gathered 35 Maroons hopefuls together for what amounted to an orientation. There, we established the principles we live by every day in camp. The list of these principles was – and still is – posted on walls around our pre-game camps. They are given to the young guns in the Emerging Origin and Queensland Academy of Sport development systems. As well as forming the philosophy for how we wanted to be seen off the field, they were central to what we wanted to do on the field as well:

T RUST

E FFORT

A GGRESSION

M ATESHIP

More personally, Mal made a point of seeking my advice on everything from the camp program to the actual game plan. He sought my input and approval on a regular basis, as he did with Petero Civoniceva and Steve Price. He wanted us to take greater ownership of the team. Of course, assuming greater ownership of a team is a double-edged sword. While the spoils of victory provide a greater sense of satisfaction, you also shoulder much more blame for a poor showing by the team.

I could barely lift my head during the long walk back to the visitors' dressing-rooms, deep in the bowels of the Olympic Stadium. I knew I had let Mal down. I had let my team-mates down. I had let myself down and I knew what was coming. In 20 years of rugby league, I had played my share of shockers but I couldn't remember ever being more upset with myself than I was after that night.

Johnathan Thurston had been so dominant at North Queensland and, given he was still pretty raw, subconsciously we both made the decision to step back and let each other do what we do best rather than have each other worry about trying to change our games. However, by taking that attitude, we both ended up waiting for the game to come to us. The speed Origin football is played at makes that almost impossible and, sure enough, before I knew it the game was over. Not only had I gone away from the game plan Mal had outlined for me, in doing so I had let the team structures crumble.

It was one–nil Blues and predictably the knives came out. While I knew the criticism was inevitable, the amount and intensity caught me off-guard. I remember Phil Gould wrote that Queensland needed to sack me. I have had very little to do with Gus over the course of my career, but certainly respect his standing in the game and his opinion – even if I don't always agree with it. Gus's ability to analyse and dissect a game is second to none. At the time, I was already hurting and he certainly didn't hold back on what he saw as some glaring and irreparable problems with my game.

He wasn't alone in calling for my head and, knowing the firestorm that was going on, I made the conscious decision to keep my head out of the papers. Instead, I poured every waking ounce of energy and focus I had into my preparation for game two. It was the only way I knew how to deal with what was in front of me. I am not and have never been someone who goes out and seeks advice or reassurance from others. Whether it was on the football field or in my personal life, I have always enjoyed problem-solving and the challenge of finding my own way through the process. More often than not in my football career, the search for an answer begins (and oftentimes finishes) at training.

In my own mind, I knew I had better in me. I knew what I had to do to put things right in game two. The coach, however, wasn't so sure and in the week before naming the squad for game two in Brisbane, Mal told me he wanted to shift me back to fullback. I was adamant that wasn't the answer and told Mal so, but he wasn't prepared to let it rest. He told me straight out that he had concerns about my ability to implement the style of play he needed at five-eighth, which was vastly different to what I was doing at the Broncos. In technical terms, at Brisbane we were playing a lot from the scrum and using two-pass shifts. In the more physical confines of Origin football, Mal wanted to play more midfield and split JT (Thurston) and me either side of the ruck. Mal kept at me, questioning whether I could make the necessary adjustments, and it started to get under my skin. I needed him to show some faith in my ability to get the job done and I told him so. I felt he and the other selectors should either pick me at five-eighth or not pick me at all. When the team was released the following Monday, Karmichael Hunt was named to make his Origin debut at fullback and I was named at number six.

The work we did on the track ahead of game two was near perfect. There was a real focus in everything we worked on and we played accordingly. We lost Greg Inglis – whose two-try effort almost single-handedly kept us in game one – but it caused barely a ripple within the camp. Adam Mogg – considered by most people as a bit of a journeyman footballer – stepped straight in and played the game of his life. The focus of the group was unshakable. Mal had been at pains to point out to us from the moment we arrived in camp that we had played well below our best yet fell only a point short. He also pushed home the need to reclaim Suncorp Stadium as a fortress for Queensland teams. His call for fans to make it as uncomfortable as possible for the visiting Blues was answered in kind. The fans that night were as loud as I have ever heard them. They knew – as we did – how much that game meant to State of Origin football.

In the end, it was a romp. Our forwards completely dominated their big men in the middle of the park. JT and Cameron Smith were outstanding controlling the play. It was a sign of the combination I believe has been the key to Queensland's subsequent dominance of Origin football. They looked poised and calm and their confidence was infectious. The final score was 30–6, but it could have been more. We played outstandingly and, while I took home the man-of-the-match award that night, half a dozen other team-mates had equally justifiable claims.

And so we came to game three.

Unfortunately a lot of the confidence we – or perhaps I should say I – had taken from the performance at home in game two was lost by the fact that we had to make a host of changes. Clinton Schifcofske, Rhys Wesser, Josh Hannay and Nate Myles all came into the side. Our backline had to be totally reshuffled and without Karmichael, Steve Bell,

Justin Hodges and Greg Inglis, questions were being raised about whether we had the necessary strike power to beat the Blues down in Melbourne.

I have never prepared more intensely for a game – at any level – than I did that week leading into game three in Melbourne. I knew what was on the line, not just for me but for the concept of Origin football, which I loved so dearly.

But the best laid plans can come unstuck in a hurry, particularly on a rugby league field. In contrast to game two, everything seemed to be going against us in the decider. The first 60 minutes was a mixture of blown chances by us and – as so often happens when things aren't going your way in general play – some horrible calls from the officials. The frustration of the boys was obvious – and in no one more so than JT.

JT's onfield persona is much like Gorden Tallis. They both wear their hearts on their sleeves. They give absolutely everything and are just so passionate and so competitive they can't help but let things spill over sometimes.

I thought JT was going to absolutely explode when Eric Grothe was awarded a try midway through the second half, despite a blatant knock-on in the lead-up. He was standing there behind the line, head down, saying things about the match officials which won't make it past the editors of this book, so I won't even try. Suffice to say, he wasn't impressed.

And neither was I. We hadn't got a call all night. But I knew how important JT was to this team and I just felt the game wasn't over. We were down 14–4, but I knew I had to give the boys some hope. As captain, that was what my job was at that moment. I told JT to lift his head. I don't talk or rant and rave too much as a captain, but in that moment I called them all in and just said: 'There is still time to win this game. We're Queenslanders, we don't f***ing give up.'

Fittingly, it was JT who then made the decisive play. With 10 minutes to go, he got the ball inside our 20-metre area and put one of his trademark steps on Luke O'Donnell and just took off. As the defenders closed in, he fed the ball to Brent Tate, who played one of the games of his life that night. This was Brent Tate before a lot of his knee problems and he had some serious wheels on him back then. When he took the ball, it was all over – the chasing pack never looked like putting a glove on him. I still consider that one of the great Origin tries.

The try was converted, so there we were, still down by two points with eight minutes left on the clock.

In that situation when the stakes are so high, I am a strong believer in playing field position and pressure. I wanted to put the ball deep into New South Wales territory and force them to carry it out. There are two reasons you do this. First, length-of-the-field tries late in the game are tough. Everyone is tired and finding the fresh legs that are going to carry the ball 100 metres can be extremely difficult. Second, and most importantly, pressure does funny things to people. When you are tired and the game is on the line and you have a crowd of 50 000 people screaming at you, your decision-making process often gets compromised and you do things you wouldn't normally do.

So I kicked the ball deep, where it was gathered on the 10-metre line by Eric Grothe. From the ensuing play-the-ball, the Blues fullback laid it off to one of his centres to bring it back upfield. Brett Hodgson is one of the toughest, safest fullbacks I ever played against. If he threw 1000 passes out of dummy-half, 999 of them would hit the designated target in the breadbasket. But with five minutes to go in an Origin decider, Hodgson's ball sailed high, well beyond Matt King's desperate lunge. I was pushing up hard in defence with the rest of the team and just happened to be in the right place at the right time: the ball bounced up perfectly for me and I scooted through to score a try. Half their team was still making their way back and I got a bit lucky. There were New South Wales players either side of the loose ball, but I was screaming through and had the momentum working in my favour.

I have always believed that if you are prepared to work hard you will get the rewards. When Petero and Tunza (Tonie Carroll) came through and hugged me, I remember thinking about all the work I had put in since game one. I still believe that was the Big Fella upstairs giving me a bit of a reward for all that.

It was a surreal feeling. There were only two minutes to go, so we were never going to lose it from there. The final score was 16–14, and we had finally won another Origin series. Lying in bed the night before the game, I had let my mind wander a bit . . . which is not like me. I had started to think about what I might say if we won – how I would feel lifting that famous Origin shield above my head. But when the moment came, the siren sounded and Grothe kicked the ball out to end the contest, everything just sort of stopped. I looked around at the crowd and at my team-mates. It was an indescribable high.

I found Petero and he grabbed me and said, 'How good is this!'

That's all I could think: *how good is this!*

ONE

In the Beginning

To START THIS story it is both necessary and appropriate I go back to the very beginning – to my beginning. Necessary because all stories start somewhere and appropriate because everything I have achieved, all the wondrous experiences and remarkable people I have encountered on my journey through life, I owe to my parents, David and Sharon.

Mum and Dad are your quintessential 'Little Aussie Battlers', a salt-of-the-earth couple whose rural ties are evident in the values by which they have lived their lives and raised their family. They never had the biggest house in the street, nor the flashest car. To them, travel was what you did to get from home to work and back again. They married young, the pair of them having just turned 20 when they took the plunge. At that time Dad was working as a front-end loader operator – one of a number of different labouring-type jobs he held as a young man. The thought of building a career was the furthest thing from his mind. As long as he brought in enough money to provide the basics for him and Mum, that was all he was after.

Beyond that, the major prerequisite for an employer was that his job not take him away from his two great loves in life – his new wife and the Morningside AFL club in the Brisbane suburb of Hawthorne. A representative soccer player through his formative years, Dad was introduced to AFL in his late teens by his brother-in-law, who was a mad Carlton fan. After seeing it played live for the first time, he fell in love with it. Dad was a pretty handy athlete and an absolutely ferocious competitor, and he took to the new code like a fish to water. His natural aptitude for the game saw him quickly rise through the ranks to the point where he was made captain of the Morningside under-19s the following year in what was just his second season at the club.

After getting a taste of senior football late in that year, he joined the State league squad on a permanent basis the next pre-season. Without the instincts of someone who had played the game since childhood, Dad found his niche in defence, with few able to match him in a man-on-man contest for the ball. In no time at all, he established himself as a regular member of Morningside's starting 18 and went on to play more than 90 matches for the Panthers, predominantly at centre half-back. In an act of loyalty most modern-day footballers would sadly struggle to even comprehend, Dad walked out of the club at the end of the

1977 season in protest at the sacking of the senior coach, leaving him agonisingly short of his 100-game milestone.

Sharon Lockyer: I guess Darren has had a way of catching people off guard since the very beginning. I think it is fair to say we were caught a little off guard. He wasn't exactly planned, Darren. David and I had been married about three years, but we didn't think we were in a position just yet to start a family. However, Darren wasn't interested in waiting and it was the same again with his birth. It was still more than two weeks before he was due when he decided he had had enough and he arrived without much noise or fuss on 24 March 1977. He was 6 pounds, 6 ounces [2.72 kilograms] and quiet as a mouse – which I guess was a bit of a sign of things to come. Darren was a very placid baby, though there were some rough patches when he was struggling with a couple of serious bouts of colic. He was active early – he was crawling and then walking and running before any of the other children around his age that we knew and he always loved being outdoors. Even as a baby, he hated being cooped up for too long. He was always going somewhere.

David Lockyer: I had all types of footballs and tennis balls around him from a very young age. He was about four years old when I gave him his first real lesson about how to kick a football and had him practising with both his left and right feet. By the time he was six, he was already able to have a reasonable kick-to-kick with me over 15 metres or so, kicking with either foot and marking the ball to his chest when I kicked it back. I got him down to the Springwood junior AFL club, where he played in the age group above his own for two straight years before we as a family packed up and headed out of the big smoke, relocating out west at a town called Wandoan, a tiny community in the Western Downs region about five hours north-west of Brisbane.

Sharon and I had been offered the chance to take over the running of a 24-hour truck stop just on the edge of the township. The plan was that I would take care of the shop and petrol, while Sharon would oversee the kitchen and dining areas. Initially, we thought we would do a two-year stint out there, earn some cash and head back to Brisbane. But in the end we were at that truck stop for more than four years before we moved to Roma when Darren was starting high school.

It's astonishing my teeth haven't fallen out yet, given my diet over the course of the four or so years we spent at Wandoan consisted of very little outside of toasted sandwiches and Mars bars. Mum was flat out cooking for the customers, but would often put some food from the diner out for me and my younger brothers, Matt and Russell – a nutritious option we routinely replaced with chocolate. It was great.

For three young boys growing up, you couldn't wish for a better landscape to have at your disposal than the vast open spaces on offer in Wandoan. That sort of freedom for a young boy is irreplaceable. We lived out the back of the diner, beside an enormous wheat silo station – an inquisitive youngster's field of dreams. We used to crawl inside different sheds and storage units surrounding the main structure. It provided countless options for games of hide and seek. If you didn't know where to look, you were facing a lengthy stint heading up the search party.

We rode motorbikes and camped out under the stars with our friends, the group of us sharing the warmth of the campfire, staying up till all hours laughing and telling jokes. As you do when you are growing up in rural areas, you learn to drive a car pretty early – Dad realising he needed to teach me after an attempt to teach myself at age 11 ended with Mum's crappy old Corolla rolling straight into the back of a trailer that was directly in front of me, only about 10 metres from where the car had been parked.

It was out at Wandoan that I got my first taste of rugby league and straightaway, I was hooked. I played anything I could – basketball, athletics, cricket, touch football, swimming . . . you name it. If it involved physical activity, I was there.

Sport was how I was able to interact socially as well, particularly in my teenage years. Because I was pretty shy and didn't have too much to say, the way I was able to find friends and my own personal niche in the grand scheme of things was through my participation in every sport imaginable. I actually had some success on the athletics track, competing for State representation in the 100 metres and the 200 metres sprints on the track, while in the field events long jump and shot-put were my strong suits. I was a reasonable basketballer and an okay cricketer.

But by the time we left Wandoan for Roma, where Dad had accepted a new position with BP, I knew rugby league was my game. Oddly enough, I was reasonably big as a 10-year-old and so I started my junior football in the centres, which I didn't mind at all as it allowed me plenty of time and space to play my football. In 1989, I got my first taste of representative football when I was selected in the Queensland under-12s squad at outside centre.

My centre partner that year was the kid most saw as the standout talent in the side. His core skills were comparable to those of a senior player. There seemed no doubt Elton Flatley would one day hit the big time. He was way ahead of me and went on to play rugby union for the Queensland Reds and the Wallabies. I was the big, fast kid who looked dominant against kids his own age, but most doubted that I could make the transition to play in the NRL.

I learned in later years that Cyril Connell first spotted me at about the age of 14 and began asking questions around the place. Typically, it was almost a full 12 months before Cyril began speaking to me and my parents. By that time we were firmly entrenched in our new home at Roma, having made the move in early January 1990.

By the midway point of high school, the halcyon days of under-12s when I towered over other players seemed a distant memory. Thankfully, my wheels were just fine though, because I had begun playing more in the halves, where agility and speed are a key part of your arsenal. Those two attributes were also of major assistance to me in playing touch football, helping me to State honours there in the under-15s.

Matt came three years behind me and was a very good footballer himself, earning regional selection in Queensland under-age teams right through his junior football. Matt was a bigger build than I was. He was always strong and in contrast to me he is really thick through his shoulders and chest. So, while Matty would have me well and truly covered on bench press, I reckon I would have had a considerable speed advantage.

But enough of petty sibling rivalry. While I am enormously proud of what I have done over the course of my playing career, I am equally as proud of the player Matt became playing five-eighth for Easts in the Queensland Cup. While being given a short opportunity at the Wests Tigers, it is unfortunate he wasn't given more of a chance by any NRL club before he chose to hang up the boots. He had such a great work ethic and has always had that poise and calmness under pressure.

David: Poor old Matt had it hard, to be honest. As a footballer, he was as honest as the day is long. He was really solid. He didn't make errors. He was a good defender. He was a very complete footballer and he should have played NRL. But he probably suffered a bit from being compared to his older brother by scouts. He didn't have the flair or the athleticism that Darren had, but he was very good in a lot of other areas.

To his credit, though, there was never a moment of bitterness or jealousy. He has always been Darren's biggest supporter and like the rest of the family is just immensely proud of Darren and all he has achieved.

Sharon: The only time we ever worried about his brothers getting a touch resentful or envious of Darren was for a time not long after we came back to Brisbane, when Russell just refused to watch his games. He didn't talk about them . . . it just seemed to come out of nowhere.

But as quickly as it came it went, and Russell comes to the home games and keeps every one of Darren's stats himself these days.

I am still not sure what it was about, though it may well have been a reaction related to his condition.

Russell was diagnosed with epilepsy not long after he went into high school. Back then there was still a real stigma attached to epilepsy and it was incredible to see the way everything changed. Russell went from being one of, if not the most popular kid in school, to being really withdrawn and isolated. I am sure some of it was how self-conscious he became. He just lost all confidence in himself when he was in public. It was really tough for everyone, because there was nothing we could say that could change the situation he was facing. His seizures became really severe and he was forced to go on some very strong drugs to minimise those sorts of episodes.

Darren had moved away when this started and I guess the significance of what Russell was trying to deal with didn't really register with him until sometime later when he saw his younger brother have an episode. His immediate reaction was to try to find a solution. In Darren's mind, there is a way to solve everything, you just have to sit down, take your time and think your way through things. He started doing some research about epilepsy and the various treatments on offer and helped get Russell down to the leading treatment centre in Melbourne. But unfortunately the specialists found they were unable to help with Russell's particular type of epilepsy because they weren't able to pinpoint the area of the brain which was being affected.

Growing up, they weren't all that close. The five years between them meant Darren was always at a much different stage in his life. By the time Russell hit high school, Darren was gone.

Today, Russell has a great job, a driver's licence and has been able to fully grow his independence.

Where Matt and I were always involved in sport of some description throughout our childhoods, Russell never really showed a great deal of interest in joining in. It wasn't until he was much older that he played any team sport at all, but there is no question his involvement with rugby league has been enormously beneficial for Russell, especially in regard to building his confidence in social settings. He actually has a really engaging personality and it's great to see the way he has come out of his shell in more recent years.

Unfortunately, though, the reality of his condition meant he needed to take a lot of strong medication following his initial diagnosis, as the doctors sought to minimise the risk of him suffering a seizure. Talking to him now, he says the impact of the drugs left him lethargic. As he describes it, he spent most of his teenage years in somewhat of a fog. It was as if he was perpetually drowsy, unable to think with any clarity and devoid of all motivation.

With my football career only allowing me a limited number of chances to get home to see my family, my relationship with Russell slowly began to dissipate. In all honesty, my relationship with both of my brothers became pretty detached after a while – a situation for which the blame falls squarely on my head.

By nature I am relatively unemotional. I have never been someone who is big on public displays of emotion – or affection, for that matter. Some people probably refer to me as being a bit cold and I think for a long time that probably had some truth to it. But as I have got older, I have started to find specific things which stir my emotions and/or evoke a passionate response. Professionally, I invest far more in the success of the teams of which I am a part, while on a personal level I have gradually become a little more open with many of the people in my life and am certainly more outgoing in public than I was in my younger days.

The catalyst for the changes I have made in this facet of my life, that experts like to tag 'emotional maturity', undoubtedly has been what I have seen and experienced since becoming part of my wife Loren's extended family. In the 17 years I spent under Mum and Dad's roof, we had what you would call semi-regular contact with my uncles, aunts and cousins on Mum's side but little to do with Dad's family. It is not that there is any bad blood between any of the siblings; they have just always lived some distance from any of the places we called home. There seemed very little emotional attachment between the members of Dad's family, but it wasn't until I had the chance to see the Pollock family gather for a celebration that I realised how precious the bond is between family members.

I have to admit I have, on occasion, found myself feeling rather envious of the wonderful relationships Loren enjoys with several of her cousins and all of her aunts and uncles. They provide so much support for one another, not to mention the endless laughs and sensational food that accompany a family gathering. I sometimes reflect that perhaps the tyranny of distance robbed my family of some of those opportunities.

They are the sorts of things I want our son, Sunny James, to experience growing up and the key to that lies in keeping the expanding Lockyer clan together. Just as Loren's family were up north, I am really keen to have Matt and Russell and their young families in close proximity to us. Matty has two young girls who are just a ball of fun, and I have told Matt how keen I am to see them be a major part of our children's lives, having seen first-hand the enormous impact they have had on Loren.

> **Loren:** Early on in our relationship, Darren really struggled with how over-the-top my family is and the way we all greet and say goodbye with hugs and kisses. We have just always been a really close, affectionate family and that is right through all the relations. It took a while before he started to come around and he is much more comfortable now when any of my cousins or crazy aunts come and give him a big hug.
>
> He's much better with that these days . . . it's nice.

We left Wandoan for Roma in the Christmas holidays prior to me starting high school. I was shattered when Mum and Dad sat me down to explain how Dad had been offered a promotion which required him to be based closer to what, after four years in Wandoan, we considered 'the big smoke'.

I don't know that I have ever been more scared than I was walking into school on the first day of grade 8. It didn't help that Mum had made sure I was wearing the full, formal school uniform, with socks pulled up and leather shoes properly shined – something which may not have been too big a deal had it not been for the fact I was the only one to do so. I almost ran out when I realised, convinced it was proof I was the odd one out and didn't belong there.

I still remember how tough those first few months of school were. I had just started to develop some really good friendships back in Wandoan and all of a sudden we had to pack up and leave all that behind and start again. Looking back over my life, there is no doubt I have always been comfortable on my own. I am not sure where it stems from, but I know that it is a part of my personality that has evolved as I have grown up.

As an adult, I guess I have become far less concerned about the fact I sometimes struggled in the big group settings. On tours, for instance, I am happy to just spend a lot of my down time doing my own thing. In fact, sometimes, I need to get away to find some peace and quiet, because there are definitely moments when it all gets too much – that is to say, all the attention and interest we receive as NRL players. I absolutely feel blessed that people do care so passionately about the game and their respective teams, but I almost get a little claustrophobic at times and need to escape.

Back in Roma, though, I was a kid and able to gain some acceptance from the other kids in my grade largely through sports. Rugby league in particular gave me a platform from which to build on my high school years and social networks.

After getting a taste of football at a higher level as part of the Queensland under-12 team, I found myself with better coaches to learn from and players to test myself against. I managed to find a way into the Cities under-16 A side as a 14-year-old. The following year, by the time I had turned 15, I was starting in the halves in the local first-grade side.

David: I guess there were maybe a couple of times early on when I worried about him playing against men at such a young age, but he had handled everything up to that point; it was just the next logical step for him. He was the star kid in the area and it probably rubbed a few of the older blokes up the wrong way, but none of them were ever able to do any damage. Darren was too quick and too smart. He saw them coming before they had even started coming themselves. His team-mates all looked after him too, but Butch Smith, who was the captain–coach of the Cities side, was his main bodyguard out there. Graham 'Butch' Smith was a genuinely hard, old country man. He knew Darren's importance to the side, but more than that he saw that Darren had the chance to really do something with his career and he wasn't about to let some country thug hurt his chances of going on with the game.

After a few years in his new position as BP's regional manager, Dad started to look for something new. Typical of folks from rural Australia, Dad placed enormous value on owning the things in his life and as such was desperate to move into business for himself. The idea of working for some faceless figurehead overseas never quite added up to my old man. He and Mum were given the tip that a convenience store in Miles was about to go on the market and they jumped at the chance.

If he had his time over, I have no doubt Dad might have taken a little more time before making such a major decision. The round trip from home to the store in Miles was a touch over three hours, a journey which became simply impossible once Dad realised the enormous number of hours he was required to be at the shop – on top of the long hours the store was open to the public, Dad was bringing in deliveries, stacking and rotating products on the shelves and cleaning the place. There were also stocktake numbers to monitor and stock order forms which needed to be fired off as required and checked closely as they came in.

So Dad made the decision to remain in Miles during the week and head home each weekend to see his wife and three boys. He continued that routine until I moved out of our home at Roma at the end of grade 12, when I headed to Brisbane, having accepted an offer to join the Broncos. It was over those last couple of years that Mum and I became particularly close. With Dad's workload keeping him away so much, it sort of fell to me to help Mum out as much as I could with things around home, as well as with taking care of Matt and Russell. Mum was holding down a job of her own, as well as running around after the three of us, but not once did I hear her complain about her lot. She just kept going and nothing we needed was ever too much trouble.

It was through Mum and Dad that I learned about values like loyalty and commitment. I saw what it was to have a strong work ethic and the importance of generosity and selflessness. Neither Mum nor Dad has ever so much as played a game of rugby league. But make no mistake, they were the best coaches I ever had.

TWO

The Gold Miner
– Cyril Connell

'He was quite simply the best man I have ever met in my time in football. My life is better for every minute I spent with Cyril Connell.' – Darren Lockyer

WHEN WAYNE DEPARTED at the end of the 2008 season, fans and media understandably focused solely on the impact his absence would have on the renowned stability upon which so much of the Broncos' success had been based.

Just as he would have wanted, Cyril Connell moved off quietly into retirement. The news barely caused a ripple outside the club, but to me it was almost as significant as Wayne leaving. Cyril was quite simply the best person I have met in my time in rugby league. Wayne was obviously an enormous influence on me, and there are many others I feel lucky to have had the chance to meet. But Cyril is without question the man I most admired. An absolute gentleman, he was humble to a fault. It wasn't until I met another former great by the name of Bobby Banks, during a trip to Toowoomba almost a year after arriving at the Broncos, that I learned what an outstanding, tough player Cyril had been in his own right. He never mentioned it – he was always more interested in other people. That sort of selflessness is all too rare these days. But like so many of Cyril's traits it is something to aspire to.

Having always promised to stick around as long as Wayne was at the club, Cyril had just turned 80 when he finally called it a day. It ended an association with rugby league that dated back more than 60 years to his days as a crafty halfback, who represented Queensland throughout the 1950s and was a Kangaroo tourist in 1956. After hanging up the boots, he began a career in Queensland's education system, where he worked his way up to the office of assistant director of Education Queensland – that is, the second in command. As a schools inspector, he spent years travelling the state meeting with teachers, principals and students – establishing an unrivalled network of contacts whose loyalty to Cyril was unshakable. At the behest of one of the Broncos' founding fathers, Paul 'Porky' Morgan, Cyril joined the football staff in 1990 to help oversee talent identification and recruitment. Wayne always said he was the best recruit the club ever made.

By the time I was finishing high school, Cyril's legend was already well and truly established. Every youngster who had been selected in a representative side knew about Mr Connell – as he was known. A tiny man, Cyril would shuffle around to watch games from behind the goalposts, occasionally dropping into the dressing-rooms to congratulate or encourage the boys. When he came in, you could hear a pin drop. He never had a harsh word to say about anyone, Cyril. He was so humble and warm. It says much about how special he was that, in a game like rugby league in which reputations are forged on physical confrontations, I know of no one who was more universally loved and respected than Cyril Connell. Over the course of my career, I have come to know the people whose opinions matter to me. It is a small group, to be honest, but all the members are people I hold in the highest regard and I worry about falling short of the expectations they have of me. Cyril and my mother, however, share a place at the very top of that list. I always felt indebted to him for the life-changing opportunity he gave me as a kid. But the beautiful nature of the man is what made him so special. I have never met a more gentle, caring or generous man than Cyril. He also had the unique ability to be able to find something good or positive to say no matter how dire the circumstances. It was a skill I drew on numerous times to get myself back in a positive frame of mind when frustration and anger, usually at myself over a mistake I have made, builds to such a level it impacts negatively on my ability to properly captain and lead a young Broncos side.

I first met Cyril at an under-15s carnival at Caboolture. I was playing for South-West region and we pretty much got poleaxed every year by the more powerful sides from

Brisbane, Gold Coast, Sunshine Coast and Darling Downs. He just congratulated me on how I was going and said he was going to be keeping an eye on me. I was pumped. For my generation of schoolboy footballers, Cyril Connell was 'the man'. He was the one you wanted to get noticed by. Those few words from him were all I needed to really start working on my football and begin dreaming about the possibility of becoming a Bronco.

Cyril stayed in regular touch with me and my parents over the next two years and put me on a scholarship with the club when I started to play some pretty good football, thanks in no small way to the well-timed and much-needed growth spurt which occurred shortly after my 16th birthday. The scholarship covered my high school tuition and the costs associated with playing junior representative football. After being selected in both the Queensland under-16 and Queensland schoolboys sides in my final two years at school, I was offered a place in the Broncos Colts for the 1995 season.

It meant relocating within a few weeks of school ending to join the main group for the start of pre-season training. I was a little apprehensive initially. Leaving my mum and brothers and all my friends in Roma was tough, but I just kept telling myself that this was the chance I had dreamt of since I was a kid. Still, I barely said a word to my dad on the drive to my new home in Brisbane with the Cranston family. They were friends of Cyril's who he felt could look after me and help me settle into my new life. My food and board were part of the first contract I signed with Brisbane at the end of 1994. As a part of that deal, I was also given a job working behind the bar at the leagues club at Red Hill and the princely sum of $2000.

Over the course of his 19 years as Broncos recruitment manager, Cyril brought dozens if not hundreds of boys to Brisbane on similar deals. He always included a job and/or education and training, no matter how talented a player you were. I remember working alongside two big, ugly-looking blokes during the pre-season of 1995 who introduced themselves as Tonie Carroll and Shane Webcke, respectively. Cyril would drop by whenever we were working to check in on all of us and see how we were adjusting. One of Cyril's most endearing traits was his ability to make you feel as if you were the most important person in the room whenever he spoke to you. He took a real interest in you and the things that were going on in your life.

He may not have been there in 1988, but I don't think many people would argue the fact that he was one of the foundation stones upon which two decades of the Broncos' unrivalled success was forged. Where Wayne provided the stability and direction on the field, Porky Morgan and Barry Maranta set new standards off it. Cyril was responsible for providing both with the personnel required to meet their respective demands. Amongst the litany of stars Cyril recruited to the club are names like Wendell Sailor, Lote Tuqiri, Justin Hodges, Shane Webcke, Petero Civoniceva, Tonie Carroll, Darius Boyd, Steve Renouf, Karmichael Hunt, Shaun Berrigan, Brad Thorn, Ashley Harrison, Carl Webb, Sam Thaiday, Corey Parker, Dane Carlaw, Brent Tate,

Berrick Barnes and Peter Ryan. In an age where players changing clubs mid-season has become commonplace, it is worth noting that 16 of the 17 members of the side which beat Melbourne in the 2006 grand final arrived at Brisbane as teenagers courtesy of one Cyril Connell.

In 2007, the club decided to honour Cyril's stunning contribution to the organisation by naming our main training facility the Cyril Connell High Performance Centre. Players past and present came to see the unveiling of a special plaque which now sits on the wall of the main entrance to the facility as a tribute to Cyril. Cyril was there, smiling as always, graciously accepting the gesture before declaring it 'too much', given he was simply doing what he loved.

By this stage, Cyril was already struggling pretty badly with a variety of health problems. While his driving skills had been the source of great amusement for a long time around the club, things had got to a point where Wayne and Paul Bunn were forced to take his keys from him. Getting around on those little bandy legs was also becoming a real strain. Not that he ever let on. I just loved the way Cyril carried himself – no complaints, no whingeing. He was dealing with things that would buckle most fit young men, but he'd just rock up every day and go about his business.

It was afternoon on Tuesday 9 June when we got word Cyril had died. I knew it was coming, but still to hear the words was incredibly deflating. I have been blessed in my life to date to have largely avoided the devastation of losing people close to me. It was a really tough week for the club and everyone in it and I freely admit as a captain I probably should have done things differently. Our preparation for what was a pretty important match against the Bulldogs had already been hit by news that a couple of boys in the team, including Karmichael, had contracted swine flu. We were ordered by Queensland Health officials to stay away from training for fear it could spread through the entire squad.

Cyril's funeral was held on Friday afternoon about six hours prior to kick-off. Wayne gave the eulogy. I saw him beforehand and he was as nervous as I have ever seen him, wanting to do his great friend justice. His words were perfect. More than 500 people, including a ton of ex-Broncos, had come to pay their respects to Cyril and Wayne had their undivided attention from first word to last.

Still, it was a very hollow feeling I carried into the change rooms later that night. I remember when the black tape made its way around to me to put on the traditional memorial armband, my thoughts immediately went to Cyril and the memories we shared. My thoughts turned to those early encounters with him when I was a teenager back in Roma and it hit home to me that I would most likely not be here had it not been for Cyril's decision. I know a few of the older boys in the squad were thinking much the same thing, so we probably weren't much help to the kids in the side that night. I have never been a big believer in the notion of using those sorts of things as motivation, either. Generally I find that, when you start trying to draw on exterior factors to motivate yourself, you lose focus on your own job and your role within the team. It's counter-productive. In the end, we were pretty flat and disjointed and found ourselves on the end of a 22-point drubbing from the visiting Bulldogs.

I have to admit it is probably the only time I have come off the field after a loss and not felt that burning frustration in the pit of my stomach.

I still miss Cyril. Just the little things, you know, like watching him shuffle across the oval to the offices and seeing him after training. He'd always come over and check up on me.

There will never be another Cyril Connell. He was one of a kind; unique in his manner. I guess it is one of those situations where you have to say to yourself, 'Don't cry because it's over, smile because it happened.'

Wayne Bennett: Cyril loved all his boys, but he and Darren were always particularly close, probably because they shared a lot of similarities as people.

A nod and a wink was worth a thousand words to the pair of them. They are both extremely generous with their time. They are calm and gentle – you won't hear them ranting and raving. But probably most of all, both are incredibly humble about their own achievements.

There's no doubt they had a special relationship. Whenever Locky was in the office, he'd make a point of going in and talking with Cyril. It was probably good for Locky at different times too, with the way he beats himself up sometimes, because Cyril was just the most accommodating person and he never had a bad word to say about anyone. There is no way he would have found a moment's fault with Locky's game.

I know he always considered Duncan Hall to be the best player he ever saw, but he just loved Darren Lockyer and always believed that by the end of his career Locky would be held in that sort of company.

That sort of praise is not to be taken lightly. Cyril Connell was part of the selection committee for the Team of the Century. There aren't many who knew the game like Cyril did. He was a special man.

THREE

The Early Years

'He was quiet and kept to himself a bit, but from the first time he came into the dressing-room he just had an air about him. From first-grade, to Origin, to Test footy . . . I have never seen anyone able to step up to higher levels in the game as quickly and easily as Locky.' – Steve Renouf

I HAD BEEN happily running around with the Broncos Colts side for about 12 weeks when Wayne wandered over to me in the middle of a training session and quietly informed me I would most likely be part of the first-grade squad to play Parramatta on Sunday. I couldn't believe what I had heard, but did my best to control my reaction. On the inside I was doing backflips, but outwardly I tried to maintain my composure, being conscious of the fact that the reality of professional sport means for every winner there is a loser. For every young bloke elevated, there are normally a couple of other guys overlooked. The last thing they need to see is a young punk jumping around the place and rubbing salt into their wounds. I floated through the rest of the day, oblivious to whatever else was going on around me. All I could think about was that in just a few days' time I was actually going to be a part of the Broncos 17.

To pull on that famous jersey in the team dressing-room before falling in tow and filing onto the ground was a dream of mine growing up out west. Even after making the move to Brisbane that year, the idea of Wayne Bennett actually selecting me in a Broncos side was, in my mind, a fantasy – an audacious goal which sat out there in the distance, well beyond my reach. Yet here I was on the verge of making my debut for the team I grew up supporting. It was totally surreal. I vividly remember lying in my bed at the Cranstons' that evening and just imagining different scenarios where I would be calling for the ball from Alfie Langer, or throwing a pass to Steve Renouf, guys I had idolised for years and here I was about to play alongside them. I did the same thing again the following night and again the night after that. Fair to say I was a touch eager about game number one!

I had been playing in the halves in the Colts side coached by Steve Calder, a long-time servant of the game who does a lot of great work these days in his role as chairman of the Men of League Foundation, a charitable organisation which offers help to members of the rugby league community who have fallen on hard times. At the same time, the eldest of the Walker brothers, Ben, was playing pivot in Ivan Henjak's reserve-grade side and making quite a name for himself, earning a number of mentions in the media as a promising ball player. Obviously, though, having Alf and Kevin Walters in the halves meant opportunities in the top grade were scarce. It was an injury to Kevie three weeks before that had opened the door for me. Without him, the Broncos suffered back-to-back losses, with the utility options Wayne tried in the role struggling to provide the necessary direction in attack. Believing an injection of youthful enthusiasm would provide his star-studded squad with the spark needed to get their season back on track, Wayne turned to Ben Walker and me. Typically concerned about keeping the media spotlight well away from me, Wayne saw to it that I was included on the reserve-grade team list when it was released mid-week. It was to be my first game in reserve grade and my first in top grade, on the same day! Ben was named to partner Alf in the halves in the first-grade squad, and the debut of the eldest member of a highly talented family ensured that he dominated the media's attention in the build-up to the match.

Funnily enough, my move into the Broncos first-grade squad began disastrously. The initial excitement of Wayne's approach had subsided and reality had set back in when the teams for round 13 were released. There I was, selected to play five-eighth in the reserve-grade team. I assumed Coach had simply come to his senses and kept me where I belonged and so I was prepared for the start of reserve-grade training at around 4 pm, immediately following the first-grade's run. But just before two o'clock, I got a panicked phone call from the team manager asking me where the hell I was, that the first-grade side was about to hit the track and I was meant to be there. And so it was that I arrived late to my very first training run under Wayne. It was the first and only time it has happened.

On game day, I started in the reserves, but was unsure whether I'd get the call-up or not until Ivan yanked me just before half-time and simply told me to hurry to the main visitors' dressing-room, where I was greeted by Glenn Lazarus, Alf, Wendell Sailor, Pearl (Steve Renouf) and the rest of the side. I was totally overawed and actually froze at the door for a couple of seconds before slipping in and making my way over to a corner, trying my best to remain inconspicuous. I watched Wayne pace around, stopping occasionally to whisper something in the ear of one of his footsoldiers. Benny Walker was bouncing around and jumping up and down on the spot until Wayne wandered over and placed a hand on his shoulder. He didn't say a word, but the message was obvious. 'Settle down, son, you have a game to play yet. Save your energy.'

I sat on the bench at Parramatta Stadium, just soaking in as much as I could. Alf put on a bit of a clinic, bamboozling the home side with his creativity and the precision of his short passing and kicking games. There was about 25 minutes left to play when the call came through for me to get ready to go on. I jumped up and took a couple of deep breaths. I started to make my way towards the touch judge when the trainer grabbed me and said, 'Wayne said just get out there and play your natural game, mate.' He patted me on the back as I made my way over to meet Benny Walker, who was coming from the field. As I was running on, I just heard someone – I don't know who – yell, 'Enjoy it, mate . . . you're here!'

That the boys had opened a 40-point lead by the time I joined the fray allowed me to do just that, with little to no pressure. As so often happens when players are able to relax and take some risks without the fear of any meaningful consequence, things just fell into place for me. I had a couple of nice touches and laid on a try for Pearl – who I must acknowledge is without any doubt the best hole runner I have ever played with or against, or seen or even heard stories about. No one ran lines like Pearl. His ability to put himself between defenders or outside his man was remarkable. He was a guy who made a lot of passes look much better than they were. I remember jogging back into place after Pearl's try. I did a little fist pump and couldn't get the smile off my face. I looked up to see the enormous frame of Glenn Lazarus looming large beside me. The big fella was never one for carry-on or speeches. He just went about his work without too much fuss and expected his team-mates to do the same. But seeing the excitement written all over my face, Lazo actually cracked a smile himself. He reached out one of those giant paws of his and patted me on the head.

'See, son, it's not that hard really, is it?' he offered, before trotting off to take his place deep in the in-goal area.

That first experience in the top grade essentially proved to be a snapshot of my first six seasons of NRL football.

Steve Renouf: My first memories of playing with Locky are seeing this kid that just had IT from the moment he was thrown into first-grade. That and his hair – he had a fair bouffant going back then.

He was quiet back then and I guess on that front not that much has changed. But there was something in the way he carried himself that made you take notice.

I had been told he was a kid that could go and when he came on he set me up for a try in the second half, it was just easy as you like. I remember thinking at the time, 'Geez, I hope I get to run off this bloke for a while yet.' History shows I did and I don't shy away from saying I benefited enormously from Locky's presence in the team.

The two of us formed a combination very quickly. He made life a dream for the blokes outside him. All you had to do was run the right line – Locky would do the rest. The ball would be on your chest at just the right moment. I actually get frustrated sometimes watching some of the lads who have played outside him since I left, because they make things look much harder out there than they need to be. I cannot for the life of me understand how blokes cannot run off Locky, because he has all the time in the world. Still, the number of times I have seen him left like a shag on a rock simply because the bloke outside couldn't get into position . . . I just sit there yelling at the screen sometimes.

I remember ringing Wayne after the opening round of 2006 and just saying to him, 'Coach, can you please pull a couple of blokes aside and just tell them how to run off Locky?'

He said, 'Pearl, I keep telling them. They won't listen.'

My arrival in the NRL coincided with the outbreak of Super League, which of course tore the game in half, to the point where two separate competitions were played in 1997, one featuring the Super League–aligned clubs – which of course included Brisbane – and another between the teams who had tied their allegiance to the ARL. Given my career was still very much in its infancy, I found a lot of the discussions and disputes of little interest to me and of even less consequence. As a Bronco, I left the decision-making to those more qualified than I and was happy to accept the decision by our club's leaders to link with the News Limited–backed Super League.

In subsequent years, I have read a lot about this turbulent period and have made a point of speaking to several of the prominent figures from the two camps – people from both sides. To be honest, sitting here today as one of the veteran members of the body of NRL players and the Rugby League Players Association, I am fairly confident that if the same offer was made to me today I would strongly oppose any action or movement which even had the potential to result in a situation where clubs might end up splitting from the main competition. Having said that, given my club had aligned itself with Super League, it would have been difficult not to support that in reality. As I have got older and matured, I have become far more concerned about the state of our game and the direction it is heading. For all the good intentions of the men responsible for Super League – and there is no doubt there was merit in their criticism of the ARL administration's lack of foresight, business nous and transparency, as well as the poor conditions and protection offered to players – the fact is, the end result was the game of rugby league and the NRL brand suffered damage so significant that its impact continues to haunt the NRL in 2011 – some 15 years after hostilities ceased.

I was in just my second full season of first-grade and as such was not part of the group of players able to leverage the warring parties against one another to secure contracts well beyond those on offer to NRL players in season 2011. Not that I completely missed out on the riches being thrown around so recklessly – on top of my relatively paltry base wage at Brisbane, I collected my share of the $1 million dollars prizemoney we collected courtesy of our Super League premiership win and our victory in the World Club Challenge competition, with the 25 members of our first-grade squad each taking home an equal share. As well, my selection in the Queensland team for the Tri Series was worth $10 000 a game, as was each appearance in the green and gold at the back end of that year. On top of that, my contract with Brisbane was laced with incentive bonuses linked to appearances for the club, representative selection and the team's on-field success. By year's end, I walked away with a total pay packet only a smidgen shy of what I was paid a decade later as captain of the club, Queensland and Australia and dual Golden Boot winner. Having used my first big cheque from the Broncos to buy Mum and Dad's place in Roma and help them out of a difficult spot they found themselves in following the collapse of one of their business ventures, the following year I used my earnings from 1997 to purchase my first house – a replica Queenslander in Rockbourne Terrace, Paddington, just a stone's throw from Red Hill.

The 1998 season is one which holds a special place in my memory. At club level, the Broncos ended any debate over the validity of the Super League title we had won 12 months previously. I have no hesitation in nominating the 1998 team as the best side I ever played in. Our 25-man squad featured no fewer than 16 State of Origin representatives, with our best 17 looking something like this: Darren Lockyer, Wendell Sailor, Darren Smith, Steve Renouf, Michael Hancock, Kevin Walters, Alf Langer, Shane Webcke, Phillip Lee, Andrew Gee, Gorden Tallis, Brad Thorn, Tonie Carroll, Kevin Campion, Petero Civoniceva, Peter Ryan, John Plath.

We took home the minor premiership, dropping just five games during the regular season and finishing the year with a points differential of +378 – a figure almost 200 points higher than that recorded by Newcastle in second place. I have never played in a side where I felt so assured of victory no matter what opposition we faced or what trouble we might find ourselves in from time to time. My job was a breeze, running off Alf and Kevie where I saw fit, or occasionally slipping in to second receiver to feed the likes of Wendell, Pearl and Darren Smith. Our forwards were unstoppable. Gordie (Tallis) was at the top of his game and with Peter Ryan, Tonie Carroll and Kevin Campion provided a genuinely intimidating presence in defence. Webcke and Thorn had already established themselves as representative mainstays and offered the ideal tutelage for a young Petero. We lost just one of our final 18 matches that season, with the sheer dominance we enjoyed reflected in the scoreline on grand final day. The seven tries to two, 38–12 demolition of the Bulldogs put an exclamation mark on what was a stunning effort by an extremely talented group of men.

The premiership win followed Queensland's commanding win in the State of Origin series earlier in the year. A 'Queensland Special' in the final moments of the series opener, courtesy of Kevin Walters, Ben Ikin and Tonie Carroll, was undoubtedly the most memorably enduring piece of play of the series. With the Blues up by five and time ticking down, Kevie went for the rugby league equivalent of a 'Hail Mary', sending a wobbly spiral punt downfield from well inside our own 30 metres. For any footy fan who only saw Ben Ikin at the back end of his playing career when the toll of multiple knee operations had robbed him of his speed and agility, go and watch Iki in full flight. He was a sensational player in his prime. Iki's chase and regather and the wonderful sleight of hand by playmaking maestros

Darren Smith and Kevie which sent Big Tunza over next to the posts was something to behold. So much of the football we watch these days is highly structured and the players' input reduced to a robotic-like regurgitation of what they practised at training that week. The NRL is poorer for the absence of creative ball-players like Smithy and Kev – players who used subtle changes of pace and timing in their passes and kicks to draw opposing defenders into an error. The way Smithy held up his pass in the final movement was the key. The New South Wales defenders were caught out, having over-committed themselves rushing out of the line. From there, it was simply a case of catch and pass until the overlap created opened a gap somewhere further down the line, with Kevie's slick hands delivering the final pass perfectly.

Queensland's last-gasp win in game one of the 1998 series is also perhaps the only occasion those south of the Tweed would concede that the result helped protect the integrity of the crown jewel of our sport. In his first taste of Origin football, Melbourne Storm prop Rodney Howe didn't just match it with the biggest, baddest men in the competition, he established himself as THE dominant presence in the middle of the park. His size and strength, coupled with a relentless workrate, earned him man-of-the-match honours in game two and he was widely acknowledged to have been the best forward from either side across the three games.

Gordie tells the story of his attempt to rattle Howe early in the series decider in the hope it might slow him down.

In mid-1998, Gordie was somewhere near the peak of his destructive powers, with his imposing physical presence, coupled with the unrivalled ferocity and intensity with which he played the game proving quite the handful for opposition sides. That the man they call the Raging Bull was also a more than handy pugilist only added to the fear factor Gordie engendered. Even from a distance in those days, Gorden Tallis cut a most intimidating figure, but the full effect wasn't felt until you got up close and personal with him and stared into those wild eyes of his.

In the build-up to game three, Gordie zeroed in on his mission to limit Howe's impact. His plan on just how to achieve this boiled down to Gordie simply racing out of the defensive line and hitting Howe with a shoulder charge as hard as humanly possible. For best effect, this 'plan' needed to be executed early. The game was still in its infancy when Gordie dutifully sought out his target, launching himself at Howe as he trucked the ball forward in the opening minutes of the match. The frightful impact of the collision left Gordie a little fuzzy upstairs and with one side of his body completely numb. According to Gordie, it was as though he'd been struck by a bolt of lightning on the point of his shoulder. 'It was like hitting a block of concrete,' Gordie said.

In contrast, Howe had barely ruffled the hair on his head.

Alarm bells should have sounded everywhere after that series. Normal bodies simply cannot do what Howe was doing across those three games. Two hit-ups each set of six, punishing tackles from start to finish. He never slowed down. Talking to Melbourne players who were at the club that year, I understand Howe actually held every single performance record available. Whether it was bench press or squats in the weights room; a 40-metre sprint or a 3-kilometre time trial; or agility and muscular endurance tests, Howe topped the rankings. It was just a few weeks after Origin III when the news came through about Howe having returned a positive reading in a random examination conducted by ASADA (Australian Sports Anti-Doping Authority) officials.

While certainly a shock, I don't know that too many of Howe's peers were surprised. Howe had enjoyed a meteoric rise over the preceding 12 months. As he tells it, he first turned to performance-enhancing drugs (PEDs) to help speed up his rehabilitation following a knee reconstruction. Clearly, he was taken by the results he got during that time and figured the potential rewards outweighed the risk and he went from being a player who was at best a fringe first-grader, to being the Blues' standout performer through the Origin series. Over that period, his body shape had undergone a dramatic transformation from that of an undersized prop forward into a musclebound powerhouse. Howe eventually admitted to using the banned anabolic steroid known as Stanozolol and was suspended from the game for 22 weeks.

There is no greater sin in professional sport than to be found guilty of such cheating. (To Howe's credit, I suppose, he battled through until the end of 2004 before hanging up the boots.) Rugby league at the highest level is a brutal and unforgiving environment which offers weekly examinations of both your physical and mental toughness. It is one of the few remaining arenas in life where a man's physical presence or stature still help determine his place within the wider community. Stature essentially comes down to the hand you are dealt by Mother Nature at birth. A man's presence, on the other hand, reflects the reputation he has forged over time.

Wayne often spoke about the reaction Cyril received whenever he entered a dressing-room. No matter which town he was in or which schoolboy side was using the room, the reaction was always the same. The room would quickly fall silent. Sound systems and iPods were stopped and conversations were put on hold so the boys could each get the chance to meet 'Mr Connell', as he was always addressed by the boys. Within the NRL's current playing ranks, players like Canberra's Alan Tongue and Preston Campbell at the Titans are illustrations of little men who command respect throughout the NRL courtesy of their willingness to consistently put their bodies on the line against much bigger men, with any thought of self-preservation a secondary consideration behind serving the best interests of the team.

Phil Gould: I have said it a number of times when Locky has hit milestones – and he has hit a number of them along the journey – the thing that stands out to me is the toughness. You don't play that many games without playing injured. I guarantee it. It may not have been advertised, but I can guarantee he has carried injuries into games. I coached Brad Fittler, who played over 300 games, and I know what he played with. Same goes for Terry Lamb. It is not well publicised, but it has got to be the same with Lockyer. There is no question about that.

Anyhow, the Storm were dismantled come finals time. The Roosters posted a big win against them in the first round of the post-season. A fortnight later and we were fairly merciless, romping to a 30–6 win to end their season. The following week it was our turn against the Roosters, the 28-point margin at full-time probably a little flattering to the tricolours, such was the dominance of possession and field position we enjoyed.

The grand final didn't throw up any surprises, much to the frustration of our friends in New South Wales. The Bulldogs fought bravely to stay in touch early and actually took a 12–10 lead into the half-time break. Unfortunately for Steve Folkes' side, there is no capacity to call a halt to proceedings at half-time and in the second 40 minutes the Broncos juggernaut slipped into gear and demolished the boys from Belmore. We crossed for five tries in the second half and I am not being arrogant when I say the 38–12 scoreline on the big day was, in my eyes, a reasonable reflection of the gap between that Broncos side and its rivals that year.

In 1999, we fell victim to the mother of all premiership hangovers, inexplicably dropping eight of the first 10 matches of the year. The low point of the run came in the aftermath of what was a dismal showing on our part against the North Queensland Cowboys in round seven. Alf, in particular, had been struggling both as a player and as captain through the early run of outs. That spark and energy he provided with his sense of humour and fun-loving attitude was nowhere to be seen. The performance against the Cowboys in the Queensland derby was the last straw for him. A couple of days later, he announced he would be retiring from the NRL effective immediately. And like that, the little champion was gone, handing the captaincy of the team over to his great friend Kevie. Under Kevie's leadership, we slowly began to drag things back on track and began rolling. From round 11 through to the end of the 26-round regular season, we were beaten only once. From last spot after 10 rounds of the competition, we somehow managed to sneak into the eighth and final play-off spot, maintaining the club's run of consecutive finals appearances dating back to 1992. The reality of our situation, though, was that we were doing little more than making up the numbers in the finals series, delaying the inevitable. We were drawn to play the Sharks on the opening weekend of the finals. Playing an exciting, expansive brand of football under coach John Lang, the boys from the Shire had clearly been the best performing team over the course of the regular season. They took home the J. J. Giltinan Shield as minor premiers for just the second time in the club's history, giving rise to hope amongst the long-suffering Sharks fans that this might indeed be their season, a drought-breaking title seemingly within their grasp. We certainly proved little challenge to them on their home ground at Shark Park, sent back to Brisbane with our tails between our legs after being trounced 42–20.

Our squad underwent a facelift in the 1999–2000 off-season, with young guns Ashley Harrison, Lote Tuqiri, Dane Carlaw, Brad Meyers and Chris Walker earning places in the senior side. Wayne also recruited established stars Ben Ikin and Harvey Howard to the club, having identified specific roles for them within the totally revamped gameplan he wanted to employ. Without Alf to steer the side around, Wayne knew things had to change. Gone were the days of ad-lib attack. In its place, Wayne implemented a far more structured offensive style, which was based around overpowering sides rather than outplaying them. Almost every player was told to pack on the kilos over the course of the pre-season. There was an increased focus on our resistance training. The intensity of the programs increased, as did the time we all spent in the club's weights room. In his planning for the 2000 season, Wayne had identified the unlimited interchange rule in place at the time as a tool he could use to great effect in developing the brand of 'power football' he had envisaged for the Broncos.

It proved to be a coaching masterstroke, with the hulking Broncos side battering opposition teams into submission. We moved into top spot on the ladder after the fourth round in season 2000 and were never seriously threatened thereafter. The minor premiership was secured with a month of football remaining in the regular season, with the final margin back to second place a more than healthy six points. There wasn't a great deal of flash about the manner in which we used the ball. The plan was simple in its design. The physicality of the team and the relentless manner in which they executed the game plan was what made it so effective. You look at the side we fielded that year and on the wings we had Lote and Wendell, who were as big and strong as any forwards in the comp. In the centres, Tunza earned his nickname courtesy of the fact he could never get his weight under three figures, while Michael De Vere tipped the scales at 96–98 kilograms. Benny Ikin was one of the strongest five-eighths in the game and weighed around 92 kilograms. Then up front in the engine room you had a monstrous rotation featuring the likes of Brad Thorn, Gorden Tallis, Shane Webcke, Dane Carlaw, Harvey Howard, Petero Civoniceva, Brad Meyers and Kevin Campion.

It was fitting that the grand final against the Roosters was a dour, rugged encounter with little in the way of free-flowing attacking movements. We were happy slugging it out over the course of 80 minutes. The moment any contest slipped into the traditional 'arm-wrestle', we felt the win was ours for the taking. No one could compete with us in a field position battle, with Wayne's superior use of the interchange ensuring the biggest, strongest forward pack in the competition was always operating at maximum output. And so it was in the decider of season 2000, a gallant Roosters side fell victim to the sledgehammer that was the Brisbane Broncos that season. I have to admit I was pleasantly surprised when I heard my name read out as the winner of the Clive Churchill Medal, as man of the match in the grand final, given we had many great contributors in our team that day. Still, it was a very nice addition to the trophy cabinet and something I treasure greatly.

Wayne Bennett: I never coached Darren . . . never had to. He had incredible instincts and natural intuition. His game sense was highly developed and the environment he came into was one which got his competitive juices flowing. The environment he arrived in with Kevie and Kerrod Walters, Pearl, Alf . . . They played tougher games against one another than what they did some weekends. Locky excelled in that environment because he is super-competitive. You won't see it but it is there.

In 1997 we had Anthony Mundine, Alf, Darren Smith, Wendell . . . You know, it was a pretty bloody good team. It was the same in 1998.

By 2000, though, he was a lot more dominant. Kevie was at the end of his career. Pearl and Alf were gone. Locky had taken on a lot more responsibility and was doing a lot more ball-playing because he was needed to do that role. That year we went about things differently . . . We just physically dominated everything around us. It was Locky who added the subtlety.

Kevin was actually out injured for much of the first half of the season. I knew I needed him back to play halfback and just guide the team around the field. I remember saying to him, 'If we can get you back on the field and keep you there, we will win the comp.' Locky was always at his best when he had a good halfback in the team.

From 2000 on, Locky was always the key. He was the go-to play – on and off the field at every level. He was the one I relied on more than anyone else.

Lying in bed at home a few days after the 2000 grand final, I had to pinch myself. In less than six years I had gone from a typical dreamy-eyed kid working behind the bar at the leagues club to being a triple-premiership-winning member of the Broncos and an incumbent member of both the Queensland State of Origin and Australian Test sides.

Lazo was right ... This really isn't that hard, I said to myself.

Just when you start to get a bit ahead of yourself with thinking like that, sport – and rugby league in particular – has a wonderful way of cutting you down to size. Over the course of the next five years, this was a lesson I would learn the hard way.

FOUR

Racetrack to Real Estate

MANAGERS ARE A part of professional sport – a necessary one. Young boys and girls looking to join the ranks of professional athletes need to focus on developing within their respective sporting fields. A manager can look after a lot of the peripheral stuff that is time-consuming and sometimes beyond the scope of the athlete themselves. Contract law with its complexities, for example, is a fairly specialised area which very few athletes of any age fully comprehend.

In rugby league, managers are also helpful in knowing market values. They have established relationships with club administrators that players do not. The good managers will help their client with securing deals outside of the game – capitalising on the short time we spend as potentially marketable figures. And they can also help protect and invest a player's earnings through his career. Given that the select few who earn relatively big bucks in the NRL generally will do so for a maximum of six or seven years, it is really important to maximise both a player's earning capacity and in turn his earnings in the time available.

I am a conservative person, so I haven't had too many blow-ups at all during my career. I know I have been lucky to earn good money and for the most part I have trusted the people I have been dealing with and have generally accepted what they have told me about what they can afford and what might be out there for me should I decide to explore other options. I am fortunate to have a really solid relationship with my manager, George Mimis. I was one of his first clients and he has been there every step of the way. The important factor from my side has been that I have always been comfortable in the belief George has worked hard for me and that he has had my best interests at heart when advising me on a decision.

Now, that doesn't always mean following the money. Development as a footballer and as a person are considerations which are as important as, if not more important than, the financial rewards at one club or another. Unfortunately, too many managers in our game are far more concerned with lining their own pockets and simply steer their player towards the biggest deal. They take their commission and that is the last time they are seen until that contract is up for renewal.

That isn't what it is about and as a game we need to protect our talented young kids from getting caught up with people who are simply there to prosper off the hard work of someone else. I know the NRL has brought in measures whereby player agents must be accredited with a central body. But I don't know how much monitoring they do of what is happening out there in the world of the NRL player market. Surely there is something the NRL can implement as part of the accreditation process which stipulates certain expectations managers must meet with regard to the welfare of their clientele. It should be part of a player–manager registration that both parties have to sign, and if a manager fails to meet the standards of that agreement they should run the risk of losing the right to represent any player in the NRL.

I arrived at the Broncos on a deal which saw me paid a lump sum of $2000 and given a job at the club which paid around $200 a week. However, by the middle of 1995, I had broken into first-grade where I earned $1500 a win before tax. I was excited to have made the step up and to have increased my modest earnings along the way.

At the end of that year, I signed a new deal. Helping me with it was a guy by the name of Peter Hickey. He was just a businessman I had crossed paths with who had offered to assist with the negotiations. I met George not all that long after. He had flown to Brisbane and basically came up to me and my parents at the club one day and introduced himself. He asked if I had official representation from a player manager. I explained that an associate had helped me with the deal and George asked if he could see it.

Now he didn't laugh, but he raised his eyebrows and after a bit of a pause told me straight that I should be earning significantly more than I was being paid. At the same time, he asked me if I had any commercial agreements outside, which I hadn't even considered. He told me he could secure me a deal worth double what I was being paid by the club and could also get me a sponsorship deal with Nike. As an impressionable 19-year-old, I liked what I was hearing, but was still wary. I gave him my number and told him that if he could deliver on those promises I would gladly agree to join the small group of players represented by his fledgling sports management company.

George Mimis: I remember sitting at home watching the Broncos and Eels play. I think it was the second half when they brought this kid on – Darren Lockyer. I am watching this and thinking, 'Who is this kid?' So I rang Darryl Mather, who runs our recruitment, and asked him if he had heard of this kid from Brisbane, Darren Lockyer. He said he hadn't and I just told him the kid looked something special. So I rang around and tracked down Darren's contact details.

I arranged to meet him and his parents at Broncos Leagues Club and chatted generally about his professional endeavours. He was receiving advice from a gentleman who wasn't a mainstream agent. He had some sort of formal arrangement in place, but the terms of the commercial arrangement he had with Brisbane weren't great. I also saw enormous scope for leveraging his obvious ability and aligning him with brands, though, if I am being honest, at that point in time I was probably selling him the potential rather than the ironclad deals. Anyhow, I was intent on getting Locky to sign on with us, so I made contact with Peter Hickey and offered him a small payment to release him. He agreed straightaway and immediately released Darren from their relationship.

Not long before that I had caught up with Steve Crowe, who was the marketing manager for Nike in Australia at the time. I met up with him again after meeting with Darren. It was in the Sydney Airport and I proposed Darren to Steve for Nike. I said, 'Steve, you have got to see this kid I have just signed by the name of Darren Lockyer. He is out of this world.' I told him if he was going to take my word on any one player in the NRL to make it in a big way, this was the one. And so sitting there in the Sydney Airport, he agreed to a deal on my advice.

The original deal was largely merchandise-based, but that quickly changed to the point that by about 1998 Darren was the highest-paid Nike athlete in rugby league and continued to be so through to the end of his career.

So, from an income perspective, Darren essentially went from a bag of nothing to something pretty significant in a very short space of time.

My first real investment was buying the family home in Roma in early 1997. Mum and Dad had run into a bit of trouble with the convenience store they were running at

Miles. With my brothers and I still in high school, Dad was forced to continue to live near the store from Monday to Friday, returning home on the weekends. Mum was working as well, but was always at home to look after her three boys, cooking, cleaning, and taking us wherever we needed to go after school. It probably wasn't until shortly before I left home that I began to comprehend just how much my parents sacrificed and how hard they worked to provide us boys with every opportunity a kid could wish for.

To be able to give a little something back at a time of need – it was the least I could do.

David Lockyer: We had got into a bit of strife with our business at Miles. It was back at a time when the interest rates were crazy – double figures. Anyhow, I just ran the business wrongly. I needed to have the family there with me, helping out. That was the only way it was going to be a success. In hindsight, it was never going to work having me running down there and running it with hired staff. I was forking out so much in wages we just couldn't even make a dent in our bills.

Sharon Lockyer: I burst into tears when Darren told us he was going to buy the family home. I felt bad as a parent that my child felt he had to do that. It was his money and I didn't want him to think he was obligated to use it to help us out. But at the same time I was a bit overwhelmed. I was so proud of the man he was becoming – and has become.

It gave us the breathing space we needed to get things back on track. But more importantly it allowed us to stay in Roma for the final years of Matt and Russell's schooling. What we went through during that period before Darren was able to help us out … it isn't something we like to talk about. It was really tough and as a family we struggled under that pressure at times.

Like so many other aspects of my life, I got my first taste of the stock market through Wayne. Coach arranged for his personal broker to come and address the team about investment and he touched on a number of potential winners, as he saw it. He pushed the impending Telstra share float as an option definitely worth our strong consideration. I went away and did a little research myself before I bought in. I followed the progress of those few shares compulsively, watching every bump and dip. While clearly unnecessary, my obsessive approach allowed me to quickly get my head around the 'fundamentals' of the stock market – the different terms, what the different indexes and figures meant, what to look for when evaluating stock options, and so on. That education process has been ongoing in the years since. As my understanding and appreciation of the stock market has gradually improved, so too has my interest and enjoyment in that world increased. Most mornings I will browse the *Australian Financial Review* before running an eye over the big Business section in *The Australian*.

I made a bit of money with my first foray into shares, which I used to build up my portfolio. Generally I am rather cautious or conservative in my approach to most things in life, but especially when it has something to do with money. The dot com boom had sent the world's markets haywire. Tiny internet-based companies were taking off and crashing at an equal rate of knots. It was just ridiculous. Getting on a winner became akin to getting a tip on the horses, at least in my eyes at that point in time.

I remember coming into training and Kevie would be there clapping his hands: 'Okay, boys, who are we getting on today?' The only difference was instead of going to a bookmaker and picking a number, we'd be picking some obscure info-tech company whose balance sheets were rubbish. By the end of 2000, though, the boom had turned bust and the fun and games were over.

Thankfully I hadn't invested too heavily in the internet phenomenon, but I still learned a valuable lesson. Well, it was more a reminder that things don't come easy in life. Nothing is free and if something appears too good to be true, it probably is. Nowadays my portfolio is loaded with 'Blue Chip' stocks – the value of which became evident during the economic downturn which struck in 2008. While the value of my mining shares was slashed in half at one stage, they rebounded faster and stronger than I anticipated. As I have been told more than once, when you are dealing in Blue Chip stocks it is more about time in the market than timing in the market.

I only ever used money my shares had made to have a bit of a play or a punt on the stock market. As is the case with most punting, I won a couple, lost a couple more and had some great stories about the one I just missed. Gambling was certainly nothing new to me. The old man was an enthusiastic punter and I spent many an afternoon at the racetrack or TAB when I was growing up. Mostly Dad was into the horses, but like plenty of Australian men he would happily take a tip on most horse races and I learned by observation.

When I arrived at the Broncos in 1995, I was of the understanding that the weekly form guide was, in fact, compulsory reading and that it was the done thing to head down to the track and have a punt basically whenever I wasn't training or playing. Certainly the environment I encountered upon my arrival at the Broncos did little to dissuade me from these beliefs. Alf and Wendell's love of a punt is well known, but Kevin and Kerrod Walters, the Walker brothers, and Michael Hancock also enjoyed a day at the track. So gambling was a popular topic of conversation around the club, which I joined into because I already knew a bit about horses – or so I told myself.

I became part of the group down at the track and went through the whole routine for more than a year before things came to a head for me. I had gone from being a country kid dropping five bucks each way on a couple of races, to putting $500 or more on different races around the country. It took a run of outs for me to finally confront the fact that I had a bit of a problem which needed addressing before it spiralled out of control.

I got home after the last time and was just shattered. I was a wreck, stressed out and angry and significantly out of pocket. That night I went for a run, to try to clear my head. I started running over things in my head. A couple of people at the club had raised some concerns about my punting – concerns I had tried to brush aside at the time. Now, though, I was asking myself why I was doing it in the first place. Was I just doing it to try to win cash? Or was there some other element that attracted me to that sort of setting? I came to the conclusion pretty quickly that this wasn't a hobby or a pastime I actually enjoyed. Nor was it one that in any way added something positive to my life. When I lost, it wrecked my day, sometimes my week, depending on how big a hit I had taken.

I worked out that my motivation was largely to do with trying to make money. But, given I was already being very well looked after playing football, there was simply no need for me to be looking to make a quick buck elsewhere. When I weighed up the potential upside of winning some cash against the stress and angst I encountered when things didn't go so well – which was more often than not . . .

Well, let's face it, there is a reason they are called punters. The fact is, when a race day ends they are the ones catching the train home. The bookies' biggest concern is making sure the leather seats in the family Jaguar are warmed adequately before they start their journey.

So, just like that, I pulled the pin and told the group I wouldn't be heading to the track with them. I wanted to see if there was something I missed about not being there with my mates. It didn't take long before the answer to that question became abundantly clear. Put succinctly, I didn't miss it at all. Life was so much less stressful not poring over the form guide every Friday and my weekends improved 1000 per cent because I wasn't losing money at the races.

I haven't looked back. I will have a punt at a pub if I am in a group that is having a bit of a novelty bet, but I am not interested in revisiting that life again.

Sharon Lockyer: There was only one time after he left home that we felt the need to ring Wayne and speak to him about what Darren was getting himself caught up in and that was when we felt his betting on the horses was getting a bit out of control. We were worried he was getting mixed up with some of the older guys at the club who were at a different stage in their personal and professional lives than Darren was. A couple of people had raised it with us and I could tell something had been on his mind, so things added up.

But we just felt a bit helpless being so far away. So I rang Wayne and asked him to do what he had to do to get Darren out of that crowd. I left it at that. I actually rang George (Mimis) as well and I know he flew up to Brisbane to see Darren. I don't know what was said, but I know Darren was himself very soon after that.

I must confess I kept a small link to my punting past via a stake I purchased in a racehorse by the name of Vietnam. There was a perception out there that I was a significant figure in the horse's career, however nothing could be further from the truth. I paid $500 for a 10 per cent stake and that was about the extent of my involvement. I was happy for the stable to use my profile to get some exposure, thinking I would have been satisfied to get out all-square. Well, in this case I was happy to be a long way off the mark. Against all odds, Vietnam collected six wins and was runner-up five times in 25 starts, amassing more than $360 000 in prizemoney.

As was the case with Vietnam, there have been widespread misconceptions about my business dealings over the years, particularly in relation to my role in the ownership structure and daily operations of a number of bars, clubs and restaurants around Brisbane. The reality is I was a minority shareholder in the venues and again was largely there for publicity, able to use my profile to get some exposure in the media and within the community itself.

My involvement with the different establishments was through the majority owner, Lyal Midgley, whom I'd known since our days together in Roma. Lyal had had some success taking over some old country pubs and modernising them. He was keen to try his luck in Brisbane and, after a lengthy search, settled on an old building in Caxton Street as the ideal place to start. The position was sensational and, while the renovation was a big job, when it was all done 'Ice Bar' on Caxton Street was a really nice-looking venue when it opened its doors in late 2003.

Knowing how restricted I was in terms of the man-hours I could commit to any business venture, I was a very minor partner in the business. What was valuable in that arrangement was the chance to see first-hand what it takes to run a business like a bar, particularly in relation to man-management with staff. Lyal ended up rolling out a couple of other 'Ice Bars' around Brisbane.

As Lyal turned his attention elsewhere, what did appeal to me was the actual property there on Caxton Street and I eventually purchased it from Lyal, which gave me sole freehold ownership of the building. I had a couple of different tenants redesign the bar. However, running a bar held very little appeal for me and as I write this I am undertaking plans to upgrade the block.

Given my nature, it probably comes as no surprise that property development is something I enjoy. To me, it is a bit like a puzzle. You need to go out and find a site that fits your requirements. To do that you need a bit of vision. You need to see through what might be in front of you and be able to see what it could be. I currently have some property that I am planning to develop, but I am in no hurry. All that sort of thing will be there waiting for me once my playing days come to an end.

I have never been the type of guy to put all my eggs in one basket, whether we are talking about playing a game of football, trading on the stock market or learning the ropes of property development. I am a big believer in the notion that you must pay your dues in life if you are going to achieve meaningful, long-term success. Nothing in football or life comes easily, and the one stand-out factor I have learned is that hard work is esssential for any level of success.

That means knowing and accepting your limitations and staying in touch with reality. My main aim over the past few years has been building a solid nest egg for me and my family. If I can provide for my family and generally be comfortable with what I am doing work-wise, that is essentially all I am looking for. I am conscious of never forgetting the principle of needing to work hard for whatever I earn in life. I never want to lose sight of that, because aside from anything else I never want to lose that motivation for life that only comes through contributing to something bigger.

I just want to be happy knowing I am doing something worthwhile with my time. Top of that list is raising a good family, contributing to the community and having a well-balanced life.

FIVE

The Pinnacle

'Of all his achievements in the game, probably the greatest legacy he will leave behind is what he has done re-instilling pride in the Kangaroos jumper.'
– Wayne Bennett

THE MOST REWARDING feeling I have experienced in my career has been in those few moments after winning a grand final. State of Origin evokes a different sort of passion. The ferocity of the Queensland–New South Wales rivalry is unrelenting and it is the toughest football I have experienced. There is an incredible sense of satisfaction which comes with victory in such an arena. But given Queensland's emotional attachment to these games, I have also felt an enormous sense of relief whenever I have been lucky enough to be part of a win.

But to pull on the green and gold jumper for Australia; to stand alongside 16 team-mates linked arm-in-arm and belt out the national anthem; to have the chance to lead the mighty Kangaroos squad – nothing can compete with the sense of pride that comes with such honours. I feel so humbled to have had the chance to represent what I consider to be the greatest country on Earth. To imagine I have captained my country more than any other player in the history of the game is difficult to put into words how much that means to me.

Being handed the Test captaincy by Chris Anderson back in 2003 not only changed me as a footballer, it changed my life in general. It probably took me a couple of years to fully comprehend the significance of the title. But the gravitas of the captaincy tag was something I grew to understand and respect enormously. I don't mind saying that I worked really hard to lift my standards and those expected of a Kangaroos skipper with a view to one day matching those of the Australian cricket captain or Wallabies skipper. A lot of the little things I adopted over the years were taken from what I had noticed either Ricky Ponting or George Gregan doing in their respective leadership roles. Their presentation, demeanour on and off the field and the statesmanlike authority with which they addressed all matters within their game are traits both men maintained throughout their time as captain. They are little things I became conscious of over time – little things I realised were so very crucial in upholding standards both within rugby league circles and in the wider community, about what the office of the captain of the Australian Kangaroos stands for.

For me, the Australian captain should be a beacon. He should be out there setting an example for every other player in the NRL to follow.

Injury and form prevailing, my career will finish at the completion of the Four Nations tournament in Great Britain at the end of 2011. If we were once again able to qualify for the final, it would take my final captaincy tally to 40 matches. If you had told me that was where my Test career would finish in the hours after my first taste of international football, I would have offered you the cab fare back to the nearest asylum for the insane.

My Test debut was memorable for all the wrong reasons. It is in the grand final for the worst game in my career. In fact, I think you'd go a long way to find a worse Test debut than my effort coming off the bench against the Kiwis in the 1998 Anzac Test. Played in typically crappy conditions at North Harbour Stadium, it was one of those games where things started badly for me and the harder I tried to do something even remotely constructive the worse it got. I had come on after Robbie O'Davis was injured early. My first involvement was poor – a dropped ball. It proved to be a sign of things to come. I wouldn't expect to drop as many balls in a season as I did that night. I had hands like feet – spilling bombs, fumbling grubbers. I got rag-dolled attempting to pull down a couple of the Kiwis' rampaging forwards. It was embarrassing.

I saw Wendell once describe it as the 'worst debut of any player at any level'. When you consider that sort of assessment has come from one of my best friends, it paints a picture for how truly woeful I was that night. That the scoreline finished 22–16 just added salt to the wound. I had literally lost my side a Test match. When I got back into the dressing-room I couldn't bring myself to look coach Bob Fulton in the eye. I already had a taste of international football playing for Australia in the Super League Tests – Test fixtures which for some reason are not included on the playing records of any of those who competed – but here I was living out a childhood dream, pulling on the famous green and gold jersey of the Kangaroos and all I could think of was that I should take extra special care with the team kit I had received at the start of the camp because it would almost certainly be the only lot I would ever receive.

I got a few pats on the back and Bob made a point of coming over to me after the match and offering some reassurance. But I had been around football long enough to know I had let a lot of people down. As I tend to do when I feel like people are out to get me, or even when I know in my own heart I have let myself down in one way or another, I withdrew from the group to think about what had gone wrong and how and when I was going to fix it. I barely said a word to anyone on the flight home, but in the hours before the plane touched down in Brisbane I had made my mind up about a number of things. As bitterly disappointed as I was with the Test match, it was done, there was nothing I could do now that would change what had happened, so when I arrived back at the Broncos I did so with my mind totally clear.

I have never been one for self-pity and I certainly am not someone who seeks comfort from others. Everyone has their issues and problems, everyone makes mistakes . . . Deal with it. When life knocks you down or you fall flat on your face, the only thing you can do is pick yourself up, dust yourself off, put one foot in front of the other and get going again.

There was only a 48-hour turnaround between the Test match and the Broncos club game against North Sydney at ANZ Stadium, but on this occasion I could not have been happier. While the body had some bumps and bruises, the 48-hour window was long enough to allow me time to digest what had happened in New Zealand and move on, but not so long that the negative emotions I was carrying following my Test debut could begin to filter back into my mind. Both Wayne and Craig Bellamy pulled me aside at different times during the team's final training run just to see where my head was at and whether there were any signs suggesting that my confidence was shot. I was adamant that wasn't the case, but could see that Craig, especially, had his doubts.

Wayne Bennett: I remember he came back to training on the Saturday. He had just flown back in and we were playing the next day. I grabbed him because I knew the media would be all over him. I just said to him that while he'd had a bad night, that wasn't him. I was walking down the field with him and I just reiterated the point – that game wasn't who he was or who he is. I remember being struck with how calm he seemed and how positive he was about playing the next day. It really impressed me and I took note. He told me he'd had a bad night and had no intention of ever letting it happen again. Sometimes you hear players say those sorts of things and you can see straight through it. They are just trying to say the right things. Not with Locky. He doesn't talk a great deal, Locky. When he does, he doesn't bother wasting words telling people what he thinks they want to hear. So when I heard that from him, that was good enough for me. I never brought it up again. I never needed to.

Craig Bellamy: One thing about Darren Lockyer is he doesn't tolerate fools. He has no time for them. And generally it takes a while for people to get his trust. I certainly found that. He is always polite and well-mannered but it takes time to earn his trust and respect. I know in my roles up there as performance director and then as assistant coach – I mean, I just don't know that Locky believed in what I was saying for a while there.

I think that's a good thing, though. He doesn't waste his time with people who are just going to stroke his ego or say what they think he would want them to.

Locky is his own hardest marker, so he knows if someone is bullshitting him. He doesn't need that, because he is smart enough and strong enough mentally to see if there is something he needs to address and then to go about addressing it.

I remember he had just had one of those foul nights that can happen for no good reason whatsoever. That it happened to him is a little reassuring because you can say with some confidence that they genuinely do happen to the best of us. It was a shocker.

I still remember him coming back and preparing for the game we had against North Sydney. I was actually thinking to myself, 'Geez, should we really be playing this kid?' Fullback is such a crucial position and there is probably no position on the field where you would have greater trouble overcoming a crisis of confidence. I actually mentioned it to Wayne and suggested we give Locky the weekend just to get his mind right. I just thought for a 21-year-old kid in his Test debut . . . I just figured there might be some baggage there.

Wayne was really confident though. He just kept telling me, 'He'll be fine, mate, he'll be fine.'

He said, 'It won't be an issue; he's a bit different, this one.'

I was still in two minds right up until kick-off. Over the next 80 minutes, Locky put on an absolute clinic. We won by 50. Locky was everywhere; they couldn't get near him. He won man of the match . . . I reckon if I had been doing the votes he might have got three, two and one.

But that effort showed me he had the will – the mental toughness – to match what we could all see was world-class athleticism and very special football-ing instincts. For a young bloke to do that . . .

It's indicative of what he has done throughout his career. It typifies the quality of the bloke.

Bob stepped down as Australian coach a short time after the mid-season Test, citing personal reasons. During his nine years in charge of the national team, the Kangaroos won 37 of the 45 Tests they played, with one draw. I still feel bad about the fact that such an outstanding career ended in such a manner and was genuinely concerned I might have blown my shot at that level.

Wayne Bennett: Given I took over from Bob, that wasn't ever something he needed to worry about. Locky was always one of those guys who was so outstanding people went looking for faults and, when they managed to find something once in a while, would sweat on it. I knew that wasn't him and to be honest I have always considered Bob Fulton to be one of the finest judges of football talent I have met. He was no fool when it came time to identifying the best of the best. So I don't imagine he would have been putting a line through anyone's name on the basis of one poor debut. Bob has seen enough football to know you don't do that.

Wayne stayed in the job long enough to help Alf complete a premiership–Origin–Test series treble as captain in 1998. Chris Anderson took over as Australian coach and had wonderful success during his four years in the job. He took a very relaxed approach. While we always worked hard on the training track under Opes (Chris Anderson), he was a firm believer in ensuring the boys let their hair down at the end of the day.

The 2000 World Cup was the first major tour I had under Opes and it was a hell of an experience. The Australian squad was: Trent Barrett (St George Illawarra), Darren Britt (Bulldogs), Jason Croker (Canberra), Brad Fittler (Sydney Roosters, captain), Bryan Fletcher (Sydney Roosters), Matthew Gidley (Newcastle), Ryan Girdler (Penrith), Craig Gower (Penrith), Scott Hill (Melbourne), Nathan Hindmarsh (Parramatta), Andrew Johns (Newcastle), Robbie Kearns (Melbourne), Ben Kennedy (Newcastle), Brett Kimmorley (Melbourne), Darren Lockyer (Brisbane), Adam MacDougall (Newcastle), Mat Rogers (Sharks), Wendell Sailor (Brisbane), Jason Stevens (Sharks), Gorden Tallis (Brisbane, vice-captain), Michael Vella (Parramatta), Shane Webcke (Brisbane).

In reality, the 16-team tournament was dominated by just a few teams. In our final 'group' match we ended up beating Russia, 110–4. Now, you won't find a bigger supporter of the international game than me. And I am a huge believer in having emerging nations involved in the international schedule. On the field we ran through the competition with relative ease. Despite this imbalance, it is still vital for the development of the game beyond the traditional strongholds.

Off the field ... well, it was a very different climate to the one in which players exist in 2011. We had blokes like Darren Britt, Jason Croker and Bryan Fletcher who were throwbacks to the 'old school'. They could pull up a seat and down beers with ease but always back it up by giving 100 per cent at training and in games. I shared a room with Trent Barrett for that tour and I want to put on the record that he was a little bit tidier than the room-mate I got handed for my first tour.

Andrew Johns: The first time I ever really met Locky was when we went to New Zealand in 1998. He was my room-mate, so I got to know him very well and we clicked pretty quickly. That said, if you can't get on with Locky you are pretty much struggling to find friends. We had a great time. I really enjoyed his company, though I got the feeling he was pretty happy when the tour was over and he no longer had to deal with the stress of having his pristine, perfectly ordered environment in such close proximity to my mess. Of course, where he sees a messy pile steadily growing in both height and diameter, I like to think I have things under control . . . organised chaos. I guess we were the resident odd couple, but we certainly had a good time.

Not many people get to know the real Darren Lockyer. I know when my mates ask what Darren Lockyer is like I always say he is sensational company. He is really funny. He loves a beer (or a vodka) and more than that he loves a dance when he has had a few. You always knew when Locky was in for a big one when he moved on to the dance floor. But he doesn't let people see that side of him unless he is in an environment where he is comfortable and isn't concerned about doing something which has the potential to be taken or twisted into something potentially offensive or damaging to the game. I found he let his guard down a lot more when we were overseas and he was out of the spotlight. But I can't really tell you too many stories about him. Like they say, what goes on tour, stays on tour. All I can say is I have had some very funny nights out with Locky and most of them revolve around dancing and dressing in women's clothes.

People who only know the Darren Lockyer they see on TV most of the time probably think he is dry and very serious. It is the discipline he has maintained for a long time now. I reckon it probably stemmed from the reaction when he made a blue early in his career. It's easy to remember, because it was the only one he made and he got carved up by the media. Some of the criticism was a bit over the top.

I hold myself responsible for the mistake Joey refers to. I was sent a text message with the joke just as I was heading into a corporate luncheon at which I was speaking. It was early March and the off-colour joke suggested the Bulldogs' premiership chances in 2004 had skyrocketed on the back of the realisation that the Dragons had won 11 in a row with only one (John) 'Raper' in the team – so imagine what the Bulldogs could do. In February all hell had broken loose when a young woman claimed to have been sexually assaulted by some Bulldogs players at the team hotel in Coffs Harbour. While the allegations were dismissed a few months later, at the time I made this joke, the investigation was in its infancy and the damage done to the game still very raw. My reign as Test captain had barely got off the ground, but immediately after the words had come out of my mouth I was hit by a wave of embarrassment and dismay. I assumed it was only a matter of time before the powers that be would deem it to have been a failed experiment.

When you are doing interviews at those sorts of functions, it is not unusual to have about half the crowd chatting amongst themselves rather than listening to anything that might be going on up the front of the room. While I had become pretty comfortable with media conferences and the like, I still wasn't at ease addressing big groups like that. I am certainly not trying to make an excuse but, given the way I just sort of blurted it out, I think it was probably a case of some nerves or anxiety momentarily getting the better of my brain. So when I said it, there were some pockets of laughter but the overwhelming reaction was the mixture of exasperated sighs and disapproving groans which you associate with the proverbial 'lead balloon' response. I got really nervous. I actually started to get the sweats up on stage – I just couldn't believe what I had done. Part of what makes up the overriding fear of failure which has driven me throughout my career is the paranoia I feel when I am embarrassed in public. Sitting on the stage, I was glancing round the room at people, certain they were all looking at and whispering about me.

As soon as I got off-stage I was greeted by a less than impressed Tony Durkin, who was the Broncos' media manager at the time. He just shook his head and said,

'Mate . . . not good. You are going to have to speak to the media and explain yourself.'

I agreed and told him to give me some time to just get myself together. I obviously wanted to apologise to anyone I had offended, but I wanted to do it properly. By the time I got down to my car I had replayed the whole thing over and still couldn't figure out what on Earth possessed me to say something like that. I started to think about the number of people I would have upset. The Raper family, obviously, and I could only imagine what the young lady involved in the situation at Coffs Harbour would have thought having me trivialise her feelings like that. More broadly, it was offensive to women in general and I just started to think about my mum and grandmother and everything they had done to help me. I felt awful that they would have to hear about it on the news again and again. They had raised me to be better than that. I knew I had let them down badly.

Sharon Lockyer: Darren rang me on the way home from the function and I could tell immediately something was wrong. He is normally so calm, but this time I could hear in his voice that he was worried about something. I said, 'Darren what's wrong? What's happened?'

He told me he had said something he shouldn't have.

He said, 'Mum, I am so sorry. The media is all over me and this is going to be in the papers and on TV for a little while.'

He was still a very young man and, while I know he shouldn't have said what he did, it was a silly mistake. There certainly wasn't any malice in it. I know he learned a lesson from it. He was always private. That is the way he is. But definitely after that he was conscious of the ramifications of everything he did and said. He was the Australian captain, so there was no escaping it. He just began to take much more care with what he told to different people. I suppose he became more guarded.

After assisting to establish the end-of-season Tri Series in a bid to help resurrect international rugby league, Wayne took over as coach of the Kangaroos in 2004 and immediately set about addressing some obvious issues with the game at that level. As much as I loved playing under Opes and rated him very highly as a representative coach, it took Wayne's arrival for some prestige to return to the Kangaroos jumper. Before then we were paid a $100 a day on Kangaroo tours and that was it. The team kit consisted of some training gear and the playing attire. That was it. There wasn't even a team photo on most occasions. It was more like a country team from Roma heading overseas to play some games, as opposed to Australia's national rugby league team.

When Wayne became national coach, that all changed. We were suited up properly. There was a team tie and other uniform clothing, so that, if nothing else, we at least looked like a team. Wayne brought some of the history back into the jersey. Since that time, the green and gold Kangaroos jumper has slowly but surely begun to reclaim the esteem in which it was once held. Players these days no longer take the option of undergoing off-season surgery straightaway if they can do so after a Kangaroo Tour. The fans have embraced the growing rivalry between Australia and New Zealand, who have emerged as a legitimate challenger. In fact, given their success in the Tri Series in 2005 and 2010 and in the World Cup in 2008, most Kiwis could present a reasonable argument that they are, in fact, already the world's best rugby league team.

The relaxed atmosphere of the previous tours also changed dramatically when Wayne took over. He had us take guided tours of a number of historic sites. We were guests at numerous functions and generally took a more professional and disciplined approach. After we romped to the 2004 title, Wayne's reign as Test coach ended in unbefitting circumstances, with the loss in the 2005 Tri Series final compounded by his infamous side door escape from the media awaiting his arrival in Brisbane afterwards.

In recognition of his rapid ascension in the ranks of National Rugby League coaches, former Canberra Raiders star and dual international, Ricky Stuart, was appointed to replace Wayne. I knew very little of Ricky outside of what I had heard from the boys from the Roosters when we were touring. I remember watching him as a player and even played a handful of games against him in his final couple of seasons of first-grade, which he spent at the Bulldogs. He had moved into coaching with immediate success, guiding the Bulldogs Jersey Flegg side to the 2001 premiership. Taking nothing away from Ricky, he had a reasonably talented bunch at his disposal including Johnathan Thurston, Rocky Elsom, Roy Asotasi, Matt Utai, Corey Hughes and Glenn Hall.

In 2002, he was appointed Roosters head coach, replacing Graham Murray. Again he enjoyed immediate success – with the likes of Brad Fittler, Craig Fitzgibbon, Luke Ricketson, Adrian Morley, Michael Crocker, Jason Cayless and Chris Flannery thriving under Ricky's high-octane and physical game plan. The Roosters were grand finalists in 2003 and 2004 before things started to slide away quickly. Ricky, though, continued to excel, guiding Country to a win over City in 2004 and helping the Blues to a come-from-behind series win in the 2005 State of Origin series.

Still, while I had no doubts about Ricky's ability, I was a little concerned about the way the Roosters had apparently simply run out of legs in 2005. After three years of relentless intensity in their training and game style, the players simply had nothing left.

We first met early in 2006 following the annual Broncos–Roosters match on Good Friday. Ricky had rung up to invite me for a beer at the Clovelly Pub to more or less break the ice and have a chat about his ideas for the role of Kangaroos coach. I could tell from that first encounter how driven he was not just to win, but to do a good job as Test coach and leave a bit of a blueprint for the future. I could see how passionate he was and it was a passion he brought to the job.

For the most part, it was a real positive. Unfortunately, though, it was also probably his undoing. In contrast to Opes, Ricky is really intense and expects his players to be similarly focused when they're out on the training track.

There was once during the 2006 Tri Series when Petero and I actually went and spoke to him about how much work we were doing, because it was starting to take its toll on some of the squad. The great thing about Ricky is he loves his players and he took on board what Petero and I had to say and wound things back just a touch. When we spoke, I remember him saying to us that come game day we should be jumping out of our skin, wanting to get out there. He told us that if ever that wasn't happening to speak to him immediately. I was really impressed with his openness and knew in that moment he was a coach I would always want to play for.

In the end, we reclaimed the Tri Series in spectacular fashion against the Kiwis. It was six minutes into extra time when Johnathan Thurston sliced through the New Zealand defence, courtesy of his patented 'show and go, baby'. I was actually outside him and started to push forward. I just had this feeling he was going to go through and I wanted to be there in support if that happened. I must say I didn't expect to be only 30 metres out from the tryline with no one ahead of me when JT was finally rounded up. All the hard work had been done, and I simply finished things off. It was a hell of a way to finish what had been a huge year for me personally and professionally. It was a long time before anyone was able to wipe the smile off my face. For one of the few times in my life, I felt content and satisfied that my world was pretty close to perfect and all the hard work had paid off.

Ricky Stuart: I hear people talk these days about blokes in the game who are tough and inevitably it is because they have thrown a few punches or can fight a bit and don't mind getting in a stink. That's not tough to me. Tough to me is a bloke who can play under fatigue . . . who can push himself when he has nothing left in the tank. I call it 'tough energy' and no one is able to draw on that tough energy when he is under fatigue like Darren Lockyer. Blokes who'd criticise him for missing one tackle here or there simply don't know the game. He is the toughest bloke – physically and mentally – I have ever come across.

If you watch a replay and you see where Locky came from to score that try in the final in 2006 . . . He ran 60 metres just to be in support of JT. This is after 86 minutes of high-pressure football. Your legs are heavy, your stomach is burning. But he pushed the pain to one side to do what the team needed. Now to me THAT is f***ing tough. It's a hell of a lot tougher than getting in a blue and belting someone. When you are absolutely spent and screaming out for oxygen and you have to sprint half a field just to get there to be an option . . . that's tough.

And that's the sort of bloke you want to follow. It is a big part of Locky's leadership. His team-mates love him because he will give absolutely everything he has for the good of the team. There is no player I have coached that I trusted more than Locky when it came to making team decisions. He never made a selfish decision. Everything he did was in the best interests of the team.

The happiest I have ever seen Locky was when he rolled up there on the outside of JT to score that try. And it was the day after that Locky and I were able to sit down and for the first time I felt as though he unwound and opened up a bit. I think that afternoon Locky began to believe a bit more of what I was preaching. It took me till then to gain his trust.

Continuing what Wayne started, Ricky did a wonderful job recognising the traditions of the past and addressing some of the things we may consider relatively minor but that play a significant part in the overall experience which should accompany the honour of representing the Kangaroos. Standing arm-in-arm before the Test and making sure we all sing the national anthem, for instance, were things Ricky said were expected of teams representing our great country.

During the 2008 World Cup, Ricky also introduced a team creed. It was something he had run past me months earlier and I was all for it. The idea was for this creed to be something special to be shared by the players following a win, similar to what the Australian cricket team do after winning a Test. Ricky employed Rupert McCall to pen the verses, which Ricky said should be read out by the captain to his team in the moments after a match before anyone else came into the dressing-room. It was meant to be something special for the players to share just amongst themselves and was to be a gentle reminder of who we are, who we represent, what we stand for and what legacy we have inherited and should pass on.

The first time we planned to read it out was prior to the 2008 World Cup final. Of course, as we all know, the Kiwis, with a touch of brilliance from Benji, some questionable referee decisions and more than a hint of Wayne Bennett's influence, upset us in front of a packed house at Suncorp Stadium. It is a result that ranks as one of the most disappointing of my career.

It was the first Test match we lost under Ricky and while as a team we were not at our best, there was no escaping the fact that I was extremely disappointed with one particular play of mine during the match. Everyone remembers Billy Slater's errant pass late in the match, but it was my fumble in the first half that ensured the Kiwis were able to stay in the game. We were up 12–0 when Cam put a little grubber through for me. I was coming through on an outside-in angle and was right there. The try was at my mercy and I let it slip through my fingers.

Not much went our way that night, though we didn't help our cause with our error rate. Looking back there are so many 'what ifs'. We changed some aspects of our preparation that week. We had dinners and official jersey presentations. Ricky was driving the parochial theme hard, which was what led to the decision to walk forward to meet the Kiwis as they did the Haka pre-match. All of it was designed to have us peaking for the 80 minutes of the game, but I wonder now whether we overdid it a little bit. We had the talent. It was a game we should have won and the loss cut deep. It played on my mind throughout the off-season. In fact, it still irks me just thinking about it now.

As much as what we did wrong, the other defining aspect was Wayne's influence on the result. Much to the chagrin of many, Wayne had accepted an offer to assist rookie Kiwi coach Stephen Kearney and, without wanting to take too much away from Mooks, the performance of the New Zealand side in the final had Wayne's fingerprints all over it. He is the master at getting his teams through the pressures of a big build-up and clearly Wayne helped build the self-belief amongst Benji's boys. It felt strange seeing him in the midst of their celebrations, wearing a black shirt.

Wayne Bennett: Coaching against Locky was really weird for me and I made a conscious decision I needed to block him out of my thinking when I was working with the New Zealand team. Any player I have coached for an extended period is off-limits in team meetings. I never talk about them, outside of offering something like, 'Darren Lockyer is extremely good at this or very good at that' – that is it. I will never talk negatively about them and if there is a weakness I am aware of, I keep it to myself. I have too much respect for someone like Darren Lockyer to start doing that sort of rubbish. One thing I did realise coaching against Locky, I just never relax. You can't because, no matter what the score is, I know he is out there doing everything he can to get his team home and no one could steer a team home under difficult circumstances like Locky.

That World Cup win – that was fate, because if Locky had scored that try to put Australia up 16–0 it was probably game over. Now, Locky never makes mistakes. His hands are as good as anyone who has ever played the game, but on this occasion the ball bobbled out of his grasp and it was game on again.

But I think it is worth noting that with three minutes to go the bloke there driving Australia and pushing them was Darren Lockyer. Jeremy Smith pulled off one of the great defensive efforts in the dying minutes to prevent Locky scoring and turning the game back in the Kangaroos' favour.

The disappointment of the loss was compounded the next day when Ricky abused then English-based referee Ashley Klein when the pair crossed paths at the team hotel. While I know Ricky was only saying what a lot of people were thinking and only had the interests of his players at heart, what he did was unacceptable and he knew it. It was a mistake – we all make them. I had hoped that, with an apology and some genuine attempts to do something constructive for the development of referees, Ricky might have seen out the storm. But it wasn't to be. A fortnight after his one and only loss as Test coach, Ricky Stuart tendered his resignation to the ARL.

I was sad to see him go and genuinely hope he gets

another crack at it at some stage down the track. Should Stick indeed get the chance to reclaim the Test coaching position, I simply pass on my best wishes to the skipper of the side. To be the first to address the Kangaroos team with the creed and begin what I think could become a very meaningful tradition . . . well, I have to admit I am a little envious. I hope he understands the significance of the moment.

THE AUSTRALIAN KANGAROOS' CREED
by Rupert McCall

Brothers in Arms – feel the crest on your heart
We stand up together! We fight from the start!
This is my dream – an Australian Rep
Like the Emu and the Roo – we take no backward step!

To those who have worn it – we honour their name
To those who support it – we carry their flame
For my family's pride – I will not waver
I've never felt stronger! I've never felt braver!

Brothers in Arms – feel it beat in your chest!
Step forward! Step forward – The best of the best
To play for my country – the ultimate vow
For the green and gold jersey – our time is now . . .

Ricky Stuart: The support I got from Locky after I did what I did is something I won't ever forget. He doesn't say too much, Locky, so for him to come out publicly and back me, it just gave me a bit of a lift at a time when I needed it.

I knew I had stuffed up as soon as I cooled down and started to think a bit more clearly. I was disappointed in myself, but there wasn't much I could do. I couldn't undo it, but I was conscious of not wanting the heat that was coming to filter onto the players. I actually went and saw them on my way to the airport in the afternoon. I was heading to a charity golf day in Canberra I had committed to attend months earlier, but made sure to swing by the pub where the boys were drowning their sorrows. I called them all over and just told them I had made a monumental blue a couple of hours ago and shit was going to hit the fan. I told them they needed to keep their heads down and said, 'For god's sake don't do something that is going to get you lumped in with me.' They couldn't put a foot out of line and I pulled Locky to one side and just said he needed to take charge. He didn't say more than a couple of words, but the respect he has from the blokes around him – a couple of words was all that was needed.

In a funny twist of fate, Ricky's old club coach Tim Sheens was appointed to the top job. The short time I have had to work with Tim has been another eye-opener. No one knows more about the technical side of the game than Tim and I am constantly amazed at what he picks up in his analysis of opposition teams. While his approach is vastly different to Ricky or Wayne, or even Opes for that matter, the thing I have come to enjoy most is the fact that every session under Tim you learn something new. He is always thinking of different trick plays or gameplay theory. It is a real education process working under Tim.

I can say with absolute conviction that I valued every second I got to spend in a Kangaroos uniform. It is not something I ever took for granted, nor is the remarkable legacy I inherited – first as a player and then as captain of the Australian rugby league side. I think there is something fitting about the fact that my final playing days will be spent in the green and gold of Australia. Of everything I have been lucky enough to share in over the course of my rugby league career, having been part of the renaissance of international rugby league and helping re-establish the Kangaroos jersey as the game's pinnacle is probably the one of which I am most proud. It is back where it belongs.

More personally, I'm still not comfortable seeing D. Lockyer alongside the likes of Gasnier, Churchill, Lewis, Irvine, Raper, and Meninga in the record books. It still seems surreal to think I have pulled on the Kangaroos jumper more times than any other player in history.

I am honoured, privileged . . . humbled.

It is the crowning achievement of my playing career.

SIX

The Times They Are a-Changin'

'The move to five-eighth exemplifies Darren Lockyer being the ultimate team man. Here he was the Test fullback and captain, one of the best to ever play that position in the history of the game, and I am asking him to turn his back on that and make the move because we were struggling in the halves and we needed to fix the problem.' – Wayne Bennett

LOOKING BACK NOW, it is fair to say the conversation Wayne had with me in the team's gymnasium one afternoon during 2004 pre-season training changed the course of my career and, over time, reshaped me as a player and a captain. At the time, however, I was more than a little apprehensive about the proposal Wayne had pitched about shifting me from fullback to five-eighth.

After a really promising start, the Broncos' 2003 season ended disastrously. Seven losses in a row to finish the regular season saw us tumble from a share of top spot down to eighth. We were cannon fodder for the Panthers, who had finished minor premiers. As was the case with the Sharks in '99, Johnny Lang was at the helm of the side which ended our year on the first weekend of finals football.

The Kangaroo tour which followed was a real bitter-sweet experience. Just a month out from leaving, Gordie made the shock announcement that he was standing down as Kangaroos skipper, due largely to problems associated with his chronic neck complaint. The other obvious candidate to lead the side, Andrew Johns, had already withdrawn because of injury, along with a staggering 18 other players. So when I was offered the captaincy, as humbled and honoured as I was, I couldn't shake the feeling that I might be inheriting a poisoned chalice. Still, you don't get offered the chance to captain your country every day, so I tried to be as positive as I could from the outset.

The media in both Australia and England, though, were giving us no chance. The Poms were pretty happy with the squad they had put together and appeared confident that up against an under-strength Kangaroos squad with a rookie at its helm and boasting less experience than any Australian touring party before it, this would be the year they would finally end their run of outs against the green and gold.

My first match in charge did little to alter that line of thinking, with New Zealand steamrolling us at North Harbour to the tune of 30–16 – their first win against us in four years. As if that wasn't enough, it was my pass that was intercepted by Francis Meli to set up Clinton Toopi for one of his three tries that turned the match in the Kiwis' favour after we had jumped out to an early lead. Not that I can remember any of that after I was knocked out badly in the second half. I still have no idea what actually happened to me. For all I know, a piano could have fallen out of the sky and landed on me. Whatever it was, it left me with little recollection of my first Test as captain.

From that low, however, things began to turn. We showed gradual improvement through our three tour game wins prior to the first Ashes Test at Wigan. The whole thing probably turned on the first tackle of the series, when Adrian Morley ironed out Robbie Kearns with a 1970s-style stiff-arm and was marched. Despite the one-man advantage, we only just scraped home. We had been scratchy with the ball all match, but a great individual run by Craig Wing, who was playing out of position in the centres, handed me the match-winner on a platter. The next two matches were equally tense. On both occasions, the home side held the lead with less than 10 minutes to play before we managed to find a way home. In the end we headed home undefeated – a perfect six wins from as many starts.

That squad was probably as tight a bunch as I have ever toured with. Opes (coach Chris Anderson) was a bit 'old school' and very much encouraged us to have a few beers together as a group. On top of that, we had a strong representation from the Roosters – Anthony Minichiello, Craig Fitzgibbon, Luke Ricketson, Mick Crocker, Craig Wing. They brought with them a really strong work ethic on the training track, but by the same token it was a work hard, do the job on the field and enjoy ourselves afterwards approach. There were a lot of funny stories to come out of that tour.

One I still cop a bit of grief over was the short-term narcolepsy I developed after the concussion in New Zealand. With some of the stuff we are starting to learn these days about managing concussions, it is something I would have taken much more seriously if it had happened in 2011. But at the time it was the source of much amusement amongst the team that after half a dozen drinks I would simply fall asleep wherever I was sitting. I have never had anything like it before or since. It was a bit bizarre, but the guys used to find it very amusing when, a couple of hours into a night out celebrating a win, people would be looking for me and find me somewhere snoozing.

Of all the tours I have been on, I will never forget that one. Obviously, being the first time I captained Australia, it was always going to be significant, but more than that, it was the feeling of achieving something very few thought we could. We won against all odds and although I don't speak regularly to those guys anymore, I know that, for most of us, it was a part of our career that will always stand out.

Individually, my year finished on a high when I was awarded the Rugby League International Federation (RLIF) Golden Boot award. I don't know that it has ever sat all that comfortably with me, this notion of being the world's best player. You need your team-mates to be effective on the football field. We play a team sport. Without them, you are nothing. I always felt like just one cog in the wheel. Still, it was a nice recognition and will be something to tell the grandkids one day.

So I was feeling reasonably good about myself and my game when Wayne hit me with his proposal about the positional switch. Obviously I had played most of my under-age football in the halves and certainly took on more playmaking duties than your average NRL fullback. But the people in the media who had been spruiking the idea for some time as if it was something you could implement on the spot with any sort of effectiveness were kidding themselves. Let me assure you, the game I played from 1995 to 2003 bears no resemblance to what I was doing in the second half of my career.

So I had my concerns, but Wayne just laid it out straight for me. He said the team needed this, but that it would take a lot of work on my part. I knew we were in a bit of a bind. Over the space of a few weeks, the Broncos had lost both the obvious playmaking options for 2004 when Ben Ikin retired having been worn down by three horrific knee injuries and Scott Prince agreed to move to the Tigers after three injury-riddled years in Brisbane.

It was what the team needed and I knew it. For any footballer worth his salt, that is all the information they should ever need.

Wayne Bennett: The move to five-eighth exemplifies Darren Lockyer being the ultimate team man. Here he was the Test fullback and captain, one of the best to ever play that position in the history of the game, and here I am asking him to turn his back on that and make the move because we were struggling in the halves and we needed to fix the problem.

We had actually set our sights on getting Brett Kimmorley to the club that year. We nearly got him too, but in the end we missed out and that hurt. We needed him badly.

I couldn't find another way to solve the problem in the short term and I thought Locky was the only one who was capable of getting the job done for us.

I asked him and, as casual as you like, he said, 'Coach, if that's what you want me to do, if that's what the team needs, I'll do it.'

I said, 'Well, that is what I need you to do, mate, and that is what will best serve the team.'

I said, 'You understand that by doing this a lot of what you have worked for is gone. There are no guarantees with Origin or Test selections. Everything will be different for you.'

He said, 'I understand all that, Coach. I am happy to do it.'

Johnathan Thurston: People underestimate the enormity of the move. They are two totally different positions.

To make the transition from the best fullback in the world to being the best five-eighth . . . well, it isn't something I could do.

Defending in the front line is obviously the big change. You get so much traffic thrown at you, and that is where they went after Locky.

In the days following my brief discussion with Wayne, I spent a lot of time and head space thinking about what exactly I had agreed to. There was no escaping the fact that the entire experiment was a major gamble for both me and Wayne. I was risking my representative jerseys. Wayne was risking his reputation, such is the unforgiving world in which professional coaches live. While physically I felt as though I was at the peak of my powers, at 27 the reality was it was very likely my career was closer to the end than the beginning. I did a fair bit of self-analysis, looking back over my career to date, and I couldn't escape the feeling I had far more to offer than I had shown up to that point. It isn't something written down anywhere or made public at any stage, but over the 2004 pre-season I settled on the idea that the move to five-eighth was the challenge I had been waiting for. If I was ever going to find out just what I was capable of in the game, it was also the challenge I needed. With that now decided, my next question to Wayne was, 'Who is going to play fullback?'

I was caught off guard when he began to talk about this 17-year-old kid he felt could take over at the back. I thought he was perhaps trying to have a lend of me. But Karmichael Hunt quickly showed he was no joke at all.

I loved playing with K. He was a remarkable kid – I have never seen someone so physically and mentally tough at such a young age. With the ball in hand, he could lift a team with his fearless charges back at the defensive line. It was also a great way to build momentum, because inevitably he would at least get a quick play-the-ball and from that we could attack almost immediately. He was equally adept at creating for his outside men. The second man sweep play became a favourite of ours and was responsible for an incredible number of Broncos tries during the six seasons K spent at the club before he was sensationally poached by the newly formed Gold Coast Suns AFL franchise.

As for the critics who wrote off K's chances of making a success of the pioneering code switch from the outset, I encourage them to meet him in person. I guarantee you will leave with your mind changed. K is blessed with brilliant hands and athleticism, but it is his mindset that will get him to where he wants to go in AFL. He simply will not let himself fail. K is so assured in every aspect of his life I don't know that the idea of him being unable to make the necessary adjustments to play AFL at the highest level would be something that ever passed through his mind.

Anyhow, things started really positively for me and the team. We won six of our first seven games and I was pleasantly surprised at the ease with which I was adjusting to life in the front line.

By Phil Gould
11 April 2004
The Sun-Herald

All those mortals battling with game plans and plays,

anxieties and nerves, would be wondering just what's so easy about playing five-eighth in the NRL.

Well, on Friday night Lockyer strode on to the field against the Roosters and backed it up. The world's greatest fullback is now the world's greatest five-eighth.

The thing I like most about him is that he is an old-fashioned five-eighth. He plays the position as it should be played and as a result the Broncos are playing the game something like the way football was played in the old days. Only much, much better.

Lockyer's game is still very much a work in progress and he is constantly making adjustments. Some players look back on a season before they make changes. Some look a week. Lockyer is modifying his game minute by minute, even play by play.

The Broncos continued to show good signs throughout the season. Unfortunately, my year was hampered by a nagging rib cartilage injury I first sustained playing for Australia against the Kiwis in the Anzac Test. I re-aggravated the torn cartilage a couple of times, the last of which saw me sidelined just a month out from the finals. It was a cruel blow, because until that point things appeared to be tracking perfectly for us to challenge for the title and give Gordie the send-off he deserved. Despite winning just one of our final four games, we finished the regular season in third spot. But with the injuries piling up and with no momentum whatsoever, we were always facing an uphill battle to progress deep into the finals. And so it was that we bowed out in straight sets, flogged by Craig Bellamy's young Melbourne Storm side first up before the Cowboys ended a 17-game winless streak against us, their 10–0 win their first against the Broncos in club history.

Despite the fact I was awarded the Dally M five-eighth of the year, by season's end there was no doubt the extra work in defence had taken a toll. I was targeted a lot and I remember having a couple of particularly sloppy games and copping a fair bit of heat about it.

Ricky Stuart: Initially I was a coach who preferred coaching against Darren Lockyer when he moved into the front line. Today I would prefer him at fullback.

From fullback he had this incredible ability to just glide across the park and create the extra man before any defensive line could adjust. I have never seen a player who was better at it, so when I heard he was moving to five-eighth I was happy.

The easy option for him would have been to stay at fullback. Now he has to make 25–30 shots – shoulder shots, not wrestles – every game. He always defended three in from the sideline, he didn't hide at two or one. So he always had big backrowers going at him. Every tap, every penalty – he knows they are coming for him first-up.

I actually created a play designed specifically for him. Whenever we got to him, from the play-the-ball, we'd run out and turn the ball straight back and go at him again. I feel shocking having to admit it now, but it shows you what opponents thought of him, because you only do that to a player because he is that good you know you are no chance if you can't find a way to curb his impact on a match.

Those who'd criticise him for missing the odd tackle here or there don't know the game.

It took courage for him to risk his standing as one of if not the best fullback the game has seen and move because his team needed him to.

For those of you wondering how I ended up with a voice which sounds like I have swallowed more gravel than it took to build the M1 freeway to the Gold Coast, it happened during a match in 2004 when I caught an accidental forearm in the throat attempting to make a tackle. As I understand it, a small bone fragment from my larynx is pushing against my vocal cords, leaving me with a voice which permanently sounds as if I have just necked a bottle of Tabasco sauce.

What was a pretty frustrating year ended on a high when we retained the Tri-Nations trophy courtesy of a 44–4 win over England in the final at Elland Road. The game was over at half-time, thanks to perhaps the most dominant half of football I have ever played in. We ran in six tries in the first 40 minutes – Willie Tonga and Mini snared two each. I got one of my own and had a hand in a few others. It was just one of those really rare occasions in sport where everything went our way. Everything we tried came off. Every bounce of the ball fell our way. I have been on the other side of a couple of matches like that. All you can do when it happens is try to limit the damage. At full-time you shake hands, tip your hat to the winner, walk off the field and forget about it. There's nothing you could have done, so don't worry about it.

By Greg Davis
5 December 2004
The Sunday-Mail

Rugby league Immortal Bob Fulton has lauded Darren Lockyer's first-half performance in last weekend's Tri-Nations final as 'the most dominant display by any player in the history of the game'.

Lockyer had a hand in each of Australia's six tries in the opening 40 minutes as the Kangaroos blitzed the British to set up a 38–0 lead by the main break.

A rampant Lockyer scored one try, set up five others and kicked six goals in a dazzling effort made all the more noteworthy because he had to nurse a long-term rib injury through the match.

Fulton – a former Kangaroos captain, coach and current Australian selector – said Lockyer was at the peak of his powers at Elland Road in a performance that rivalled the vintage displays of Lewis during the 1980s.

'That first 40 minutes was unbelievable. It was the most dominant display by any player in the history of the game,' said Fulton, who coached the Roma product in his Test debut in 1998.

'He was that good that if he were in the Great Britain side the other night, they would have won.'

So, I arrived for pre-season training with the Broncos in 2005 pretty confident I was on the right track with my development as a five-eighth. The return of Justin Hodges from the Roosters and Brad Thorn after a stint in rugby union, which saw him earn All Black honours, helped fill the enormous void left by Gordie's retirement and I certainly appreciated having their class, experience and size in what was my first year as Broncos captain.

Wayne Bennett: I knew when Locky was 19 that he was going to captain the Broncos one day. You could just see the talent but also the calmness he had about him even when all the blokes around him were hitting the panic button.

There are a lot of things you can see in Darren and his rock-type stature. He is a strong person and leads from the front. He has all the skills you need to be a captain, what he doesn't have is the extroverted personality of a lot of the captains you see out there. It isn't that you have to be an extrovert to be a good captain, it is just holding that position requires you to do a lot of things and put yourself out there. Sometimes you have to say things you don't want to say, speak on behalf of the team when that is the last thing you feel like doing. So he had to develop all that stuff and he did because he wanted to be a captain and he wanted to be a bloody good captain.

My tenure started on a positive note with a solid 29–16 win over the Cowboys in the first Queensland derby season-opener. Over the next few weeks, though, we struggled for consistency, with a win over the Roosters in round three sandwiched between losses to the Warriors at Suncorp Stadium and Melbourne at Olympic Park, the latter defeat a 50–4 drubbing, the worst ever loss by a Broncos side.

We bounced back in the best possible fashion, however, going 12–2 over the next 14 weeks. Heading into round 20, a top two spot appeared assured. Once again, though, injury struck at the worst possible time – a torn hamstring suffered in our round 22 loss to the Dragons ruling me out for the remaining matches in the regular season. There was something eerily familiar about how things finished up. I was again stuck on the sidelines when my team needed me most. As a group, we just looked to be running on empty and coupled with a lack of direction we again limped into the finals on the back of a run of defeats.

Again we finished the year ranked third and again we found ourselves hosting a young, in-form Melbourne Storm side. Not surprisingly, the result was the same as it was 12 months earlier, the 24–18 loss at home forcing us to head to Sydney in week two to face Scotty Prince's red-hot Tigers outfit. On a warm Sunday afternoon at the Sydney Football Stadium, Princey reminded us what we had lost when he left the Broncos, combining with boom youngster Benji Marshall and his band of fleet-footed team-mates to simply run us off our feet to win 34–6. We were barely a speed bump for the Tigers on their way to their first premiership as a joint venture club. Speaking after the match, Wayne wasn't hiding from the criticism we both knew was coming. Since winning the competition in 2000, the Broncos had recorded just two wins from 10 finals matches, with worrying form slumps seeing us exit meekly four years in a row.

'Success is a little elusive at the moment,' he said after the game. 'We had it in our grasp two and a half months ago. To finish here today in the manner that it did, you couldn't have foreseen that a couple of months ago.'

I have probably sat alongside Wayne in post-match media conferences on 120 or more occasions. Often entertaining, occasionally uncomfortable, but always interesting is the best way I could describe the experience. Odd as it may sound, he tends to be more open and affable after a loss – unless it was a really bad one. It probably reflected the philosophy Wayne had about the coach–player–media relationship. Knowing that consistency is the key to ongoing success, Wayne always believed it was up to a coach to convince a player he wasn't quite as good as he thought he was when he was going well. But nor was he as bad as others might say he was when he was struggling.

There have been times when I would just cringe even before Wayne responded – sometimes afterwards – because

I knew the response that was coming. I wasn't there for the famous monosyllabic media conference he held after a game against Manly in 2007. It was the first time one of his media conferences was shown live, as is the case with Monday Night Football. It wasn't pretty, as he fired one-word replies to every question. I was glad to be watching that from my hotel room at Origin camp and not from the seat next to him. I would have been squirming.

Wayne is very quick-witted. I have seen him cut an awful lot of blokes down when they have tried to come at him. Not too many journalists take him on in those public forums, because it is difficult to fluster him. He always comes prepared – it is all pre-planned. He gathers his thoughts and settles on what he does and doesn't want to say a long time before he sits down. So I was more than a little surprised with his response when asked if the loss to the Tigers which ended our 2005 campaign supported the suggestion from critics the club was in need of a new coaching style or even a new coach.

'Yeah, well they may be right . . . ,' he said. After a pause, he added: 'They may be wrong too, but . . . Perhaps we play too hard at the beginning of the season. You just can't do it for 26 weeks; it's too long a season. We've just got to keep going the way we are going and hope we can get it right.'

He had been around long enough to know there needed to be a significant change to some of the systems he had been employing. I knew he would be poring over just what he needed to do to fix the problem and it would be weighing heavily on him. I expected change, I did not expect what went down shortly before we took off on the Kangaroo tour, on 7 October 2005, tagged 'The Day of the Long Knives' by the major Queensland newspaper. Wayne sacked club legends Kevin Walters and Glenn Lazarus as assistant coaches. Another long-time servant and coach of the Clydesdales Queensland Cup side, John Dixon, was also let go, as was performance director, Gary Belcher, whose relationship with Wayne dated back to their days together at Souths in Brisbane in the mid-1980s. In their place, Ivan Henjak returned to the coaching staff after a few years away. Allan Langer and another Queensland Origin halfback, Paul Green, were also brought on as assistants, with Peter Ryan coming on too as defensive coach.

Each would play a major role in the club's resurgence; however, it was the appointment of Dean Benton as performance director which really shook things up. A leader in the strength and conditioning field, Dean was a protégé of renowned former Broncos conditioner, Kelvin Giles, and had a résumé which included stints with the Australian Institute of Sport, the Australian track and field team and the Australian Rugby Union. He was and is at the very top of his field.

If Wayne thought the Kangaroo tour would help see the furore pass, he couldn't have been more wrong. Rather than easing the pressure, things went from bad to worse after he presided over Australia's first international rugby league series defeat in 32 years. Having broken a bone in my foot early in the tour, I was forced to watch on helplessly as the Kiwis romped to a 24–0 win in the final of the Tri-Nations. Wayne's decision to take a back exit upon his return to Brisbane rather than confront the waiting media at the main terminal was something he has admitted was a serious error in judgement. It left Petero Civoniceva to face the music and I know Wayne regrets putting a player in his charge in such a situation. It served to further inflame the ongoing feud which existed between Wayne and some sections of the media.

People were lining up to have a go at him, with the Broncos sackings still fairly fresh in the memory. I remember about 12 months later having a chat with him and just saying, 'That must have been really hard to give that news to guys who are your friends.'

He said, 'It is the hardest thing about my job as a coach. I absolutely hate it. I hate having to do it. To have to tell a player or a member of your staff – people I care about – that they are no longer required, it's an awful thing to have to do. But the fact is there are times when you have to do it. It comes with the territory and if you can't do it, you need to find a new profession.'

There is no doubt there are a number of ex-Broncos who remain disappointed about how their respective careers finished at Red Hill, and generally that disappointment is directed at Wayne. I have to say I am glad I will be able to hang up the boots at season's end loving the club as much as, if not more than, the day I first stepped foot in it 17 years ago. I would like to think if I had come to a situation where Wayne gave me the tap on the shoulder that I would understand he has only ever wanted the best for the club. He is the one who has had to make the tough calls and it's not something he revels in.

I can look back now and say it is a credit to Wayne to have had the guts to make those tough calls, because it is what the team needs. A lot of the critics who called him selfish or arrogant fail to acknowledge how tough it was for Wayne to risk long-time personal friendships for the good of the team. In doing it, he also knew the buck now stopped with him. If 2006 delivered more of the same, it would fall on him.

Still, at the time, I wasn't thinking like that. All I was thinking about was Kevie, Badge and Lazo and how tough they were doing it. Around the club, it was as if there had been a death in the family. No one was speaking. There were heads down everywhere. Like a lot of the team, I felt a real sense of responsibility for what had occurred. After all, it was our performances on the field that demanded things change. I spent a lot of hours wondering if I had let them down personally. As captain, I went over times where I maybe could have or should have spoken up and chose not to.

It was probably the start of some pretty serious self-analysis. I did plenty more over the months ahead and I think it would be fair to say that, when I was honest enough to hold up a mirror, I wasn't entirely happy with the reflection. There's no doubt for part of 2004 and for most of 2005, I wasn't getting the best out of myself. I certainly wasn't doing everything I could for the teams in which I was playing. I was Queensland and Australian captain and I think I fell into the trap of believing I no longer needed to do the sort of work I had done early in my career. I was performing at an Australian level but, in reality, that was probably the easiest of the three levels simply because of the quality of players around me. I didn't have to take responsibility for other blokes. I could cruise through just worrying about myself and looking good doing it. But there's a poem Wayne loves called 'Guy in the Glass', by Dale Wimbrow, that perfectly sums up what I am talking about.

When you get what you want in your struggle for pelf,
And the world makes you King for a day,
Then go to the mirror and look at yourself,
And see what that guy has to say.

For it isn't your Father, or Mother, or Wife,
Who judgement upon you must pass.
The feller whose verdict counts most in your life
Is the guy staring back from the glass.

He's the feller to please, never mind all the rest,
For he's with you clear up to the end,
And you've passed your most dangerous, difficult test
If the guy in the glass is your friend.

You may be like Jack Horner and 'chisel' a plum,
And think you're a wonderful guy,
But the man in the glass says you're only a bum
If you can't look him straight in the eye.

You can fool the whole world down the pathway of years,
And get pats on the back as you pass,
But your final reward will be heartaches and tears
If you've cheated the guy in the glass.

I had just allowed my mindset to become too relaxed and needed a reality check to bring my focus back completely to where it needed to be.

I guess it isn't a big surprise that this period of change in my mindset came just after I split with my girlfriend of seven years, whom I had been living with for quite a while. We had started seeing each other when I was only 19, so essentially since coming into first-grade I had always had a steady girlfriend. Given that, a lot of the things my mates did in those three or four years after leaving school – partying and enjoying their newfound independence – was something I missed completely. I am not complaining. I missed it because I had a lot of other great things in my life which took precedence. But I think when the time came that I was unattached, my perspective changed a little. My priorities got all mixed up. The losses in Origin in 2004 and 2005, the Broncos' poor finals efforts ... they hurt, sure. But I know now, they didn't hurt enough.

SEVEN

Dreams Really Do Come True

BY THE TIME the opening round of the 2006 NRL season arrived, one thing had become abundantly clear. If the Broncos were to slump late in the season, as had happened every year since 2002, it wasn't going to be because of a lack of fitness.

While all the changes made over the 2005 off-season had a positive impact, Dean Benton's arrival had by far the biggest. It probably wasn't until he came that Wayne realised how far the club had regressed since the days of Kelvin Giles and Steve Nance, who had seen the Broncos sit at the cutting edge of performance throughout the 1990s. Dean brought a totally new approach to our training – far more scientific – and from my perspective it was a breath of fresh air. Due to the broken foot I suffered on tour, I missed the seven-day 'boot camp' run by Chris Haseman, but Justin

Hodges and Brad Thorn had no hesitation in nominating it as the toughest they have ever experienced. That foot injury really hampered me through the early months of training, making a tough task even more difficult as Dean then picked up right where the boot camp finished.

Dean came in with a big stick – as Wayne wanted him to do. He made it clear to us from the outset that he wasn't there to make friends. Where we had fallen behind in our training methodology, Dean set out to drag the group back to the top. It was brutal and relentless. He granted us just four days break over Christmas. Having got to know Dean in the years since, I realise his attitude and approach were necessary to change many of the bad habits which had crept into our training over recent years. He is one of the smartest men I have ever met and very opinionated. He is confident in his ability to do his job and during that pre-season, in particular, was unwilling to negotiate or compromise on anything. Understandably, that approach led to some clashes with some players and other staff, but nothing was going to deter him. Personally, I really enjoyed the training. It was different and I found it interesting. Other blokes in the squad weren't so open-minded.

Wayne Bennett: Dean worked them so hard that pre-season he almost broke a lot of them. But he and I had discussed what was needed and I knew that his approach was what we required. It was the foundation we built the rest of the year on. Physically we had fallen behind. Dean brought a whole new level of professionalism with his experience and expertise in sports science. He overhauled our approach to sports medicine, injury prevention and treatment . . . the whole thing changed. Dean was the ideal bloke for the job because he didn't come looking for friends or to have a joke. He came to get the team fit. And there is no doubt we were the fittest team in the competition that year. No doubt at all.

When the first competition round arrived, we were a bit of a rabble. I had only started full-time training a week out from round one, and we had done so much work on our physical preparation that we had limited ballwork, and gameplan and defensive patterns were still very much a work in progress. We were duly trounced by the Cowboys on a sunny, Sunday afternoon at Suncorp Stadium. The knives came out straightaway. I was copping more heat over my defence and now the calls began for Wayne to shift me back to fullback. I knew that wasn't the answer. I had committed to playing five-eighth and I was going to make it work, so I started working double time on my tackling with Peter Ryan and Tonie Carroll – two of the best defenders to have played the game.

A few days after the loss to the Cowboys, Wayne was asked about my performance and how long he intended to persist with having me in the front line if I continued to defend as I had against the Cowboys. Perhaps thinking I needed a bit of a kick in the pants, he responded with:

'If we can't get it right in that defensive area and it's not happening for us I can't just keep committing suicide with the rest of the guys and putting my head in the sand and hope it's going to fix itself and go away.

'We've either got to get it right or we've got to make another decision.'

Where many in the media assumed 'another decision' meant switching me back to fullback – that was never an option.

Wayne Bennett: We were committed to it. The criticism was like water off a duck's back to me and I just had to keep him strong. Not that that was a tough ask. When Darren Lockyer commits to something, that's it.

I knew he could handle the position, but what he did have to do was teach himself to tackle. And to his credit, that is what he has done. He is a very solid defender these days, but it took some time. His technique is good and his football nous is so far advanced he is able to shut down opponents when they are building an attack.

Moving him never entered either of our heads. He needed to fix the problem, sure. But 'another decision' referred to how we set up our defensive line. We made the call to put Tonie Carroll in beside him, because he was just getting hammered. He isn't a big guy and he was being asked to bring down opposition forwards 20 and 30 kilos heavier than him 30 times a game. As a coach, I needed to do something. So I gave him Tunza.

Tonie Carroll is the best hitter I have seen. Everyone

knew what Tunza's job was. He was there to protect Locky a bit. Locky would always put his body on the line. He was too brave for his own good. He wouldn't hear talk about moving wider, so I took the attitude, 'Well, if blokes want to get at him, you have to get past Big Tunza first.' If they could do that, good luck to them.

Tunza was a hitting machine. I once heard Wayne say that if he could build the perfect tackling specimen from the ground up, it would pretty much look like Tunza. He was remarkably light on his feet for a man his size, which always allowed him to get in the right position when lining up a ball carrier. He had thick powerful legs, a barrel chest and a solid trunk. While not as broad as some of your more athletic backrowers, Tunza had enormous strength through his upper back and shoulders, which he used to great effect laying out victim after victim. Tunza was voted the game's 'hardest hitter' five times in *Rugby League Week*'s annual player poll – oddly enough though, in 2006, Sonny Bill Williams edged him for top spot.

We were clearly the fittest team in the competition that year and, coupled with our big, experienced pack of forwards, we were able to grind our way through the opening two months of the competition and were nicely placed at 7–3 after 10 rounds.

Then Origin I happened. The fallout was intense and my name was at the eye of the storm, with past players taking their shots, not least Greg Dowling. While I am all for blokes saying and doing what they like in the media,

I didn't think much of Dowling's column, which criticised my leadership and called for me to be sacked. It wasn't that I had any great drama with the content – everyone is entitled to their opinion. I just thought it was poor form given that Dowling was part of our camp leading into game one.

Ricky Stuart: After that loss in game one, the Maroons were staring down the barrel of a fourth straight series loss and it rattled the entire Queensland Origin empire. For the first time since State of Origin began back in 1980, the Queenslanders turned on their own – Locky most of all. As a proud New South Welshman, I have to admit I never thought I would see the day. But they did, and people always turn on the best first, so Locky wore it.

It was a column by Phil Gould in Sydney, however, that resonated most strongly with me. This is just some of what Gus had to say.

Is it time for Lockyer to consider his Origin future?
by Phil Gould
28 May 2006
The Courier-Mail

It's time for Queensland to ask Darren to step down from their State of Origin team. It's always dangerous to criticise a champion and I'm not going to.

I wouldn't drop him, either, but I'd have a serious talk to him about his future and the future of the Queensland team.

The Maroons need to think long and hard about the development of their team and I can't see Lockyer being part of this process. I have many reasons to support this suggestion but consider these:

Lockyer looks stressed. He's trying but not much is working. I know he threw a couple of good passes late in the game on Wednesday night but it wasn't one of his better performances.

Lockyer's presence gives the Queensland team an air of predictability. It seems their plan on Wednesday was a couple of hit-ups before throwing the ball two passes wide to Lockyer.

He's a great player but he has only a couple of tricks in his game. NSW players know them well and that makes it very difficult for him to have an impact. The bad passes, dropped ball and gang tackles on his ball-runners all came from his being heavily marked.

His kicking game is also predictable and easily pressured . . . Many great players have had to retire. Who knows, maybe in two years, with the series on the line, Lockyer could make a brief comeback, as Allan Langer, Brad Fittler and Andrew Johns did, and produce the fairytale finish the greats truly deserve. It's a tough call but it needs to be considered.

Phil Gould: There have only been one or two times in his career where I have questioned Darren Lockyer. I remember he had struggled a little through the early rounds and actually came off the ground early in one match and the body language I saw from him on that occasion looked very similar to the body language of Alfie Langer in those weeks just before he retired. You get an eye for when a senior player is starting to lose focus or has other things on his mind. I didn't know what was troubling him but I suspected something was up. I remember when he came off the field that day, he was sitting on the bench looking a little frustrated, I made the comment that, 'Even the great ones have to make a decision at some time.'

It is very hard sometimes for great players to come to terms with things when they can no longer do what made them great. I had the very same conversation with Johnathan Thurston recently. He is at about the same age Lockyer was in 2006. I said to him, 'You need to learn how to manage the back end of your career.' I have had similar conversations with some of the best players of this generation – Freddie Fittler in particular.

A lot of great players struggle with the transition from being a great rep player and star to a great senior player. For whatever reason, at that time Lockyer was struggling with that. I could see it in his play in the little things he wasn't doing that he always used to do. The cutting of half a corner here and there which I had never, ever seen from him in the past. It just said to me that there was something else in his life that was distracting him. So I said what I said. Players respond to that one of two ways. Plenty will prove you right, others though will go out to prove you wrong.

To win that series the way we did, it was just such an enormous relief for me personally. I put so much into those matches, well aware of just how much was riding on the results.

I have said maybe a dozen words total to Gus across the entirety of my career, but I respect his opinions enormously. For most of the 17 seasons I have enjoyed as a professional footballer, I have made a point of avoiding the sports section in any newspaper. It is such an easy trap to fall into – to start hanging on every word that is spoken or written about you, to take it all far too personally. I made the decision very early in my career that I just didn't want that stress in my life. It is the job of a journalist to write stories that will sell papers. The correlation to my job as a footballer is zero. Obviously there is interaction. Both sides need the other in a business sense. But just as I have no say over the editorial content of *The Courier-Mail*, nor should the opinions offered on the sports pages impact how players or coaching staff go about their business.

Maybe it was fate that led me to break my sports section ban on the same day Gus's piece ran. Hand on heart, I came across the article by chance, but can look back now and say I am glad I did. The personal criticism forced me to take stock and re-evaluate exactly where I was at in my playing career. It sat me back on my arse a bit and forced me to start working a bit harder to get things right. It is one thing I am steadfast about for all NRL players, no matter how old or young they may be, that you can always get better. Your skills can always improve, provided you put in the work. The more you practise a particular skill, the better you are going to become. If there is a deficiency in your game, one thing I can guarantee you is that it won't fix itself. If you ignore it and aren't prepared to put in extra work to address things, it will forever be a flaw opponents will identify and exploit. If you are going through periods where you are falling off tackles or your passing isn't as crisp or accurate as it needs to be, you just stay behind after the rest of training has finished and you go to work. I am a big believer in the idea of reward for effort. I know I have had a few weeks over the course of my career when I have defended poorly and every day I would stay behind to do extra defensive work with Rhino (Peter Ryan) or Tunza. Hoping and praying things will work themselves out won't change anything.

I have never worked harder preparing for a game than I did for the second and third Origin matches in 2006. I have never been more focused nor as driven to win as I was during that six-week period. Obviously I am always striving to win and I have always taken pride in being meticulous in my training and preparation for games, whether at club level with the Broncos, or representative level for Queensland or Australia. No one is perfect, but I always felt perfection is what you should be striving to achieve. That way you always have work to do – there will always be an area of your game that isn't perfect. But the pressure and intensity of those weeks was unlike anything I had ever encountered and nothing has matched it in the years since.

The Origin representatives from both the Broncos and the Storm backed up a few days after Queensland's win in game three in Melbourne. The home side ground out a 10–4 win in freezing, wet conditions at Olympic Park. It was our third loss in five matches, but Wayne was far more interested in the matches to come than those that had been.

It was after the loss to Melbourne, with the bye round coming up, that Wayne enacted the next part of his strategy to arrest the issues we had encountered late in the season, ordering all players and staff away from the club for eight days. The brainchild of our genius weights coach, Dan Baker, and Dean, the mid-season break was designed to help us recharge batteries that were running on empty following the demands of the pre-season and another full representative schedule. Some blokes went to the coast. A few just put their feet up at home. Darius Boyd and Karmichael Hunt actually flew to Thailand for a holiday. It was open slather, the only rule being we were not allowed to enter the Broncos football club premises until training recommenced the following Monday ahead of our local derby clash against the Cowboys at Dairy Farmers Stadium.

As much as I enjoyed the time off, when we got back to training I was concerned about our ability to slip straight back into the timing and speed expected in round 20. All season, the teams coming off the bye round had struggled with their intensity and precision. To go an entire week without passing or kicking a football left us lacking cohesion and the Cowboys made us pay. Not even the absence of JT, who limped from the field with a knee injury after just five minutes, helped us, as Matt Sing crossed for a hat-trick in the 26–10 romp. While I knew the break would serve its purpose further down the track, I was fearful there might not be a 'further track' to worry about when I saw the damage the performance in Townsville did to the confidence of the playing group.

The talk started straightaway – we'd changed so much but the result appeared to be heading in the same direction. Further losses to Canberra and Wests Tigers saw each player within the group put under the microscope. Careers would be defined by how we dealt with the situation, or slide, or whatever it was. What it wasn't, as Wayne so emphatically declared, was a slump. Personally, I was pretty happy with how I was playing, but it counted for very little with the team battling as we were. While Wayne wouldn't buckle in his game of chicken with the media in relation to their use of the word 'slump', to me it was a non-issue. Call it a slump, a slide, a stutter, I couldn't care less. To me they are all one and the same – a team down on confidence. Simple as that. Certainly that was us at the time.

Finding your way out of a slump is tough work in a competition as unrelenting as the NRL. There are no 'gimme' games, no easybeats. That is especially true for the Broncos. The profile and success of the club has long made us the team every other club wants to beat and lift themselves for.

Matthew Johns: One of the things you can't quantify in Locky's record is the fact that playing for the Broncos

– the biggest club in the NRL – every single game he has played has been a big game. That includes a few of the trial matches he was part of as well. Let me tell you, having been a part of a number of clubs around the competition as a player and in a coaching capacity, I have seen the way teams take things up a notch when the Brisbane Broncos roll into town. Every game you play when you are at the Broncos is a big game. You might be a South Sydney of the early 1990s or a North Queensland Cowboys in their formative years in the competition and find yourself well down the ladder, but when the Broncos are in town you get your A game on and you set yourself, because you can see a big target. Every team is up for the Broncos – they want that scalp. It is something you can hang your hat on at the end of the year even if not much else has gone right. Well, the season might have been a total disaster, but hey, we beat the Broncos so it's not all doom and gloom. That is some sort of test to have to combat every week.

It is not uncommon in cricket to see a bloke able to 'hit' his way out of a form slump. That is, he clears his mind, opens the shoulders and backs his eye and his technique to get the scoreboard ticking over. Some of the most exhilarating innings in cricket history have come courtesy of this cavalier, throw caution to the wind approach. Unfortunately in the NRL things are never that simple. It is almost unheard of to have a side snap out of a lengthy losing streak by registering a 40-point win. To break the cycle you need to grind a game out. It is the effort and application required in matches like that which can often see them become 'turning points' in a season. Our round 23 loss to Melbourne was exactly the sort of performance to which I refer. The scoreboard may not have ended up in our favour, but that mattered little in the grand scheme of things. We competed throughout and pushed them right to the end. If a couple of things had gone our way, we could even have snared the two competition points.

There were a few other pieces which fell into place around the same time. Shaun Berrigan's move from the centre into hooker in round 22 gave us some spark around the ruck area – something which we had lacked after Michael Ennis was injured early in the year. Similarly, Justin Hodges' move to fullback to cover for Karmichael, who had broken his foot, added a new dimension to our offence. When Hodgo is fit and firing, he is the sort of bloke who just needs to have the football in his hands. How often that occurs in a game has a direct correlation to his team's chances of victory. The more times Hodgo is involved, the steeper the upward curve becomes.

Matthew Johns: I don't necessarily think it was strictly the move to five-eighth which Locky had problems with, it was the adjustments he had to make after moving there as defensive lines found different ways to get at him.

All of a sudden his run, run, run style was just pushing him sideways and it took him quite a period of time to take a step back and work out what he needed to do to start engaging the defence again. He had to make a monumental adjustment to his ball-playing and I don't reckon he was able to get his head around it until about a month out from the 2006 finals series. I was working at Melbourne at the time and we played the Broncos up at Suncorp Stadium late in the season. They were coming off a string of losses, but what I saw that night had me worried immediately. Where Locky's game had been suffering because he was doing too much running and not using his finesse enough, out of nowhere it was like 'bang' he changed. A lot of other players and factors helped Brisbane that year, but the change Locky was able to implement mid-season to his attack was the defining factor in them coming good in the lead-up to the finals. The way he attacked the defence did a 180. His instinct was to just run at the target defender and skim across the face of him because in the past he was always able to burn them with his speed and footwork. Now he had to pull back a bit and run on the inside of defenders to pull the defensive line out of shape. It is only a subtle shift when you say it like that, but it is bloody hard to do. It is hard to change your natural instinct. But it is the subtleties that separate the good from the great. Melbourne won that game in Brisbane (18–12). But it took a great second half to get the points and I remember walking away from that game and thinking that was a worry – they were on the way back. Locky was leading the way.

To go down in such a spirited manner to the runaway competition leaders was a huge confidence boost for the entire group. You could see it in our training the following week. All of a sudden the belief was back. Still, as we were reminded on numerous occasions in the build-up to our clash with the Bulldogs in Sydney, it had still been seven weeks since we last tasted victory. The boys from Belmore were riding high, on a six-game winning streak courtesy of a forward pack which had been brutalising their opponents in the middle of the park. Mark O'Meley, Willie Mason, Roy Asotasi, Sonny Bill Williams, Nate Myles, Andrew Ryan, Reni Maitua ... it was certainly some pack of forwards. However, while we were rank underdogs, I was strangely confident about our chances. To me it was the ideal match-up for us. We had a big pack of veteran forwards that year – Webcke, Civoniceva, Carlaw, Carroll, Thorn, Thaiday and Corey Parker. These are not men who were ever going to be intimidated by the young Dogs. Teams who could challenge them with speed and agility around the ruck were of far greater concern than one which wanted to slug it out. Webbie and Pet and Thorny ... they chew that sort of stuff up.

And that is what they did to their younger opponents that evening – chewed them up and spat them out. Steve Folkes' men were battered from pillar to post and finished the game with a bunch of injuries. Our 30–0 win turned the competition on its head. We reeled off two more wins to finish the regular season in third spot. We hosted the Dragons in week one of the finals series. They have always been a side we have struggled against and the 20–4 loss saw the critics emerge once again as we prepared for an elimination final meeting with Joey and the Newcastle Knights. It was the only time I ever played against Joey in a final and the 50–6 result in our favour suggested we were hitting form at just the right time. However, given Newcastle came into the match without Bedsy Buderus, who had been suspended for a spear tackle, and their best forward, backrower Steve Simpson, I wasn't getting too carried away with the victory – our first win in the finals since beating the Eels in a qualifying finals match in 2002 – some 1,464 days before.

The win over the Knights set up a preliminary final clash with Bulldogs at the Sydney Football Stadium (SFS) – a match that I consider one of the finest I have been a part of in my years wearing the Broncos colours. Boosted by the return from injury of Asotasi, the Dogs quickly established ascendancy in the battle for possession and field position. Shaun Berrigan opened the scoring against the run of play, but the Bulldogs found a reply just minutes later. Brent Sherwin and Matt Utai added their names to the score sheet as the Bulldogs opened a 20–6 half-time advantage on the back of a 60–40 split of possession. At the end of the first 40 minutes, we had made 60 more tackles than the Dogs.

As we headed to the dressing-room, I can still see Willie looking over at us with a smirk. He started clapping his hands together and yelling at the top of his lungs, 'Here we go boys, off to another grand final.' He kept at it, mouthing off until we separated to go into our respective rooms. Now, I am all for characters and have no problem with blokes showing a bit of confidence in themselves and their team, but as a captain I would never let a player on my side go on like that. Why give your opponents anything they could potentially use as a motivational catalyst? I shudder to think what Wayne would have done had that been one of his players doing that. It certainly fired up some of our most experienced guys.

But the reality staring us in the face as we headed out for the resumption of play was that the scoreline and weight of possession meant the Bulldogs probably needed only to hold us out for the first 10 or 15 minutes and it was game over. Wayne's first words during the break were to reassure us that the game was not over. Not if we didn't want it to be. To be any chance, however, we had to be the first to score in the second half.

Knowing we needed a spark, he switched Justin Hodges back to fullback and pushed Karmichael out onto a wing. It took just four minutes to pay dividends, Hodgo fielding a ball a couple of metres behind the tryline before brushing past the Bulldogs chasers and dashing 60 metres downfield and handing off to Berro, who somehow managed to get the ball down in the corner despite Mason's best attempt to bundle him into touch. It ranks up there with the best tries I have ever seen and was a defining moment of our season. That play put us in the Grand Final.

On their next possession, the Bulldogs coughed up the ball close to their line and Dane Carlaw barged his way over from close range. With the momentum now firmly in our favour, it became a procession. Darius, Tatey, Corey Parker and even the old bloke in the number six got over for tries.

By the time the 80 minutes was up we had run away with the match, piling on 31 unanswered points after half-time to finish 37–20 winners. The incredible turnaround was the third-biggest comeback in a final in NRL history. A careless high tackle by Petero which left Sonny Bill a little worse for wear was our only concern as we turned our attention to the grand final.

To see what lay before us in the form of Craig Bellamy's Melbourne machine – it was rugby league's equivalent of scaling Mount Everest. They had recorded just four losses all season – just two from round five onwards – on their way to claiming the minor premiership by a staggering eight points. Their +201 points differential for the year was 96 points better than we managed (+105) in finishing third.

I know a lot of people look at some of the great Broncos teams and marvel at the number of representative players they have had in teams at different times. But, while several would have to wait a few years before getting the call-up, a brief run through the grand final team-sheet shows 16 of those 17 Storm players have gone on to play Origin or Test football in their careers. The only one to miss out was classy rake Nathan Friend – someone who'd surely rank amongst the best players in the modern era never to have earned representative honours.

While there was plenty of skill and class in our side as well, there is no escaping the fact that talent-wise they had us well and truly covered. Looking back at it, the Broncos squad that year was a bit of a mish-mash of vastly different individuals. You had Darius and Benny Hannant who were just finding their way. Webbie was at the end of his stellar career. We had one of our centres (Hodges) playing fullback. Our fullback (Karmichael) was on a wing. Our other centre (Berrigan) was playing hooker, while our lock, (Stagg), filled the gap in the centres. Two of our backrowers (Carroll and Thorn) were re-establishing themselves in the NRL after spending time in the English Super League and New Zealand rugby union, respectively. Shane Perry was a journeyman who'd been called-up from the QRL and handed the task of looking after the forwards. He was a bloke who has never got the credit he deserves for what he did for us that year.

Wayne Bennett: When we missed out on signing Brett Kimmorley, we missed two or three premierships. I say that without hesitation. We desperately needed a player who could play to Locky. There are certain players who are at their best when they have their hands on the ball every other play. That isn't Locky. He isn't at his best when he takes on too much responsibility. One of his problems is the fact that when Locky sees something not working he wants to get in there and do it himself and lift everyone around him. That is wonderful in some circumstances, but when it is happening week after week, month after month, it isn't good. It is not sustainable. Unfortunately, with the exception of 2002 when Alf came back, we didn't have the halfbacks who were able to go in and take control of the forwards and bark out directions.

Just while I am there, let me say what a tragedy that 2002 season was. That premiership was ours for the taking. To be robbed of the chance by someone other than an opponent . . . it was a tragedy.

Anyhow, as I was saying, Locky is at his best when he has a halfback who can take care of steering the forwards around the park and maybe serve as an option kicker. That way Locky doesn't get over-committed and can sit back, do his job and when the time is right, seize the moment. We had been through a bunch of halfbacks between 2001 and 2006. Brett Seymour had actually started the year as the first-choice number seven, but of course we had to cut him and Neville Costigan mid-season.

Then along comes Shane Perry. The bloke has been plying his trade in the Queensland Cup for years and he is a mature 30-something-year-old, so what he brought was a willingness to do the job – to yell at the forwards and get them around the park. But more than that, he knew his role and was happy to simply get the ball to Locky when Locky wanted it. It's why he got the job done.

Going into that 2006 grand final, I knew we were up against it. The Storm had been the standout side all season. We couldn't beat them in a shootout. We needed to reduce the game to a physical battle – a test of wills, if you like. We couldn't be the flashy Broncos of the past, we had to be the Broncos of 2000. We had to be brutal and relentless – it was the only way to counter the Storm's methodical style. We had to pressure them with our willingness to engage in the physical battles. I just knew that if we could get into the 'arm-wrestle' we had a big strong pack of forwards – guys with big game experience – guys who have forged their reputation with their performances in the furnace-like intensity of Test and State of Origin football. Still, Locky was the key. We needed him there to win it.

The game itself was tailor-made for Darren Lockyer. When he first came to the Broncos, we used to play a lot of football off the top of our heads. It's what Alfie and Kevie and Pearl and Willie Carne and those guys all did so well. They had such wonderful instincts, so we just let them use that flair and creativity. It was a different era and the game was played differently, and Locky excelled in that sort of style. It is a big part of who he is.

But then when he started going away on Kangaroos tours and spending time with Fittler and Johns and talking with them about the game, he started to learn about structure and about being patient. He'd watch those guys and study them – the way they moved around the training field. The way they moved the ball into the field position they wanted before demanding it.

Locky is a wonderful observer. He watched all this and started to bring it back with him to the Broncos and worked on adding it to his game. He really took to this studious approach to the game and learning about the game's intricacies at NRL level. All of a sudden then we had this guy who could take the moment by the scruff of the neck, but was equally comfortable sitting back and waiting patiently, just trading set after set because the moment wasn't there – happy building a platform slowly, knowing the try that will break the game open will come from that platform.

That was what he did that day. He was on the ball from start to finish. His kicking game was brilliant. It helped keep Billy Slater out of the game. Neither side was giving an inch that day. You earned every metre. In the end, the difference was Locky's ability to capitalise on the opportunities we did get to attack their line. He was the bloke who threw the last pass to Hodges to score first. The pick-up and pass he pulled off for Tate's try in the second half . . . there's not many other blokes in the game that could have done that. He also kicked a couple of goals for us. We were taking whatever we could get that day.

When he slotted that field goal, though, that was when I knew we had it. He wasn't going to let us lose from there.

Craig Bellamy: I was asked about coaching against Locky the other day and whether he was always the bloke I focused on stopping when my teams were playing against him. He was and still is. He will be till the day he finally does hang them up.

I have had the opportunity to coach some exceptional players, but I don't think I have ever seen someone who can read the game as quickly as Locky. From my earliest meetings with him when I started working at the Broncos, I couldn't believe how well he knew the game. Some of that stuff is obviously learned, but the instincts and ability to read a game the way he can – I think some of that you are born with. I guess the best comparison I can make is to a musician. When I see a sheet of music I see a bunch of lines and dots on a page. A great musician sees the same sheet and they see a song. I think when Locky looks at a defensive line or watches a game, he sees things very differently to the average person. Because of that he knows when to pass or when to go. As a coach, I always found him a difficult bloke to plan for, because you want to cut down the time he has the ball in his hands. If you give him too much time and space, he will pick the right option every time. Every single time. And he will cut you to shreds.

I know there have been a few times over the years at Melbourne where we have tried to change a couple of things with our defensive structures because we were playing against Darren that week. And when you haven't practised something enough, it gets exposed under match conditions – as often happened with these plans. Locky was just so hard to handle because he was one of the very, very few guys who was equally as dangerous running the ball himself as he was passing and kicking. The number of players that got caught grasping at thin air after shooting out of the line trying to pressure Darren . . . That was where you had to find the right balance, because he was so good on his feet, when you forced him to run he would beat you one-on-one, which would immediately create an overlap he could exploit.

Preparing for that '06 grand final, he was our big concern. He had a big pack of old hard-heads in front of him and the thing that struck us was the way he had learned to work off the back of them, just picking his moment when to kick. Sometimes he'd shoot into dummy-half and just speed things up when he felt it necessary. He just seemed in total command of the tempo the game was being played at.

Trying to prevent him taking control of the game was something we spoke about in the week. But it is one thing to talk about it. It is another thing trying to get out there and actually try to contain Darren Lockyer's impact on a game. Unfortunately we couldn't and in the end he was probably the difference between the two teams. Watching that field goal sail through – and it never looked like missing – I just remember the sinking feeling which hit me straightaway. When I saw him lining it up, I initially felt a sense of relief. I thought it was a good result we had forced him into a Hail Mary field goal attempt. There was no way he would slot it from over 40 metres out. Not with how heavy his legs would have been feeling after 73 minutes of the hardest football imaginable.

The thing was, when I looked down and realised who it was who did it, I wasn't surprised or angry. It's the sort of thing he does. That final 10 minutes of the game – that is where Locky comes into his own.

As the week progressed, I became more and more confident about our chances. Our gameplan was pretty simple. We wanted to condense the field and have our big blokes roll at them through the middle over and over and over again. We wanted to exhaust their forward pack. Berro and I would simply sniff around behind them. Where during the year we had relied on structured shift a lot in our attack, during the finals we were a little more ad-lib style, with the team concentrating on working the ball down the middle of the park and waiting for some broken field we could attack. Tatie's try in the second half was the perfect example of what I mean. A quick play-the-ball by Petero allowed Berro to beat the markers. A series of short sharp passes, highlighted by an over-the-head speculator by Casey McGuire, somehow ended up in my hands. I handed off to Tunza who in turn found Tatie who scored in the corner.

To be honest, I knew at that moment the game was ours, but the pessimist in me ensured I celebrated nothing until that siren sounded at full-time.

When I heard it ring out across the Olympic Stadium in Sydney, I remember just being overwhelmed by a sense of excitement and I guess joy, for want of a better term. It was decidedly different to the feelings I had experienced after winning grand finals previously. I suppose in '97, '98 and 2000 we went into the big game expected and expecting to win. To do so was more a combination of satisfaction and relief. This time around we had been given little chance.

The win gave my great friend and teammate Shane Webcke the fairytale finish to his outstanding career all players dream about. I had the chance to call him onto the stage before lifting the famous NRL trophy depicting the muddy embrace of combatants Arthur Summons and Norm Provan. No one worked harder for us to achieve that win than Shane Webcke. And I am not just talking about that day or even that year. Webbie had led that team with unrivalled determination and commitment. I may have had the captaincy tag, but Webbie was the spiritual leader of the group. He was the bloke the young blokes were terrified of upsetting and he was my first port of call whenever I needed to address an issue within the playing group. He was always a bit more mature than me and was extremely well read and well educated. He and Thorny had such great values and were wonderful mentors to all the boys off the field. A lot of Webbie's traits are what you want from a captain. What probably held him back from getting those gigs, however, was the fact he wasn't really interested in footy. He didn't know much about it. He didn't know opposition players because whoever they were made no difference to him. His job remained the same. Run and tackle as hard as possible. When he was stuffed, he came off, had a breather and got stuck back into it.

Wayne Bennett: Webcke should have captained the Broncos. He would have been an outstanding leader of the club. But the fact is Darren Lockyer was the man for the job. Webbie knew it. No one resented the decision when I made it. Doing what he did, calling Webbie on stage there – says it all about the man and why he is a great leader. He's always thinking of the team and his team-mates.

We had been written off several times throughout the year – both the team and me personally – so I have to admit I found it really fulfilling to be able to prove I was capable of achieving something many believed was beyond me. I think sometimes people out there – be it fans in the crowd, journalists and reporters, whoever – think we don't hear what they yell or even hear the rumours they whisper about us. But rest assured, we do and I think it is only human that amongst the happiness and elation, there is also a little part of you desperately hoping those same people are watching. Often it will only shut them up for a short period of time, but as they say in the classics, silence is golden.

EIGHT

Coach

'Clearly, Darren Lockyer is held in the highest regard by his coach – and let's be serious, Wayne is Darren Lockyer's coach. He knows him better than anyone.'
– Phil Gould

As LOREN WILL tell you, I am anything but a hopeless romantic. I have never been the sentimental type and I don't think I am divulging state secrets telling you Wayne Bennett isn't big on sentimentality either, so I will do my best to avoid getting too mushy in the pages ahead.

I wanted to just put that on the record before I get into this chapter about the man we know affectionately as 'Longneck' – a coach who became a friend, confidant and guide through my career in rugby league and my life outside of it.

Wayne's status as a legend of the game was well and truly established before I arrived on the scene. So too his reputation for being able to get the best out of players by the unique relationships he formed with men in his charge – becoming more a father figure than simply a football coach.

Like any young Queensland rugby league player, I can vividly remember the first time I saw Wayne in the flesh. It is funny to say now, given all that we have shared in the years since, but I was as scared and intimidated as the rest of my team-mates in the Queensland under-12s side who had played at Lang Park earlier that day, the curtain-raiser to the main game between Brisbane and Parramatta. I thought all my Christmases had come at once when I found out we were going to get the chance to go into the Broncos' sheds after the first-grade match and meet Wayne and the players.

I remember reading former premiership-winning coach and leading journalist Roy Masters once writing that Wayne ranked somewhere 'just beneath Jack Gibson', which in rugby league circles put him 'somewhere just above God'. Well, being a kid born north of the Tweed, who was raised on rugby league in the 1980s and early 1990s, I didn't know a great deal about big Jack. And given I wasn't raised a Christian, Wayne Bennett was the nearest thing to a deity that existed in my little world. I couldn't even bring myself to shake his hand. I just looked at him across the room and then tried to shrink towards the back of the group, out of sight.

The next time we crossed paths was early in 1993, when Wayne and some members from the Broncos squad brought the NSWRL Premiership Trophy to Roma during their state-wide tour, following the club's inaugural grand final win against St George in 1992. Dad had brought me and my brothers into town, where it appeared the entire population of Roma had gathered to get a glimpse of the team.

In finishing the regular season as minor premiers before sweeping through the post-season to claim the major prize with a comprehensive victory over traditional powerhouse St George in Brisbane's first appearance in a grand final, the Broncos had turned rugby league in this country on its head. The dominance Queensland had enjoyed in State of Origin football during the 1980s, when Wally Lewis, Mal Meninga, Geno Miles, Fatty Vautin and the boys were taking it to the Cockroaches wearing sky blue was one thing. It was entirely another to have the interlopers from up north so brazenly usurp the powerbase of Sydney clubs.

With Alf, who was awarded the Rothmans Medal (the equivalent of the Dally M at the time) as the competition's best player, directing a brilliant backline featuring young stars Julian O'Neill, Steve Renouf, Willie Carne and Michael Hancock, Brisbane shredded the book on conventional wisdom within rugby league. They showed little regard for long-held beliefs about defence being the key to winning titles and attacking-minded teams unravelling under the pressure of semi-final football. Watching that side as a youngster, I never felt as though the game was out of reach of the Broncos, such was their capacity for piling on points in quick bursts. They appeared to play with an attitude whereby, no matter how many tries an opponent scored, they backed themselves to score more.

And they could and would attack from anywhere, as evidenced by Steve Renouf's famous length-of-the-field effort in the second half to seal the win. The Dragons had actually been pressing Brisbane's line just one play before and their halfback Noel Goldthorpe put in a useful grubber which looked certain to earn his side a repeat set. Carne was facing the dead ball line and collected the ball deep in the in-goal, but rather than simply submit to the chasers or carry the ball out of play, he propped, spun and took off. After a 15-metre burst running parallel with the dead ball line, he straightened and somehow made it into the field of play. It was an incredible piece of football and typified the confidence that the team was playing with by that stage in the year. From the ensuing play-the-ball, Kevie Walters actually raced up and pushed his brother, Kerrod, out of the way at dummy-half. He slung it out to Alf, who in turn sent a long spiral out to Pearl, who was in space, with just one hapless defender coming across in cover. The poor bloke nearly broke an ankle trying to adjust when Pearl stepped inside and set sail.

They were unstoppable and it was so much fun to watch. Those days were what made me want to be a Bronco. The adage that a team must lose a grand final before it wins one was trampled beneath the hooves of those rampaging Broncos in their 28–8 win in the decider.

Wayne had added a World Club Challenge trophy and a second premiership in 1993 to his already imposing résumé when I finally met him. It was 1994 and I was playing in an under-16s representative carnival at Ipswich. I assumed

Cyril Connell would be there, but he hadn't mentioned Wayne would be coming with him.

Cyril would always take up a position behind the goalposts at one end of the ground, preferably elevated slightly above ground level. He always felt that was the best spot to watch games develop and, more importantly, analyse how different boys read a game both in attack and defence. Could they see when one side was stacked or short? Could they spot and attack a potential overlap? Could they see when their side was short in defence and did they work hard to help out? Your best chance to see all this is from an elevated position behind the posts and that is exactly where I saw Cyril and Wayne sitting at North Ipswich Reserve.

When they saw me, Cyril came over and told me he wanted to introduce me. I was really nervous. All I knew of Wayne at that time was what I had seen in the snippets of him on the news. The stern face and piercing stare of his don't exactly give off a relaxed or friendly vibe, but after shaking hands we spoke and within moments settled into a fairly comfortable rapport. The end result of that conversation was Wayne offering me a full-time place at the Broncos the following year, but we certainly covered a variety of topics before we got around to that.

In the 18 years since that meeting, I have watched countless players of all ages go through the same moments of trepidation before their first meeting with Wayne. As recently as this year, I spoke to a number of the boys who were part of the 2011 Queensland Emerging Origin squad, which gathered in Brisbane in January for the annual induction-type camp designed to introduce promising young Queensland players to the philosophies and culture of the Maroons. Its formation was part of the restructure Wayne had implemented following the debacle of the 2000 State of Origin series and, as the head of the program, Wayne oversees the camp. Jharal Yow Yeh and Matty Gillett both came back from that stunned at how open and engaging Wayne was and were taken aback by just how much he knew about them. The general public's perception of Wayne is a far cry from the reality of the man . . . not that he is the least bit perturbed by such misconceptions.

I think one of the keys to his coaching philosophy is the fact that he takes a genuine interest in you and your life. I remember during my first year at the club when I'd be training with the under-19s and it would be quite late. The way it worked back then was the first-grade squad would train, followed by reserve grade, then the under-21s, and the under-19s went on last. On several occasions I would come in and shower and Wayne would still be at the club. He would wander over casually and see how I was going. And it wasn't just me, he did the same with all the young blokes at different times. He knew where we were staying; he knew our background – the different places we each hailed from. He knew the girlfriends and wives, the parents and siblings.

His recall for that sort of thing is quite staggering, actually. It might not sound like much, but in my opinion, this trait has formed the backbone of Wayne's success as a coach. I remember the feeling after one of those post-training encounters with Wayne – it was as if I was 10 feet tall and bulletproof. Here was the senior coach talking to a kid in the under-19s and taking an interest, not just in my game but in me. It just made you feel important. That is the sort of coach I want to play for and I think that is the key to success for any coach – having a group of players desperate not to let you down.

Having now had the chance to work under a variety of coaches at both club and representative level, I have come to a few conclusions about the role of a head coach in the modern game. I think there are a number of NRL coaches who get consumed by the video room. The number of hours some spend poring over videos and devising structures, strategies and set moves to fit every conceivable scenario the team may encounter over the course of an 80-minute match is staggering and can often see them lose focus on what I consider to be the fundamental responsibilities of a head coach.

At the very top of that list is the need for a coach to create an environment players want to be a part of when they arrive at work each day. If you get to a stage in the season where a number of blokes simply are not enjoying coming in to training each day, things will fall apart quickly. Wayne understands this balance better than any other coach I have encountered. He has a harsh, dry sense of humour we all enjoy. He almost always dropped a couple of sarcastic cracks at different blokes to break up review sessions – I guess over time he just figured out the right balance between needing to be serious and focused and having the odd laugh to ensure we didn't get too intense.

Then there were the times he had us in stitches through his penchant for mixing up the names of players during match analysis and planning sessions. Wayne actually possesses an incredible recall of facts, dates, players and names, which really made the semi-regular gaffes even more amusing to us. Just strange little ones, like referring to 'The Chief', Newcastle's Paul Harragon, as Paul Harrington for 30 minutes before Webby or Petero piped up with something along the lines of, 'Okay, Coach, I understand all that, but who the f*** is Paul Harrington?' There was another occasion when he continuously referred to Andrew Johns as Chris Johns. I think it was Shaun Berrigan who took the chance once Wayne's spiel was complete, raising his hand querying the need for employing such intense plans to curtail the impact of a bloke in his mid-forties who hadn't laced on a boot for more than a decade. Wayne would wave us away, 'F*** off, Berro, you know who I am talking about.'

I have often heard people talk about Wayne's man-management skills as his greatest asset. That is, his ability to get each and every individual within his squad pulling in the same direction. To me, that stems from a combination of Wayne's uncanny ability to 'read' people and the unique relationship he is able to form with his players. Wayne knows when he needs to put an arm around a bloke and similarly when he needs to give a bloke a rocket. He demands that players train and prepare with the necessary intensity, but understands the importance of down time. As I mentioned earlier, he is well aware of the value of a laugh and a joke within the team dynamic. I have no doubt it was his relationship with Allan Langer that left an indelible imprint on Wayne in this department.

I know Wayne will probably insist he doesn't have favourites. But make no mistake, Alf was his favourite. Alf could get away with saying anything to Wayne. Actually, Alf could and still can get away with putting shit on pretty much anyone. When he turned his attention to Wayne, Wayne would just laugh. Being so introverted and reserved himself, he just loved being part of the fun – even if it was at his expense. More than once during the latter stages of Mad Monday celebrations, Alf decided to ring Coach – who is probably the most famous teetotaller in the game – to warn him our festivities were moving out to his place at Mt Ommaney in Brisbane's western suburbs.

And so, at the back-end of a solid day of celebrating, we'd all pile into cabs, head over to Benny's house and simply wander up and knock on the front door. It must have been quite the sight for other people in the street to have 20–30 young men, decked out in an array of bizarre costumes and clearly a little under the weather, standing there waiting to be let in. The door would always open and in we'd go and, while most boys thought it wise to be a little more reserved at the boss's place, Alf did nothing of the sort. Usually he'd locate the stockpile of alcohol Wayne always has at his place – unused gifts people have given him over time.

Wayne would just laugh – he could sit there and watch Alf playing up and joking around all day. He'd just sit there and laugh and it was the same with Kevie. To this day, Alf will pepper Wayne with calls at all hours of the day or night, needling him, singing – doing what it is Alf does. I had to laugh when, as Wayne joined the rest of the Dragons players and staff in the dressing-room celebrations following the 2010 grand final, I saw him asked whether he had heard from his little friend in Brisbane.

See, after winning the 1993 premiership, Alf had caused quite a stir when he got up on stage, grabbed the microphone and started chanting, 'St George can't play' – a putdown aimed squarely at Dragons coach Brian Smith, who had riled a number of Broncos players in the lead-up to the match after tip sheets on each Broncos player were leaked. The sheets featured some stinging criticisms of each individual – criticisms we now know came courtesy of Wayne himself. It was a coaching masterstroke, the players' response to the harsh words akin to that of a bull's when it catches a crimson glint in its sights. The Broncos' 14–6 win in the '93 grand final secured the club a place in history as the first team to be crowned premiers after finishing the minor premiership outside the top four. The fifth of five teams in the finals that year, Brisbane also became the first and, to date, only team to have won the title from the lowest qualifying position.

It is interesting that Wayne has always embraced the characters within the team. Wendell, Kevie, Alf, Gordie, Justin Hodges – these were the blokes Wayne really tended to gravitate towards. I guess I share some similar traits – I think we both just enjoy sitting back watching and listening to them when they take centre court. The way Wayne always took a seat right in the middle of the back row on the team bus is the perfect example of what I am talking about. As with any bus ride you go on, from your days in primary school onwards, you have the people who prefer to sit at the front of the bus and those who move straight to the back. The Broncos team bus split in much the same manner as your typical school bus, with the blokes who wanted to keep to themselves taking residence near the front while the louder and more rowdy boys scrambled for positions at the rear. The middle seat in the back row, however, was always left for Wayne. He loved listening to the stories and being 'one of the boys' – being right in the middle of it all. I think it helped him stay in touch with his players. Having been a part of first-grade football teams for almost 50 years, Wayne has some great anecdotes himself. Mostly, though, he just listens and I have no doubt that is part of what has allowed him to stay relevant for so long. He educates himself on different generations and knows what their interests are.

As much as Wayne had his favourites, we still joke about the blokes he loved to pick on and spray when they stuffed up at training. Craig Frawley was one, Dane Carlaw used to cop it and Dave Taylor was Wayne's worst nightmare with his cut-out passes and chip kicks. Then there was Tunza who was a source of constant amusement in the latter part of his career. His ability to recover from what appeared to be a serious injury time and again bemused the coach and became the stuff of legend at the club.

Wayne's ability to adjust and to change with the times and keep pace with the world around him is what has allowed him to coach for as long as he has. Over the years, he has no doubt changed the way he addresses issues with players. But his core principles have remained the same. At its heart is the belief that the team always comes first – without exception. And like the old saying about a chain only being as strong as its weakest link, Wayne expects every member to do their bit, to play their role. It only takes one person to ignore or disregard their role and the entire unit is left vulnerable. The strength of the group is determined largely by the discipline of those within it. Discipline is something that can be taught but is not something that can be employed in one area of your life and not others. You can't try to be disciplined on the football field if you have no discipline in your everyday life. So that is where it begins. He sets standards he expects every member of the group to meet. He will not compromise on these. Basic things like, if you are staying with the team at the team hotel and want to eat in public, you wear proper shoes and an appropriate shirt. Hats are not allowed. A lot of the boys of this generation want to wear caps and singlets and thongs. That is fine when they are on their own time. But when they are representing the team they fall in line with some pretty simple rules. The need to be punctual is probably the fundamental discipline Wayne enforces most strictly. He is a firm believer in the benefits of maintaining a routine in day-to-day life. There are so many examples of young guys who arrive at the Broncos with bad habits – turning up late, presenting poorly, and so on. He teaches them some basics for life and gives them some structure.

Sammy Thaiday is a wonderful example of a guy who arrived and was a bit rough around the edges. He needed to make changes in his approach to his life if he was going to fulfil his potential as a footballer. It took some time, but I think the fact Sam is one of the leading candidates to take over as Broncos captain in 2012 is a testament to how far he has come.

Another of Wayne's core principles that feeds into the over-arching team-first philosophy is developing an atmosphere of relentless competition within the playing group itself. When I first arrived at the Broncos, I couldn't believe the way in which senior blokes at the club – representative players – would turn everything into a competition. Whether it was getting through a tough gym circuit or simply signing a pile of autographs, everything was a race. We'd get through all our drills at training, but Wayne would always find time to incorporate some games into each session and he'd watch to see who thrived in the competitive environment. If you have 17 blokes who turn up each week willing to compete as hard as they can for the full 80 minutes, half the battle is already won. That willingness to compete till the very end is a trademark shared by all sides coached by Wayne Bennett and reflects Wayne's own fierce and unwavering competitive streak.

It probably wasn't until the early 2000s that I started to develop a relationship with Wayne beyond that which normally exists between a coach and any young player. The departures of Alf and Kevie changed the dynamic of the club enormously and looking back I think it is fair to say we, as a club, probably didn't cope with the change as well as we had hoped. Gordie was handed the captaincy and I was made his deputy. It was a position which demanded I take on a far more prominent role within the football department and I began interacting with the other leaders of the organisation far more regularly than I had done previously. By our nature, Wayne and I are both pretty quiet and reserved so, while we shared plenty in common, we were never going to find ourselves sitting down and talking for hours in an attempt to build some sort of emotional attachment. I remember having some concerns about how Wayne and the rest of the club would adjust to having very different personalities leading the playing group. I was never going to have the sort of relationship with Wayne that he and Alf shared, because Alf and I are vastly different people. I know there have been rumours at different times suggesting Wayne and I didn't get on, which isn't true. But by the same token, there was definitely a period there after I was appointed vice-captain when we were a little stand-offish. It was just a little awkward, perhaps because we are both more accustomed to, and more comfortable with, sitting back and allowing others to initiate conversations. But as time passed I think we began to enjoy our mutual affection for non-verbal communication.

Of course, as is required of an NRL coach, Wayne certainly didn't hesitate in directing some stern words my way when he saw fit. If I had a quiet half at five-eighth or had just struggled to get the team rolling, almost inevitably I would be greeted at half-time by Wayne, hands on hips, shaking his head.

'Are you here today, Locky? Are you even here? Seriously. Go and make a f***ing tackle or something. Do *something*!'

It was a slight alteration on what I used to cop if I had spilled a couple of balls when playing fullback.

'Locky, it's not hard. Catch the f***ing ball.'

As close as the two of us became working alongside each other for more than 300 games for club, state and country, Wayne always maintained the ability to put you firmly in your place when he believed it was required.

It didn't happen to me often, though I will never forget one phone call late in 2001. A furore had erupted after Wayne demoted promising youngster Justin Hodges after revelations he had agreed to join the Sydney Roosters the following year. In Hodges' place, Wayne promoted another teenager by the name of Brent Tate. Given the future of the club lay with Tate, Wayne was keen to give him a good taste of NRL action, adamant it would prove enormously beneficial when Tate returned for pre-season training. It just so happened that Wayne's controversial decision coincided with a poor finish to the year and, as the losses began to pile up, the pressure began to mount. The push to have Hodgo reinstated became somewhat of a campaign in the media and it gained plenty of traction amongst the fans, such was Justin's popularity. After a couple of weeks, Wayne declared the matter dead and refused to answer any questions relating to it. He ordered the squad to follow suit – an instruction I failed to adhere to when contacted by a journalist about a week later.

I think some of the ink on the paper was still drying when my phone rang the next morning.

'Darren,' Wayne said in a most severe tone.

'Yeah.'

'Did you speak to a journalist yesterday about Justin?'

'Yeah, I did actually. I didn't reall–'

'Well, f***ing don't. I told you not to.'

With that, he slammed down the phone and I was immediately hit by a wave of anxiety. I paced around my place for ages just freaking out, thinking, 'Shit, what have I done here?' I was actually scared to go to training the next day and tried to duck in quietly. But I needn't have worried. As is his way, Wayne had said his piece and moved on. He never mentioned it again.

Neither of us is especially argumentative, so we actually haven't had many blues worthy of note. Probably the only major one came during the 2008 season, when I was coming back after the knee reconstruction I underwent as a result of rupturing my anterior cruciate ligament (ACL) during a match against the Cowboys at Dairy Farmers Stadium in late July 2007. Actually, it wasn't so much a rupturing as it was a complete destruction of my right knee. The first damage came as we were attacking the Cowboys line about 15 metres out, directly in front of the sticks. I just went to pass the ball from left to right and something pinched. I felt sharp and intense stabbing pain and fell down for a second, but regained my composure pretty quickly and got back in line. About five minutes later, we were down the other end of the field and got trapped in goal. I had been hitting my drop-outs especially well for quite a while. I was hitting the ball really sweetly and more often than not was landing the ball well inside opposition territory. On this occasion, however, my plant leg buckled and the ball skewed off my boot. That's when I started to think there might really be something wrong but stupidly kept going until a couple of minutes later when I was tackled. My knee twisted abnormally and the crunching noise that followed was not one your body should make.

I found out later that the first wrench probably partially tore the ACL, along with a few ligaments. With the knee joint loose, planting the foot to pivot for the drop-out tore the ACL completely. With nothing to stabilise my knee, the final one just ripped all the cartilage away – which is what significantly slowed the rehabilitation process. I was back running in early 2008, but was forced to go in for clean-up surgery – using an arthroscope – to remove some loose cartilage from behind the kneecap that was making things particularly uncomfortable. The timing couldn't have been much worse, as it cost me a place in the historic Centenary Test between Australia and New Zealand on 9 May of that year. The opening Origin match less than two weeks later was also out of the question and, while the medical advice was that I should be taking every precaution with my recovery, I had already circled Origin II in Sydney on 11 June. I intended to be fit and firing for that match and wouldn't hear anything to the contrary.

The reality was, however, that my rehabilitation was pretty sluggish. The atrophy that occurred while my leg had been in the brace following the reconstruction was still glaringly obvious and meant I still heavily favoured my left side when I was walking or running. I knew I needed some footy before game two and told Wayne I was right to go for our clash with the Eels at Suncorp Stadium on 30 May. Wayne wasn't sold on the idea and said I needed more time. He called me into his office the day before the match and told me I needed more time to get the knee right. I was adamant I was ready to play. The exchange went back and forth a couple of times until eventually I just lost it. The frustration and anxiety which had been gnawing at me for almost a year now simply became too much.

'This is bullshit. I will prove all you bastards wrong,' I yelled, before storming out of there in a huff.

Wayne Bennett: Huge battles were going on with that knee. He was rehabbing like crazy – no one rehabs more professionally than Locky – but things just weren't coming together and Origin was coming around. I knew how much he wanted to be a part of Origin and I could see what he was trying to do and I let him do it. I owed him that much. After all he had done – all he had given to me and to the club – if it meant that much to him I wasn't going to make a prick out of myself by standing in his way. At the same time, I didn't want the knee to be re-damaged. I had seen the struggles he had been through just getting to that point, and I wasn't sure he could do that again.

We had been to-ing and fro-ing all week about

whether or not he would play this game. He doesn't talk to many people, Locky, but at the time he would speak to someone one day and make a decision. An hour later, he'd have changed his mind. By week's end I had just had enough. He was limping around the place and I had spoken to the doctors, who had made it clear he really needed the time off. He needed complete rest – which isn't something Darren Lockyer is good at.

He came up to my office and I said to him, 'This is the scenario, mate. You are out this week. You need the time off. It's for your own good.'

'No, Coach, I can play,' he told me.

I just said, 'No, Darren, you can't play.'

I reckon it was the first time I ever told him he couldn't do something. Locky is the most respectful guy you'll meet, but he swore at me for the first time after I said that.

'I f***ing can play.'

'Darren,' I said, 'you're a wonderful man. You can do what you want, but you cannot do this.'

'I'll f***ing prove you bastards wrong.'

'I'd love you to prove me wrong,' I told him. 'I don't want to be right about this issue. But I am telling you now that is the way it is and that is the way it is f***ing going to be. Okay?'

He stormed out of my office and slammed the door. I had to stop from laughing out loud, because Locky being angry just doesn't scare you that much. He doesn't do cranky all that well.

I came back and spoke to Wayne on game day and he finally relented. I wore number 19 that day and I was reasonably optimistic about my chances of getting through. The knee had improved steadily over the two previous weeks, but I needed to put it through the rigours of an NRL match before I would even dream of putting my hand up for Origin football. Things had been going fine until, with about 10 minutes left to play in the game, the Eels put a chip in not too far from our line. I went to turn and chase and I felt a burning pain down the inside of my knee. At that second, I knew I was gone for the series. In State of Origin football, everything is amplified. To carry a little niggle like that into a match is to put at risk all the hard work of the other 16 blokes in the team. There is nowhere to hide if you aren't 100 per cent focused on the job at hand and I knew in my heart that if I played I would be thinking about the knee throughout.

Funnily enough, I was actually part of a famous finish against the Eels that afternoon. Denan Kemp had a field day, crossing for four tries – the fourth of which came right on the full-time siren. I spotted some space wide out on the left behind the winger marking Denan, who was clearly the quickest player at the club at that time.

All the boys were celebrating, but when I came off the field I was pretty down in the dumps. I saw Coach in the dressing-room and just shook my head. He wandered over and patted me on the back. He didn't say a word and he didn't have to. I knew he had been right – like he normally is.

I watched on from the coach's box as JT and Cameron Smith took control of the side. Greg Inglis turned it on in Game II after Mark Gasnier got the better of him in the series opener and, along with another emerging backline giant by the name of Israel Folau, helped Queensland secure a third straight series win.

The 2008 season was Wayne's final season as head coach of the Broncos. What he has done since his departure has, in my mind, ended any lingering doubts anyone may have had about his position atop the list of the game's greatest coaches. He is it. End of discussion.

Wayne's leaving, to me, was a tragedy. From top to bottom it was handled badly and there is no question he deserved better than he got – that is both off the field and on it. As always, though, Wayne did the best with the cards he was dealt and proved a lot of people wrong.

In the end he had the last laugh.

That's why Wayne Bennett is who he is and there will never be another like him.

Phil Gould: Let's start with the fact that Darren Lockyer has been very well coached. His basics have always been solid. Playing fullback, he always did everything his team needed, just when they needed it. The same when he went to five-eighth, and Wayne Bennett has to take a lot of credit for that. Lockyer has obviously been very well schooled, but by the same token, you don't do what he has done for as long as he has done it unless you are a bloody good student.

I was at a function in early 2011. It was before Lockyer had confirmed he was going to retire at the end of the year, but there was a fair bit of speculation suggesting he was going to do just that. Wayne was there with me and we were looking up at the list of Immortals, which was being projected onto a big screen there. Almost out of the side of his mouth and totally unprompted, he leant over to me and said, 'Lockyer should be up there.'

I just nodded and said, 'He will be.'

Then Wayne sort of looked at me and said, 'He's better than the lot of them, you know.'

'He may well be,' I replied.

Now, Wayne Bennett isn't the sort of guy who throws around comments like that without thinking. He doesn't praise blokes who haven't earned it. Clearly, Darren Lockyer is held in the highest regard by his coach – and let's be serious, Wayne is Darren Lockyer's coach. He knows him better than anyone.

For him to say he is the best of the lot of them, well . . . I will just say Wayne has had some good ones. Some very good ones.

Ben Ikin: They have a relationship that is built on mutual respect. It has been built over time and on a foundation of an enormous amount of shared success. But I don't think you are ever going to see them sitting down for three or four hours having lunch . . . if they did, it wouldn't be the most riveting conversation to listen in on, put it that way.

That is why they love having those characters like Alf and Kevie, Wendell – to come in and take centre stage and make those environments entertaining and enjoyable. The pair of them are classic introverts, happy to just sit back and observe things. They will pipe up when they believe they can add something, but neither of them will use two words when one will suffice.

I suppose the other trait they share is what I call emotional discipline. I think this has oftentimes been mistaken for a lack of interest or care – but to those who know them, Wayne and Locky are as fierce competitors as you could ever hope to meet. They take enormous pride in what they do and they hurt when things don't go to plan. They feel as much emotion as anyone else – maybe more, sometimes. Locky doesn't feel the need to share how he is feeling with the world through some elaborate post-try celebration. Wayne often appears more open to media post-match after a loss.

Neither of them feels the need to be loved by everyone. They understand very clearly whose opinions are important. These are the people who form their circle of trust and comments passed from outside ceased being important to Wayne and Locky a long time ago. That is particularly important when you are in an environment like the NRL, where there is such a vast array of people passing their thoughts and opinions on what it is you do. You need to be able to differentiate between the voices you need to listen to and those you do not.

That sort of emotional discipline is very rare. I know I really struggled with it – I took everything personally no matter where it came from. I struggled with the expectations others had of me. In the end that very issue was a big part of why I retired from the game. Physically I had gotten to a stage where I couldn't do the things I once could and I just couldn't deal with the fact there were some people out there who believed I shouldn't have been there – that I was no longer adding value. The ability to maintain a level head is the key to performing consistently, which is what all rugby league players and coaches are after. The ones who struggle with that are the blokes who have the big form slumps. They ride the roller-coaster of emotions and eventually those lows become too low to come back from.

I have always felt longevity is the true test of greatness. By that measure, Wayne and Locky are in a league of their own.

Ricky Stuart: I see a hell of a lot of Wayne Bennett in Darren, which only happens when an individual decides he wants to be like his role model or mentor. Everyone has role models or mentors – people who are major influences on their lives. Some choose the right ones, others obviously don't.

But let me add I see some of Darren in Wayne too. When you see the way blokes look at one another after a win – it tells a story. You see where the coach goes first. The self-confidence Wayne displays much more openly these days, I just feel a lot of that has come from having had Darren in his team for so long and having Darren's confidence in him. I think it reflects the regard in which he holds Darren.

They both have a quiet competitiveness. Neither likes to give much away, but they are winners . . . both of them.

NINE
Friends, Foes, Fun

ONE OF THE great things about hanging around the game as long as I have, is getting the chance to share the field with so many wonderful players – both as team-mates and opponents. Over the course of my 17 years I have farewelled some of the game's true champions. On the flip side, though, I have taken great pleasure in watching new stars emerge and stake their own claim for a place in the NRL history books.

In my debut season in 1995, it was a very different landscape. In the grand final that year, two of the all-time great five-eighths and iconic club men did battle on the big stage for the final time in their glittering careers, with Lamb taking the points. To see Des Hasler's name on the Manly team-sheet for the same game reminds me just how old I am getting, given 2011 is Dessy's eighth season as coach of the Sea Eagles. Back in those days, Brad Fittler was still a Panther, playing under the captaincy of current Gold Coast Titans mentor, John Cartwright. The South Queensland Crushers, Western Reds, North Sydney Bears and Gold Coast Seagulls were all part of the Australian Rugby League's 20-team competition, but have since bitten the dust. Similarly the West Tigers and Western Suburbs Magpies and St George Dragons and Illawarra Steelers were still individual entities at that stage.

Of course, for those of us hailing from the Sunshine State, 1995 is remembered as one of the Maroons' finest hours. The decision to ban players aligned to Super League from the series had ravaged the Queensland side to the point where Maroons selectors struggled to cobble together a team of 17 regular first-graders. My great friend Benny Ikin became the youngest player in Origin history when he was named on the bench for the series opener at 18 years of age. He had been plucked from obscurity, having played only a handful of first-grade games with the Seagulls prior to his inclusion in Paul Vautin's squad. So left-field was his selection that when he arrived at the team hotel for the first day of camp he went to get on a lift with the coach and some of his new team-mates. As Iki tells it, Fatty, believing Ikin was an autograph hunter, put out his arm in an apologetic manner and explained the lift was for people involved with the State of Origin squad.

'I'm in your team,' Benny replied.

How that mish-mash Queensland side routed the star-studded Blues side that coach Phil Gould had at his disposal – to the tune of 3–0 no less – remains one of the great mysteries in rugby league's proud history.

Starting when I did, I only caught the tail end of Canberra's era of dominance, which ran from the later 1980s through to the mid-'90s. Still I saw enough to appreciate the quality of some of those teams, which featured superstars like Ricky Stuart, Laurie Daley, Brett Mullins, Big Mal and Brad Clyde, amongst others. Manly also had some great sides through the 1990s, while the Knights emerged as a force late in the decade on the back of the brilliant hooker–halfback combination of Danny Buderus and Andrew Johns. After the turn of the century, the Roosters joined the Knights as a force to be reckoned with, before Craig Bellamy's Melbourne Storm side assumed the mantle as the team to beat.

All those sides brought different facets to the game which separated them from the rest of the competition. The bullet-like long passing of Ricky and Laurie brought greater width to Canberra's attack than any team before them had displayed; the speed with which they were able to move the ball from one side of the field to the other allowed them to make best use of the array of strike weapons in the side.

Bedsy Buderus and Joey Johns revolutionised the game with their work as a dummy-half–first receiver combination. Before them, rugby league offence was built around the men with number six or seven on their back. Traditionally the halfback took position at first receiver from the ruck area, with the five-eighth one position wider. But Bedsy was so dynamic and creative the Knights attack came at you from dummy-half and first receiver, meaning it was more direct than basically any other offensive unit we had seen.

I know some blokes get a little belligerent when they are asked how they rate different team-mates and opponents, or how players of today stack up against those who have gone before, but I can never understand why. Those are the sorts of topics we want the media and our fans talking, even arguing, about. While I think things have improved significantly over the past two years, the so-called 'NRL soap opera' – which refers to the seemingly endless number of off-field dramas involving NRL clubs, players or officials – still occupies an unhealthy percentage of the time and or space media outlets dedicate to their coverage of rugby league.

When you compare the coverage of the NRL with that of the AFL or rugby union, there is an obvious lack of intelligent debate or critical analysis of what is happening on the field each week. As a game, we need to work harder to promote that sort of coverage. Similarly, we need to better embrace the proud history of our game. I think that needs to start with the NRL doing more to acknowledge the prominent figures and significant moments of yesteryear. In doing so, we could begin to better educate our fans, as well as the people working within our game, about how the code has grown into what we enjoy today.

I love watching some of the Channel 9 intros to State of Origin matches which show footage of games with legends of the game from the 1960s, '70s and '80s. I loved seeing clips of those great Dragons sides with blokes like Graeme

'Changa' Langlands and Reg Gasnier or the champion Eels outfits of the early 1980s, when Mick Cronin was tearing teams apart. We don't do it enough. The NRL should have access to a video library, because I think it would be the best promotional tool available to them. They certainly managed to dig up some wonderful footage at different times through the Centenary celebrations in 2008. Langlands, Gasnier and Cronin were names that were famous to me when I was growing up, even though I saw very little of them on the field.

Those names need to be famous for every generation and the only way to do that is by having their faces and names shown regularly to today's players and fans. The Americans can sometimes go over the top, but more often than not they do a wonderful job of romanticising major sporting events. The way the NFL, for instance, remembers the incredible moments or games of yesteryear gives me goosebumps. As a viewer, you just become engaged. There is so much more we can do in this department – capturing the imagination of the public and taking them into the moments. We continue to undersell so many aspects of our game – our wonderful history, perhaps, most of all.

I actually really enjoy talking about my experiences sharing a field with genuine champions of our game. Certainly, Benji Marshall is forging a career which is on track to secure him a place in such company and I loved the chance I had to train with and play alongside Benji as part of the NRL All-Stars side in 2010 and 2011. The first time around we never really got a chance to see how things worked with the two of us out the calling the shots, because I was injured in the very first tackle of the match attempting to bring down a rampaging Georgie Rose. It was much better second time around. By the second training run together in the lead-up to the 2011 NRL All-Stars match, the two of us had found some rhythm – our groove, so to speak.

The thing that struck me about Benji is the way he can create or imagine something in his head, but then has the skill and athleticism to go out onto a field and attempt the play in a game situation. I once heard it said of Tiger Woods that when he was at his best, tearing apart the world's best courses and destroying quality playing fields, what set him apart from the other exceptional golfers on the PGA tour was his imagination. Tiger could visualise a ball doing things other golfers couldn't and possessed the necessary skill to turn those dreams into reality. Benji is like that out there on a grassy field with a rugby league ball in his hands.

The other part of his game which really impressed me and is something I just love watching is his sleight of hand. Of course, he is capable of pulling off plays that defy logic, but what I like is the way he just uses changes of pace to get defenders off-balance. I don't mean only the changes to his footspeed when he is carrying the ball, but I also saw him use variations in the speed of his passes and the release of his pass. In fact, the opening try of the game came on the back of Benji holding up his pass to a runner sweeping deep to the left and drawing two defenders into error.

It had shades of the great Jason Smith about it. Smithy was the master of subtle trickery out on the field – he built his career on it. An athlete Jason Smith was not. He wasn't particularly big or strong and definitely wasn't the quickest bloke going around. But put a football in his hands and he was something special. In a game which is so dominated by powerful athletes carrying out the instructions their coach has set for them, Smith was a throwback. An old-school 'footballer' who was at his best playing what was in front of him, probing for cracks in the defensive line, trying to plant a seed of doubt in the mind of his opponents which he would look to exploit at the most opportune time. He was one of the blokes fans enjoyed going to watch and earned cult hero status at every club of which he was a part.

The scary prospect for Benji Marshall's opponents is knowing that he has the skills and touch of an 'old-school' footballer, as well as having been blessed with a level of athleticism only a select few within the NRL possess.

Anyhow, without further ado here is my attempt at my favourite 17. Just to clarify, it is not me saying these are the greatest players in their respective positions the game has seen. No, these are blokes I have played with and against at various levels of the game and learned to value their presence on the field. These are the ones I would want beside me in a crisis.

My All-Time 17: Billy Slater, Wendell Sailor, Steve Renouf, Justin Hodges, Greg Inglis, Andrew Johns, Allan Langer, Glenn Lazarus, Cameron Smith, Shane Webcke, Gorden Tallis, Tonie Carroll, Brad Fittler; interchange Danny Buderus, Johnathan Thurston, Petero Civoniceva, Jason Smith.

I am fully aware that some of those selections will raise eyebrows, and that is fair enough. This is one topic where there is no right answer. It is just my contribution to the debate.

From the top, I went for Billy, but I also have great memories of playing with Karmichael Hunt and also Anthony Minichiello. Billy is a fantastic competitor and athlete, and he has a knack for scoring tries when games are on the line.

On the wings, Dell was great. He was like an extra forward, but then was a sensational finisher as well. He also had a bit of an intimidating presence about him. It was a little like Gordie, where you just felt safer having them in the side. I remember a few times towards the end of his career when Gordie would miss a match and opposition teams would try to bully us. No one tried to bully a team with Gorden Tallis in it.

What happened to poor old Casey McGuire against the Warriors back in 2004, when Awen Guttenbeil and Monty Betham each had a crack, would never have gone down with Gordie there. At worst it might have been a bit of a mêlée. There are just certain blokes when they are in the dressing-room with you, you just feel a bit more confident about things. Gordie and Dell both brought that to the table.

GI is the most natural footballer I have seen, so he can fill the other wing. Pearl would be in every team I ever picked. The fastest bloke off the mark I have ever seen, he burnt that many blokes with his first three steps it was ridiculous.

Hodgo would be my other centre. When he is on, he is just unstoppable one on one.

Joey and Alf complement each other nicely. Joey was the most skilful player I have ever seen. Freddie was big and powerful and could throw those beautiful long spirals either way, whereas Alf was the master of deception with his agility, short passes and grubbers. No one could work in confined spaces like Alf. He could create something out of nothing.

In the forwards, Jason Smith would get a start off the bench for all the reasons I mentioned earlier. Gordie picks himself and I would put Tunza alongside him. I am always surprised at how few of Tunza's tackles seem to make it on show reels depicting the NRL's biggest hits. Tunza was the biggest and best tackler I have ever seen. You could chalk him down for three or four bone-rattlers every match. Having had him alongside me for much of my time at five-eighth, I have seen with my own eyes big-name NRL forwards literally change the side of the field they were running because of Tunza.

I have appreciated how complete and composed a player Cameron Smith is, having played with him over the last six years, particularly at Origin level. Danny Buderus is someone I really enjoyed playing with at Test level. They don't come any tougher than Bedsy.

Either side of Cam, we have the bookends, Glenn Lazarus and Shane Webcke. While Petero was on my bench, he is very much in the same league as those guys. It would be fair to say that at the end of 80 minutes, the blokes on the other side of this forward rotation would know they'd been in a game. That is, provided they had made it through the 80 minutes in one piece.

JT gets the final spot on the bench because to me he is every bit as good as the other playmakers I already have in the team. He is something special, JT.

He, Benji and Cam are the blokes who will assume leadership roles within the NRL playing ranks in the years ahead. They are the blokes young viewers these days aspire to become.

Given that I started watching rugby league about 1986–87, my hero was, not surprisingly, Wally Lewis. I loved sitting at home and watching The King play either for Queensland in State of Origin or for Wynnum in the Brisbane competition, which was on TV every Saturday afternoon. When the Broncos came into the competition in 1988, I jumped on that bandwagon and Alf was obviously the star.

But if I am being honest, my real idol as a youngster was Hawthorn captain Leigh Matthews – the AFL's greatest ever player. My old man had got me into the AFL and the Hawks were my team. They were some sort of side through the 1980s, with stars right across the ground. But 'Lethal' was something else again.

He actually had a fairly similar build to Wally, relatively short and stocky. Both were exceptionally strong men, who played the game with the sort of physicality which instilled fear in opponents. Wally's defence was, at times, brutal. I still wince at replays of the shot he put on Michael O'Connor in an Origin match when he somehow found himself defending at fullback. There was another where he picked up a charging Gary Jack around the waist one night and flung him into the turf in a move I have seen replicated on a few occasion by various WWE wrestlers.

Matthews' hip and shoulder was equally as devastating but what separated him and Wally from other 'tough guys, in their respective codes, was the skill and finesse they also possessed in spades. That combination gave each man the extremely rare ability to be able to single-handedly change the course of a match. Their presence and ability was such they could win matches with very little support from their team-mates.

I don't think I am being disrespectful in saying that Leigh is probably best known up here in Queensland for his deeds as coach of the Brisbane Lions, leading them on their run of four consecutive grand final appearances from 2001 to 2004, which saw them claim a hat-trick of premierships (2001–2003). Leigh was well into his tenure with the Lions when I actually got the chance to meet him. He was very impressive and still had that presence about him. He still had those thick shoulders and piercing eyes I remember, but was very knowledgeable and articulate. If I was to equate him to someone in league circles, I guess you would say Phil Gould has that same sense of authority.

Over the years, I got to know a few of the boys from the Lions, particularly Michael Voss and Jonathan Brown, when I crossed paths with them a number of times at functions where we, as captains, were representing our respective clubs. Vossy and I were roughly about the same age and had inherited captaincy positions at a young age, so we had plenty in common other than our skin colour. The funny thing I found with those guys was that, while you don't see them all that often, there is a mutual respect that exists and when you get into a conversation it's almost like you both know what to talk about – and for the most part it is something other than footy. Football might be the ice-breaker, but really we know the last thing the other guy wants to talk about is footy.

I also crossed paths with Jason Akermanis quite a number of times, which was certainly an experience. He is a unique individual, Aker, and while he sometimes leaves you questioning the strength of the link between his mouth and brain, you cannot deny he could play. He was different and happy to be different. He loves stirring the pot and I actually remember one night at the now-defunct City Rowers nightclub a debate between one Gorden Tallis and Aker which concluded with an agreement for the need to stage a head-to-head longest-kick contest between me and Aker. It never eventuated, but I remain pessimistic about how I'd have fared had it ever gone down.

I also had a bit to do with George Gregan during his time as Wallabies captain and really enjoyed his company. We had a couple of great nights out over in Europe when the Kangaroos and Wallabies crossed paths. I enjoyed comparing notes with him. Same with Ricky Ponting, when I have had the chance to have a number of chats with him at different times. Ricky and George obviously have much bigger international profiles than I did as Kangaroos skipper.

Dad and me, taken shortly after my second birthday on one of my first trips to see my paternal grandparents, who lived on the water at Hastings Point. The 'Dennis Lillee' moustache and disco jacket Dad is sporting are reminders I was a child of the '70s.

I am not ashamed to say that I was a bit of a mama's boy – she is the most selfless person I have ever met. Here we are together at our Stone's Corner home in February 1980. While Sunny James has yet to turn two, the resemblance between my son and his old man at that age is uncanny.

The Lockyers at home – Mum and Dad with the three boys not long after Russell's arrival. It was early 1983 and we had recently moved into a new home at Rochedale on Brisbane's Southside.

Visiting Nana and Grandad at Hastings Point in 1983. The family holidays we spent there are among my most treasured childhood memories. My affection for that whole region is still with me today, and I now holiday there with my own family.

A bit of fun in the sun with my brothers. The homemade Slip 'n' Slide used to get a fair work-out during the long, hot summer months out at Wandoan. That's me in the middle with Matt (*right*) about to race back to the top of the tarp we doused with water and detergent. Russell is displaying perfect technique.

Splashing around in the creek again at Hastings Point. Grandad and Nana's place here was magic. The position was incredible. I could actually drop my fishing line into the water from my bedroom window – now *that* is waterfrontage!

The Lockyer boys at our home at Rochedale in 1985, shortly before we packed up our lives and headed out west to Wandoan. Matt (*right*) and I dutifully say 'cheese' for the photo. Russell is far more interested in something happening off to the side.

All grown up. The Lockyer lads: (*from left to right*) Russell, me and Matt at my place at Rockbourne Terrace in 2001.

Stretching out during my days as a Springwood Puma. I believe my grounding in AFL was an enormous help throughout my rugby league career. The foot skills and peripheral vision in particular were very beneficial to me playing rugby league.

Breaking away from the pack during an under-7s match against Morningside in 1984. I always wondered how I would have gone had I continued playing AFL or even switched codes mid-career. Before Karmichael Hunt, though, I never thought I would see someone actually try.

My first ever rugby league carnival – the 1987 regional primary schools' championship at Condamine. I lined up in the centres for Wandoan State School. The matches were played between makeshift goalposts on the flattest fairway they could find on the local golf course.

The 1986 Western Downs under-35kg squad that competed in the annual Zone 5 Carnival. That's me centre row, third from the right – a strapping outside centre. Despite being up against the likes of Wynumn, Redcliffe and Central Downs, we managed to get all the way through to the final. Unfortunately, Redcliffe had our measure, thanks largely to their star half, Shane Drahm, who went on to play professional rugby for Queensland before heading to England and Japan.

Once he was settled in his role managing the truck stop, Dad became the major sponsor of the local senior team, the Taroom–Wandoan Battlers. As part of the deal, I was made the 'official' team mascot and got to lead the team onto the flint-hard dustbowls they called fields in the Roma competition. I thought I was the luckiest kid on Earth. Note the captain with both knees strapped – a common sight across the league. Those country blokes played a seriously tough game.

The 1989 Queensland Primary Schools side. I (*far left*) played in the centres alongside future Wallaby Elton Flatley. Mark Tookey, who played plenty of NRL football, was a beast at that age. But our star was Andrew Meads, who ended up playing 21 first-grade games during stints at North Queensland, Balmain and Parramatta. My first taste of interstate football was a good one, with Queensland recording a 3–0 series whitewash against the Blues.

Ready, Set . . . ! Shortly before being called up to the starting blocks for the 100m final at the 1991 track State Titles. (I'm the one in yellow and blue.) Representing South-West, I also competed in the 200m sprint and long jump events. It was my first visit to QEII Stadium in Brisbane – a venue I would become very familiar with in the years ahead.

The 1991 Roma Cities Under-16As, which played in the Roma and Districts rugby league competition. I am in the back row, second player from the right. I was only 14 years old at the time, so I was often the slightest player on the field. Thankfully, though, I had a bit of speed and more often than not was able to avoid taking too much punishment.

Here I am during our round 19 clash with the Wests Magpies at Campbelltown in 1995, my debut season. It was still very surreal at that stage – things had happened so fast. I remember this game because I put in a cross-field kick for Willie Carne to score. Carne had been an inspiration and hero of mine for years. Having also come from Roma, his success at the highest level was proof it was possible. (Photo: Action Photographics)

The 1997 Super League Grand Final played at ANZ Stadium. We ran through Cronulla 26–8 in front of a sell-out crowd. We had an awesome side back then. You couldn't swing your arms in the dressing room without hitting a Test and Origin representative. Fair to say, I don't know if we would have been able to squeeze them into the salary cap in place today. (Photo: Col Whelan/ Action Photographics)

On a kick-return back in 1998. Hostilities had ceased and the competition reunited following the Super League war that split the competition in 1997. I was still a fresh-faced kid when it all happened, but it has probably taken the remaining 15 years of my career to repair a lot of the damage that the entire affair caused. (Photo: Rob Cox/ Action Photographics)

My first Origin profile pic, taken before game one in 1998. The hair is a little thinner these days, and that once fresh face is sporting more than a few battle wounds. But that is a small price to pay for the memories I've collected over the course of my 36 matches for the Maroons. (PHOTO: NEWSPIX/GREG PORTEOUS)

YES!! After Tonie Carroll had locked the scores up with a try on full-time, it was up to me to slot the conversion to win the match and give us a 1–0 lead in the 1998 State of Origin series. It was a sitter, but I was as nervous as I have ever been lining up the ball. The game is such a blur, but it was a memorable debut winning in those circumstances. (PHOTO: NEWSPIX/PHIL HILLYARD)

Getting the traditional 'champagne shower' from the Prince of Centre, Steve Renouf, after our win in the 1998 Grand Final. I loved playing with Pearl. He was a phenomenal player, freakish with the ball and devastating in defence. He'd be in every team I pick – whatever the criteria.

(PHOTO: ROB COX/ACTION PHOTOGRAPHICS)

It wasn't the Broncos the fans have come to know, but the Broncos of 2000 still delivered where it mattered most. Playing behind the pack of forwards that Wayne had at his disposal back then made life pretty easy for me, and I was fortunate to win the Clive Churchill Medal. It could have gone to a number of blokes. (PHOTO: CHRIS LANE/ACTION PHOTOGRAPHICS)

Mum has been there for me every step of the way, at every big match. She always cries when she sees me after a big win – the 2000 Grand Final was no exception. Mum is my number one supporter, and I owe much of the success I've enjoyed to her and Dad.

In 2004 I managed to break Andrew Johns' stronghold on the Provan-Summons Medal, which recognises the game's best player as voted by the fans. Joey had taken it home six times in a row between 1998 and 2003. Unfortunately, I only managed to receive it once before Nathan Hindmarsh began his own run, taking the award home four years straight. (PHOTO: GRANT TROUVILLE/ ACTION PHOTOGRAPHICS)

I have to admit I was stunned when I was named the Dally M Five-eighth of the Year in 2004. It was my first season as a full-time playmaker and, while I was happy with my progress, I was under no illusions about how much I still had to learn about playing at six. (PHOTO: COL WHELAN/ACTION PHOTOGRAPHICS)

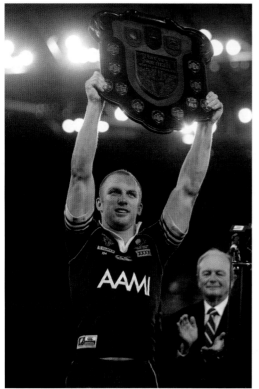

Game three, 2006, Telstra Dome, Melbourne. By any measure it was the definitive match of my career, and it has since proven to be a defining moment in the history of State of Origin football. (Photo: Newpix/Kelly Barnes)

A humble servant standing before The King. Wally was always my idol growing up, and it has been wonderful getting to know him over the years. I struggle to get my head around the fact that I am friends with my childhood hero. (Photo: Brett Crockford/Action Photographics)

What a ride. It was sensational. It's such a relief that we won my last Origin Series. It takes a big effort to win six years running. I'm going to miss it, that's for sure. I want to thank every coach I've worked with over my Origin career, every player that I've played with – it's been a helluva ride and I will never forget these times playing for Queensland. To the Queensland people, it has been a privilege to play for you – thank you and goodbye.

(PHOTO: NEWSPX/PETER WALLIS)

My personal ride to Sydney for the Manly semi-final match, courtesy of my pilot mate, Jack.

But I certainly took a lot from watching the way they went about things and their approach to the responsibility.

One of the best things about professional sport is that it doesn't discriminate. Performing in the heat of the battle is all that you can be judged upon. When the bell sounds at the start of a boxing match, it is a great leveller. When you are toe-to-toe with another man in the ring, where you come from, how much money you have, how popular you may be or what race or religion you belong to all count for naught . . . especially if you can't fight!

It is the same on the footy field. The son of a rural Queensland truck stop owner and his wife, rugby league has taken me around this country as well as abroad and allowed me to rub shoulders with people the like of whom I would once only have dreamt. Premiers and prime ministers by the bucketload, actors, singers, some of the world's best known sports stars . . . There was even an afternoon spent with royalty. That once-in-a-lifetime opportunity came during the 2001 Kangaroo tour of Great Britain, when we were taken to meet Prince Andrew at one of his spectacular dwellings.

Bono, the U2 frontman, actually came over and had a chat to me when I was out at a lunch with a number of sponsors. Apparently someone had pointed me out to him when he happened to be eating at the same Brisbane City restaurant. A rugby devotee, he came over and introduced himself – as if he needed to – and we talked Irish rugby and Brian O'Driscoll (the champion Irish centre) for a good 20 minutes or more.

On the Broncos end-of-season trip in 1996, I had one of my cooler celebrity meetings in New Orleans, aboard the Floating Casino which winds down the famous Mississippi River. Young and game, Ben Walker and I sauntered up to the blackjack table and I laid my money down. The dealer did his thing and I looked towards the first player to see what he was going to do and there in his Kangol beret was none other than Samuel L. Jackson – and before you ask, yes he is as cool in real life as he appears on the big screen.

The late, great Steve 'The Crocodile Hunter' Irwin came to a Broncos training session one day. He was just as loud and over-the-top as the bloke the world fell in love with on television. Steve was actually a big footy fan and played a fair bit growing up. When the cameras were down and we were just able to chat normally, he was a fascinating guy. I remember as part of a bit of a PR stunt they got Gordie to run at Steve, who duly executed a textbook legs tackle. Playing along, Gordie was going at half pace and got to his feet having a laugh.

What inspired Steve to ask Shane Webcke to go next, I will never know. Anyone who has trained or played with Webbie will tell you the bloke doesn't operate at half pace with anything. With Webbie it is 0 or it is 400. There is no in between. Young forwards at the Broncos used to trip over themselves trying to avoid being paired up with Webbie for anything at training. Wayne actually used to punish blokes by making them partner Webbie for tackling, wrestling and hit-up drills. Steve set himself nicely, but as more than a few opposition forwards discovered, pulling down the human cannonball is much easier in theory than in practice. Typically, Steve bounced back to his feet after being sent sprawling backwards. 'Crikey. What about that?' he yelled enthusiastically. With a bit of a snigger and a smile, Webbie extended a hand Steve's way. Steve accepted and actually thanked Webbie. For what, I am not sure.

He was a larger than life character, Steve. What happened to him was a tragedy. He was one of a kind.

On the sporting front, the chance to go to Old Trafford and meet with Manchester United manager Sir Alex Ferguson and tour the English Premier League powerhouse's training facility was incredible. Wayne and Sir Alex get on quite well, having met on numerous occasions over the years. While the Man U boss's pay packet is in a different stratosphere, the pair certainly have much in common in terms of serving long, incredibly successful tenures at one club. Neither are big talkers, though what they do say is normally worth listening to.

After the tour, we were invited to watch the Premier League squad train. I can still remember the staff pointing out a teenager they thought was going to be something totally out of the box. Cristiano Ronaldo was dribbling the ball up and down the field on his own, practising all those dazzling moves fans have marvelled at in the years since. In the gym, I had a good chat with club captain and renowned hard man Roy Keane, who was great.

In the States, I got to spend some time with Denver Broncos quarterback John Elway, which was fascinating. But no doubt my favourite experience with another athlete was when I got to meet Lance Armstrong. It was in Adelaide as part of his Livestrong campaign. Nike set everything up and we filmed an ad and did some pieces to camera. I made a point of not pestering him too much, but in the time we did get to chat he just exuded an intensity and a steel unlike anyone else I have met.

To summarise, I guess this chapter is for all those kids out there growing up in rural parts of Australia. They need to know anything is possible. That there would one day be a time when this bandy-legged kid from Wandoan would be approached by the lead singer from the world's biggest rock band for a chat; or would share an advertising billboard with a seven-time Tour de France winner who is considered one of the greatest athletes in history . . . That isn't even dreams coming true, because my mind couldn't extend that far. I am living proof that anything is possible.

TEN

The Deal
That Changed
the Game

'The lack of professionalism and respect for all Big Bulla had done for the Brisbane Broncos organisation and the NRL was staggering. The whole thing was a tragedy.' – Darren Lockyer

IF I EVER need reminding of how long I have been part of the rugby league circus, I need only look around Broncos Headquarters at Red Hill to realise just how much things have changed. Over the course of my career, I have worked under the only four administrations in the Broncos' history. John Ribot was at the helm when I arrived in 1995 before handing over to Shane Edwards, who held the post from 1996 to 2002. In 2003, Bruno Cullen took over and held the top job for seven years before it was announced that Paul White, a former policeman turned mining executive,

185

would assume the role from January 2011. Over that same period of time, I was lucky enough to be one of only four men chosen to captain this great club; the baton passed from Allan Langer to Kevin Walters on to Gorden Tallis, who turned it over to me.

Such stability was, for the longest time, exemplified by Wayne's constant presence as head coach. But it ran right through the organisation, with people like renowned weights trainer Dan Baker, team medic Kenny Rach, dietician Holly Frail, strapper/groundsman/BBQ maestro Tony 'Springer' Spencer and Paul Bunn in recruiting considered part of the furniture they have been there so long.

The notion of stability through loyalty was also a key philosophy Brisbane players bought into and passed down to each new generation of Broncos over the course of the first 20 years of the club's existence. For much of my career, Brisbane had a well-earned reputation for being able to retain and occasionally recruit players with contracts well below market value. The lure of on-field success – and the understanding that members of the 'family' would always be taken care of – was more than enough to convince many players, myself included, to ignore the riches on offer elsewhere and commit to Brisbane.

While over the years there were undoubtedly a few players that, in a perfect world, Wayne would have preferred to retain, it probably wasn't until the Roosters lured Justin Hodges down south at the end of 2001 that the Broncos genuinely 'lost' a player they desperately wanted to keep. The following year, another youngster destined for big things, versatile forward Ashley Harrison, was pinched from the Broncos' stable by Souths. But it was Lote Tuqiri's defection to the Australian Rugby Union that same year which really stung and signalled a change in the dynamic of the club.

It wasn't as though Lote was the first Bronco targeted by rugby. Willie Carne, Peter Ryan and Brad Thorn all made the switch. And it was only 12 months since the turnstile spinner himself, Wendell Sailor, had made the leap. Dell was 28 when the ARU had made him a multi-million-dollar offer that was simply too good to refuse. He departed at the end of 2001, having already played 189 first-grade games, 14 State of Origins for Queensland and the same number of Test matches for Australia. He also had three premiership rings and a swag of individual awards to his name. People sometimes forget how good Big Dell was in his prime. Chris Anderson is not one for hyperbole and he also knows a thing or two about wingers, having represented New South Wales and Australia in that position. That he saw fit to put Wendell up alongside legendary Parramatta flyer Eric Grothe Snr as the very best the game has ever seen is quite the compliment.

Obviously his final days in rugby union were marred by the two-year suspension he received after he tested positive for cocaine following the Waratahs–Brumbies clash in April 2006. Much was written and spoken of the incident around this time, and I know that it was the lowest point in Dell's stellar career. The two-year ban he copped under the mandatory World Anti-Doping Authority's guidelines is what the rules clearly state, but one wonders how much higher Dell's career could have reached had he not missed the two years through suspension.

In his hearing, Wendell presented a stack of medical evidence stating unequivocally that, if anything, cocaine would inhibit a player's performance in sports like rugby union and rugby league. Yet, because it is classed as a stimulant, the governing authorities impose the same suspension as they would in the case of an athlete who returns a sample positive for growth hormone, anabolic steroids or testosterone use. Just a couple of months later, American cyclist Floyd Landis returned a test positive for use of synthetic testosterone following a stage win in the Tour de France. By the time the news came to light, Le Tour was over and Landis had claimed a famous victory. There were years of legal battles surrounding this case, yet the end result was that Landis's positive test stood. While the magnitude of each situation seems worlds apart, the punishment for both, a two-year ban from competition, was the same.

Somehow, I managed to get roped into the drama surrounding Wendell's suspension. Wendell admitted that the positive reading he returned after the match against the Brumbies on Sunday 16 April – Easter Sunday – stemmed from the Wednesday night prior, when he had been out partying in Sydney. But that didn't stop some reporters jumping to a far different conclusion when it became known that Loren and I had stayed with Wendell and Tara the night after the Broncos' traditional Good Friday match against the Roosters, which we won handsomely. The Saturday evening was a very quiet, low-key affair. The four of us grabbed a bite at a restaurant in Bondi around seven and were back home and asleep before 10 pm. I watched the Big Fella play on Sunday and flew back to Brisbane early Monday morning for training. There was really nothing more to my stay than that. Wendell came out to say as much, but some people just didn't want to hear it.

Loren Lockyer: The media hysteria about Wendell after he tested positive in 2006, and the insinuation of Darren's guilt by association, was probably the most hurtful and distressing stuff we have dealt with in terms of Darren being such a public figure. Most of the time they wouldn't say it straight out – there weren't any direct accusations – but the insinuations were obvious. 'Oh my God, you people really have no idea whatsoever.'

That was really hurtful – I mean I got associated with it all too and there just wasn't any truth in it. We'd go down to see Darren's parents after something had been written or said and they would be there all worried, asking about what they had read. I mean, what do you say to your parents in a situation like that? The journalists responsible for printing some of that stuff either have no clue or no conscience. They are certainly not thinking about the people they may hurt with their little gossip column items. Darren just got a little annoyed and a bit disappointed at different times, but whenever he hit some drama he just rode it out until the news cycle passed.

Wendell Sailor: At the end of the day, I put my hand up and am accountable for my own actions. I made the error and paid a price for it. As hard as that was, what I felt worst about was the impact my actions ended up having on my family and my friends – particularly Locky and Loren.

Locky is the sort of bloke who takes a while to get to know, but once you get to know him he is such good company and as loyal a friend as you could ever hope to meet. He had been that to me right through the ups and downs of my career – through some really tough times too, like when my dad died. I took that really hard and lost my way a bit. Locky was one of the guys who was there helping me get back on track and that is something I will never forget.

It was tough, but he dealt with it like he does. He stood there and answered the questions – he didn't let them get to him too much. Better people than those blokes have tried to get under his skin and failed.

I was so pleased Dell got to come back and finish his career in the manner he did with the Dragons in 2008 and 2009. To have Wayne there in his final year was so fitting. Coach had been one of the blokes who had really helped Dell when he was struggling to cope with the sudden change to his life as a professional footballer.

It was a pity club management at the Broncos couldn't find a way to bring him back to Red Hill – I know he was desperate to come back to Brisbane. It was his first choice and I really believe he could have added something to the young group Ivan Henjak inherited in 2009. All Dell needed was a little bit of direction and some support and he got that from a number of different parties within the NRL. To see the smiling, gregarious character on Dellavision these days shows the value of not just offering guys a second chance, but putting the right people around them to ensure they are able to grab hold of such opportunities. When we as a game act with that sort of community understanding and spirit, everyone benefits.

Speaking of opportunities – let me get back to the one which lay before Lote in 2002. At just 21, he was already an established member of the Queensland and Australian sides. He was an incredible physical specimen. A touch under six foot four by the old scale (1.93 metres), Lote was a taller, leaner version of Dell. While he wasn't quite as big, at over 100 kilos Lote was plenty big enough and his speed and athleticism were something to behold. In the end, the NRL salary cap meant Brisbane couldn't get near the dollars on offer for Lote in rugby. He confirmed the move late in the year, just prior to being named NRL winger of the year. He finished the year at the top of our try-scoring list for the second year running and set the club single-game point-scoring record in round nine against the Northern Eagles, crossing three times and slotting seven shots at goal for a final tally of 26 points. In game two of the 2002 Origin series, Lote became just the fourth player to score a hat-trick of tries in a match.

Wayne was livid to have lost such a talent and his

anger grew exponentially when the Broncos' pleas for some assistance in the fight to keep Lote in rugby league were met with a response from Sydney-based officials suggesting he 'get over it' and focus on finding the 'next Lote Tuqiri' amongst the plethora of young talent coming into the NRL. It was an ignorant and arrogant reaction. In the time since he left, probably only Greg Inglis, Israel Folau and perhaps Jarryd Hayne could match the special blend of size, skill, speed and power of a young Lote Tuqiri. Athletes like that don't grow on trees and, when you have them in your game, you should be doing your best to keep them there.

To me, this was probably the first sign of a properly enforced salary cap having the desired impact on talent equalisation among the 16 teams. I should state up front that I am a fan of talent distribution in the game. I do, however, think there are a number of areas within the salary cap framework which need to be addressed due to the restrictions it places on players' income potential, given that careers are generally very short. At present, the cap simply punishes excellence. There is no recognition for developing a club culture which breeds loyalty, nor is there reward for clubs investing in development pathways for emerging talent.

There is something inherently amiss with the idea of dragging the best back to the pack rather than creating a system which encourages all teams to find the improvement necessary to rise to the level set by the best team/s. You only need to glance back at the grand finals line-ups of teams like the Bulldogs (2004), Tigers (2005), Broncos (2006) and Manly (2008) to understand what I am talking about. At the start of the 2011 season, Andrew Ryan was the sole survivor in the Bulldogs side from the 2004 premiership. Tigers duo Benji Marshall and Robbie Farah are the only remaining members of the starting 13 from the 2005 decider. The return of Ben Hannant and Dane Carlaw takes to six the number of current Broncos who played in the 2006 grand final against Melbourne.

The salary cap scandal which devastated the Storm in April 2010 reaffirmed the belief of many NRL coaches and administrators that the salary cap in its present form leads to clubs striving for mediocrity, such is the reality of what happens to the clubs following premiership success. There needs to be a change of ethos, because that cannot be the core ideal behind such a key component of the NRL competition. Don't get me wrong, I realise that the league needs to put in place measures to prevent the separation of the 16 teams into 'haves' and 'have nots'.

I say all this with an understanding that it is what is best for the game, however, there is little doubt in my mind that curtailing the Broncos' success was a key factor in the NRL's more stringent monitoring of its salary cap. You look through some of those Brisbane sides in the late 1990s through to the turn of the century – there is just no doubt the Broncos would have been front and centre of discussions when the game's officials began discussing the need for tighter control of club expenditure.

By the time I was handed the club captaincy for the 2005

season, following Gorden Tallis's retirement at the end of the previous winter, the strict salary cap laws were in full effect. NRL officials spruiked the fact that in the eight seasons since the reformation of the competition, seven different clubs – Brisbane (twice), Melbourne, Newcastle, Sydney Roosters, Bulldogs, Wests and Penrith – had taken home the premiership trophy. The Wests Tigers' triumph over the Cowboys in 2005 made it eight different winners in nine years – proof enough, according to the powers that be, that the NRL's combination of a free player market and a carefully policed salary cap was delivering the spread of talent necessary to at least give the impression all 16 teams begin the year on a level playing field.

After the ridiculous excesses seen during the Super League war, player earnings dipped. It has been 15 years since rugby league's heart was split in two and wages are only just beginning to reach the heights achieved with frightening regularity when the Packers and Murdochs opened their chequebooks.

The cap continued to bite hard at the Broncos. Berrick Barnes was a schoolboy prodigy, earning comparisons with 'The King' Wally Lewis at the same age. However, in a bitter blow, Barnes was tempted back to the 15-man game, linking with the struggling Reds for 2006. Big Tom Learoyd-Lahrs was another of the young guns Cyril Connell had recruited to the Broncos, only to see him leave when Canberra offered the giant prop the sort of deal typically reserved for the very elite of NRL forwards – blokes like Shane Webcke, Ben Kennedy, Steve Price and Ruben Wiki.

In my mind, however, even more than all the young talent the Broncos have had to bid farewell to, it was the club's abysmal handling of its negotiations with Petero Civoniceva in 2007 which left the most significant scar. It was a disappointing outcome and no doubt did some damage to the relationship between the club and Petero. Petero's status was such that all players were left to question the idea of loyalty in the modern game.

It's a problem administrators at every club will forever carry into contract negotiations. It is a delicate balance between looking after players who have contributed to your club over a long period and trying to build what administrators feel is the best roster for the future. With the dynamics of the player market so volatile these days, it is easy for contract negotiation to turn into a game of cat and mouse if not handled carefully. Pet was of the belief that his contract negotiations were headed in a certain direction and, having given 10 years of loyal service, was hopeful the club would fulfil its promise to recognise him with the club's marquee forward contracts which Shane Webcke and Gorden Tallis had held in previous years.

The club's decision to go out and buy Joel Clinton understandably had Petero questioning how they could afford to do that, but could not afford to give him the upgrade he had long hoped for – and one he had undoubtedly earned. I know that Petero, like most players in that situation, was extremely disappointed when informed, on the eve of State of Origin II, that the club had withdrawn its contract offer. No doubt as difficult as the decision would have been, to have it conveyed via email made it all the more shattering. I guess in hindsight everyone learned a lot from that experience, and hopefully we will never have to see such a tragedy again.

During the negotiation process, clearly the parties lost sight of the objective, which was to ensure Petero remained at the Broncos, where he belonged. With a guy like Petero, you just find a way. Within the rules, of course, but you find a way. There shouldn't be another option. I have no doubt Petero's manager was playing a bit of a game – it comes with the territory. As I understand it, he claimed to have big-money offers from elsewhere that didn't necessarily exist. It seems that the whole process spiralled out of control, and sadly Petero was the loser. Obviously, Petero was an Origin and Test prop at the time, probably the best in the game. So, when things came to a bit of a stalemate, someone just needed to be there to again refocus the relevant parties. If someone needed to swallow their pride, so be it. We all knew that and the inescapable fact is that Petero *should* have been a Bronco for life.

Personally, it was gut-wrenching to watch Bulla go through all that. We had been friends since meeting as team-mates in the Broncos Colts side way back in 1995. The Broncos was in his blood. It was home to him and he was an irreplaceable part of not just the playing group but the entire club. Everyone loved Petero.

With Ruben Wiki, Petero was the game's most beloved and respected figure. Both those guys were cut from the same cloth. Tough as teak on the field, they played the game in a brutal, unforgiving manner. And yet, while the odd tackle may have gone astray over the years, both were renowned for their sportsmanship. They played hard but fair. Neither needed to throw punches to be intimidating. Make no mistake, they were the two blokes against whom you measured your own resolve or toughness. Whether carrying the ball or in the defensive line, Petero and Ruben hit hard and hit often.

If you want clarification on this point, go and ask Jason Ryles about what it is like to run into Petero. Bulla hit Ryles in an Origin match back in 2004 with as much force as I have witnessed on a football field. Ryles is a big, strong bloke but he just buckled on impact. He was carried off and didn't return. It turned out he had suffered a shoulder/clavicle injury so serious it almost ended his career.

Pet is one of those rare blokes who are just so physically hard it doesn't matter which side of the collision you are on – whether you are tackling him or he is tackling you – you come away feeling sore and sorry. Ryles certainly wasn't the only player in the game who came off second-best following a collision with the big man. Beau Champion's memories of the 2010 All Stars match would likely be just that – all stars – courtesy of Petero's less than forgiving hip bone. When Beau got his head in the wrong place in front of a charging P. Civoniceva, there was only going to be one outcome. Champion was knocked out cold. Thankfully, by the time the season proper began, Beau was able to take his place in the Melbourne Storm line-up.

Pet did claim a scalp in round one, however, sidelining Neville Costigan for three months. This time, it was his knee that did the damage. A team-mate of Pet's and mine at the Broncos and for Queensland, Neville snapped his forearm in two in the early minutes of his debut for Newcastle when he looked to cut down the big Fijian. Nev is rightly recognised as one of the game's genuinely hard men. When he is on, there are few more ferocious hitters in the NRL today.

And of course you can't talk about Petero's victims without talking about former Warriors captain Monty Betham. Betham and Gorden Tallis were essentially interchangeable in positions one and two on the annual most-feared player in the NRL list. Monty didn't have the size of a lot of blokes, but he had a worryingly short fuse and could genuinely throw them. His old man won a Commonwealth Games Gold Medal as a boxer, and Monty himself was a world junior karate champion. In the end, he retired from footy to have a crack in the ring and had a perfect 7–0 record as a professional. I am told he simply couldn't find the fights needed to progress through the ranks. He did quite a number on former Wallaby Sam Scott-Young at one of those charity boxing events in Brisbane in 2008. Sam had a significant size advantage, which counted for very little when Monty actually switched into fight mode following Sam's decision to come in swinging from the rafters. When you are in the ring with a professional, doing that sort of thing is considered disrespectful and they generally cut offenders back down to size quick smart. Monty did just that.

Unfortunately, there was no such justification for the ugly swinging arm he threw with bad intentions in the first round match-up of the 2004 season between Brisbane and the Warriors. Petero's arms were pinned by a couple of other guys trying to tackle him when Monty let fly. Perhaps it was the Football Gods frowning on what was a really cheap shot against one of the game's true gentlemen, perhaps it was a bit of karma looking after Bulla; whatever it was, the result of Monty's hit was not what the rugged Kiwi would have anticipated. While Pet was certainly less than pleased, he wasn't rattled too badly by the hit at all. Monty, though, reeled away in pain, cradling his arm. After being placed on report, he immediately left the field nursing the arm which had come in contact with Pet's sizeable cranium. Now I could be wrong, but I am led to believe some scientific tests indicate the constitution of Pet's melon is harder even than diamond. So the five-week suspension handed to Betham by the NRL judiciary mattered little, given that team medics were expecting him to miss a minimum of 10 weeks following the surgery he required to realign the bones in his arm which had splintered when he collected Bulla high.

Petero is a rock of a man in every sense of the word. He didn't ever give too much away through what was a really tough time for him and his family. He didn't want the boys to know it was affecting him, but I know Bulla well enough to know how much it hurt him. Like all one-club players, having to move on is extremely distressing as you are leaving behind everything you love about footy. I know

I speak for everyone in thinking it would have been terrific for Petero to have been a Bronco for life.

There is no doubt in my mind that what happened with Petero during this time has ramifications for the whole of the NRL. I can speak with some certainty when I say there is no player in the game whose presence or words carry the gravitas of Petero Civoniceva. That is doubly so for the already significant but growing number of Polynesian boys in the NRL. To them, Petero is a God. We often hear in the modern game that loyalty is dead and that the NRL is a big business. I like to be a little old-fashioned and feel that in some instances loyalty is alive and well. Sadly, for both Petero and the Broncos, this old-fashioned thought just did not prevail.

The decision by the club to cease talks with Petero shook the players up a bit. There were rumblings of discontent in the Club, which was extraordinary to me given we were the reigning champions. Sadly, the way the game is structured forces change on teams that are successful. That is not a coincidence – it is by design that clubs are forced to make tough roster decisions. As a result, the club decided to sever ties with a number of other long-serving players – including Brent Tate, Brad Thorn, Shaun Berrigan and Dane Carlaw – but Petero's situation brought things to a head and I called a 'players only' team meeting in the lead-up to our round 14 match against the Bulldogs. I could tell a number of boys were pretty disillusioned. I said to them that I sympathised, and of course we were all disappointed to lose our team-mates. It seemed very un-Bronco-like, but I wanted them to get clear that we were in this together and we needed to be playing for each other. I wanted to make sure they had something to play for each week. If they were disappointed to lose their team-mates, fair enough, but they shouldn't ever let that get in the way of playing for each other.

We went on a bit of a run after that, chalking up six wins in the following seven starts. While my season ended abruptly at Dairy Farmers Stadium, that was the start of a miserable descent for the team. We dropped four of the final five regular season fixtures. Rather ridiculously, the 11–13 finish was good enough to sneak into eighth spot again. The 40–0 drubbing Melbourne handed us was hard to watch. Petero deserved a much more dignified departure.

The first time Petero came to Brisbane in his new colours, we trounced his Panthers. I watched Big Pet throughout the game and I have to admit it is probably the only time I have felt sorry for an opposition player. The fans at Suncorp Stadium made it clear what they thought – more than once standing and applauding to acknowledge Bulla, even if that Panthers jersey didn't look quite right.

Petero Civoniceva: To this day, Locky and I have yet to sit down and talk over what went down behind closed doors that led to my leaving Brisbane. I think we both probably assumed it was a deal that would just get done. It just would – as it had with other players in similar circumstances numerous times in the past. But from my perspective, the talks were getting progressively worse, not better. I really didn't like a lot of what I heard coming from the other side of the desk and in the end I wasn't left with any option other than to leave.

It broke my heart, but no doubt the hardest part of it was leaving Locky. We'd just been through so much over the years. It didn't feel right to be walking out. Ever since I first got the call-up to first grade, I played my best football largely because of the responsibility I felt towards Locky – to protect him and do whatever he needed done. Rest assured, if anything ever happened to him I would be the first one in there. Not that it would. The bloke is too well respected for anyone to try it on. There would be a huge fallout if someone did. The entire league community would be calling for his head.

My sense of responsibility grew as I became a more senior member of the Broncos squad and in those final years it was something I held very near and dear to my heart, not only because it was my job as leader of the pack to do that, but more so because of how much I valued the genuine mateship Locky and I share.

I have reflected on that time a lot and, in some respects, I felt I let him down a bit. I have asked myself a million times in the days since I left whether I had done the right thing or whether I could have sacrificed a little or just done something more to get the deal done.

I tried once to go and talk to him after the season was all over before we relocated. But as I approached him, I realised I was going to break down. So I turned around and walked over to something else. Like I said,

I felt I owed Locky a lot. It was my job to look after him. It's what I had committed myself to doing and I guess I felt as though I was leaving before the job was done.

For what it's worth, there were a few times when I was propositioned to leave the Broncos. When Dell and Lote left, the ARU was looking around at league players and for a time it was an idea that was presented to me, although I never pursued any serious discussions. I tried to imagine what position I would play in union and figured that, with a reasonable left boot on me, I would go okay as a fullback. In the end, my loyalty was always going to be way too strong, and I thought I was at the peak of my powers – why risk all that I had set up in my NRL career for myself, my club and my supporters. But as I sit here now with the end of my NRL career imminent, I do sometimes think about how I would have gone in a different code, how my skills might have translated to AFL or rugby union. I watch their games and wonder whether I could make the necessary adjustments to be successful. It's all hypothetical, pie in the sky stuff for me. For Karmichael Hunt and Israel Folau, however, it is very real and my curiosity has probably meant I have watched with even greater interest than I would normally have for a close friend. They are pioneers and, if they pull it off, the entire football landscape in Australia changes. I am sure that in years to come K will make the transition a real success. K has not got the credit he deserves at this time for the courage he showed even attempting the switch. He is holding himself up for public criticism because he wants to see if he can do something no one else has done before. That's pretty special in my book (and this is my book). I am not sure if I would have had the guts K has shown by walking away from his comfort zone and testing himself.

George Gregan: I am a bit of a rugby league tragic. I grew up a Balmain Tigers fan. Living in Canberra after the 1989 grand final . . . it was a nightmare. But anyway, I have seen Locky play since he burst onto the scene back in the mid-1990s and the thing he has always had, which all truly great sportsmen and women have, is an ability to make the very difficult appear very easy. They have time, they see things others don't, and they are always perfectly balanced. Armed with such weapons, champions can relax and focus amid chaos. That is what players are talking about when they refer to someone 'having time'. The champions never appear rushed. Darren Lockyer typifies all those qualities. More often than not, he chooses the right option – again it's the mark of a champion.

I heard whispers at different times about the ARU possibly making a play for Locky. It was one of the few gossip column pars I actually hoped would come to fruition. He would have been an absolute sensation either at fullback or playing at 10. He would have been an amazing playing out one or two passes off the ruck, because he has the tools that keep defensive lines worried. You cannot rush him, his footwork is too good. But at the same time you can't give him too much time with the ball in his hands because his passing and kicking skills are exceptional and he'll make you pay.

I have seen him compared with Stephen Larkham, who also made the move from fullback to five-eighth in the second stage of his career. For both, it proved a brilliant move because they were simply involved in the play more and when you can do what they can on the field, you want them involved as much as possible. Locky's left boot is that extra piece he brings to the table. Short or very long, Locky has a spectacular kicking game. If I could have a bit of a hybrid, I guess you'd say there is a little bit of Joe Roff and Mat Rogers in his game – particularly when he was playing fullback. Dan Carter is probably the closest thing rugby has got in terms of guys who can control and steer an entire match around the place with relative ease.

I loved watching the way Locky could construct a set of six and just work his team around and into the position he wanted. He had a wonderful discipline in executing gameplans and sticking to them no matter how dire things got. But then he still had the game sense and athletic ability to change the pace of the game if his side got a couple of quick play-the-balls. It's a rare beast that can swing so easily between a controlled, structured offensive gameplan and high-tempo ad-lib attack. He could.

Locky is just a special player – that is the biggest rap I can give him.

I wish he had made the move!

There were other fleeting moments. Around 2003, I investigated the logistics around making a move to the Roosters, who had expressed interest and where a few of my good mates from the 2003 Australian Tour were playing. I was also approached about playing a stint in the English Super League. The closest I came was when Leeds put an enormous offer on the table for me. It was around 2004 and the contract was worth a touch over $1 million a season, but my love of the Aussie climate and the obligation I felt to do right by my club and the Australian captaincy, which Chris Anderson had handed me by default the previous year, was too much to walk away from.

There is no escaping the fact that the game is a business these days and clubs are run as such. Players are professional and moving between clubs is becoming less and less of an issue. That is reality and I am happy enough working in that environment. By the same token, from a young age I was taught the value of loyalty. It is a quality I value and I think the game and society in general are the poorer for its steady demise. Above many of the records, awards and trophies, the fact that I can walk away from the game a one-club player is something of which I am genuinely proud.

ELEVEN

In Need of Direction

THERE ISN'T MUCH I don't love about Queensland. North of the Tweed really is God's country and I couldn't imagine ever living anywhere else. The south-east corner has really matured as a region in the years since I arrived. Brisbane, especially, is a far more sophisticated city these days. It will never be as cosmopolitan as Melbourne, nor will it ever exude the pulsating intensity and ambition of a genuinely big city like Sydney. But it is certainly a genuine business and economic hub, supported by a rapidly growing population base.

In my mind, though, the thing that makes Brisbane such a wonderful place to live and particularly to raise a family, is its balance. While the region and its citizens have embraced the enormous commercial development of the past 15 years and the physical transformation that has followed, Brissy has still managed to retain its unique character. The beautiful parks and gardens; the homes with genuine backyards for children to play in; and the huge number of swimming pools and sporting fields spread throughout the suburbs allow us to take advantage of the incredible weather we generally enjoy and the crisp, clean air we breathe. Brisbane is no longer a big country town, but thankfully it has retained a little of that traditional rural charm. Certainly the more travelling I do to different places around the world, the more I have come to value the typically laid-back, friendly and hospitable nature of Brisbane residents.

I still enjoy heading out west on the odd occasion. I just love the people you meet travelling through areas like the Darling Downs and out to my old stomping ground at Roma. They are just hard-working, salt-of-the-earth types who love their footy and almost always possess a sense of humour as dry as a desert.

Loren hails from Mackay, so we have spent plenty of time up north as well, visiting different members of the family, particularly her parents. Airlie Beach, the Whitsundays, Hamilton, Daydream and Magnetic Islands and, of course, the Great Barrier Reef are all sensational holiday destinations. It is a special part of the world, the eastern coastline of Australia, and the further north towards the tropics you go the more serene and idyllic the surrounds seemingly become. When the weather is clear and the sun is beating down, that region is as close as you'll get to experiencing Heaven on Earth.

With that in mind, it seems somewhat fitting that situated a short drive inland is a place that has given me hell over the years. I am sure I must have upset north Queensland's Football Gods in a past life because Dairy Farmers Stadium – the homeground of Johnathan Thurston and his Cowboys – has been most unkind to me throughout my playing days.

It was where I suffered my first major injury, courtesy of Fijian powerhouse Noa Nadruku. It was round eight of the 1999 NRL season and our title defence was already in ruins. Given the dominant manner of our premiership win in 1998, the speed and enormity with which things had completely unravelled was inexplicable and inexcusable. We arrived in Townsville for the Queensland Derby in last place on the ladder, with a victory against a pretty average Souths outfit in round six our solitary win for the season to that point.

About 10 minutes into the game, a Cowboys error presented us with a great attacking opportunity. The backline was stacked deep and wide. I was stationed out wide, in behind our outside centre. The ball came out of the scrum and if I recall correctly went to Kevie, who floated across field and hit me with an 'out ball', which is a pass thrown not to where the recipient is, but rather to where he will be – that is about half a metre wider than where he is standing at the point of release. With the out ball, the recipient essentially moves with the flight of the ball, which should put them outside of the defender marking them. The out ball works best on a sliding defence, and Steve Renouf was the best at receiving it.

The effectiveness of the play is reliant on good communication and timing between the ball carrier and his intended target, who makes the slight adjustment to the line he is running while the ball is in the air. It is one of the little subtle plays in rugby league I love so much. Its effectiveness is reliant on the two players involved being perfectly in sync. Timing is everything with this sort of play, which is used a lot by some of the NRL's best strike centres. Mark Gasnier, Greg Inglis and Justin Hodges all utilise out balls regularly and with great effect. Provided the work has been done on the training track, it takes no time at all to set up.

A nod from Hodgo is all that is needed to know what he is looking for. The end game is to give Hodgo about an arm's length break from his direct opponent. At that distance the size and strength of blokes like Hodgo and GI come into play through their ability to palm away from would-be tacklers. Hodgo's big step can also be a handful at close quarters. I have never seen anyone else able to come out of dummy-half and be able to step back so he ends up cutting back in between the bloke who played the ball and the first marker. But Hodgo does it every time he gets into dummy-half, to help the forwards out. Everyone knows what is coming when Hodgo saunters up and elbows Andrew McCullough out of dummy-half. But knowing what is coming and stopping it are two vastly different beasts.

The other option is to simply use the space as the start you are looking for to beat your opponent and simply take off, backing your pace. With his pace off the mark, this is what Gaz will normally do and it is what I attempted to do on the night in question against the Cowboys. What I failed to account for was a hard-boned Fijian winger picking the play early. Noa came spearing in at a million miles an hour and took flight. He hit me like a missile, head first – a collision which was only going to have one winner. I came away with a number of depressed fractures in my cheekbone and eye socket, grounding me for about a month. Given this match was the night which brought the curtain down on Alf's amazing club career, however, it isn't surprising my little bump failed to gain a great deal of attention.

I have done my rib cartilage twice, including the occasion which ruined the back end of my 2010 season and then there was the little knee injury I picked up there in round 18, 2007 – when I shredded my anterior cruciate ligament.

As I mentioned earlier, I wrecked the knee properly. By staying on the field after suffering the initial damage and wrenching it on two further occasions, I not only ruptured the ACL but also tore away the surrounding connective tissue, dramatically increasing the significance of the operation required to mend the joint and, in turn, the period of time needed to fully rehabilitate the knee and the muscles surrounding and supporting it. I knew what I had done, but was hoping against hope that scans would show something other than what every medical officer was telling me. I just didn't want to face it. I was as fit as I had ever been and was in career-best form. The Broncos were flying, with our win against the Cowboys that evening our sixth victory in seven starts. Andrew Gee was the football manager at the time and organised for me to fly home early the following morning for scans and a consultation with the team doctor.

Loren Lockyer: That night and the time immediately after Darren did his knee is by far the worst time we have had in our time together. He had been playing brilliantly. I had organised a dinner and drinks night at Gambaro's restaurant for all the wives and girlfriends and I was on my way to having a nice night out with the girls when I got a tap on the shoulder. I was actually on the dance floor when my phone rang. It was Darren and he just said straight out, 'Babe, I think I have done my cruciate.' He kept telling me he felt all right, but then told me to put one of our friends, who is a physio, on the line.

The conversation went

'Okay, so did you hear a noise?'

'Yep.'

'Is the knee loose? Can it move forward and back?'

'Yep.'

'Yeah, you've done the cruciate.'

'Nah, nah . . . it feels okay.'

He just wouldn't believe it. Anyway, he flew home early and went for a scan straightaway. After the scans came back we actually drove to (Broncos doctor) Matt Hislop's place. We didn't even get inside. He had a sliver of light up the side of his place and he held the X-ray up to the light, looked at it and just went, 'Yep, done, done, done.'

Well, after that things just spiralled badly. It was like someone had died. Everything Darren had known in his adult life had been pulled from under him and he went into what seemed like a depression. It was really tough, but if you want to know how much this game means to him and what these guys go through . . . that was the time that it was really rammed home to me. We didn't even sleep in the same bed for days. He went and slept in the spare bed because he was awake all night, I think, with a combination of pain and distress. I lay there each night and would listen to him moaning and wincing. It is the most helpless I have ever felt.

But after a few days, I just went to him and told him he needed to snap out of it. I told him we would get through it together. It wasn't terminal, it was just a knee injury.

That was a day or so before he went in for surgery. When he came out, though, it was still a real struggle. He wasn't even able to move for a few months, which was just infuriating for him. He is such an active guy. He can't sit still at the best of times, but here he was not able to put any weight on his leg at all for almost three months.

It took its toll. He totally lost his appetite. By the time our wedding came around in October, Darren was down to 75 kilos. I look at our photos from that day and I still can't believe how skinny he was.

I reckon it took a full year before he was back feeling like himself again. He still used to rub his knee and just say, 'Babe, it's just not right.' I think it was 2009 before it stopped playing on his mind.

I remember I had committed to an appearance for a bloke out at Samford the day after my surgery. I am really big on fulfilling everything I have agreed to do. I was in a bit of pain as a Broncos staff member drove me out, and a couple of hours into the trip I was starting to feel even more ordinary. I am not a big fan of painkillers or sleeping tablets. When I was trying to find ways, other than downing a few beers, to calm down and get some sleep after a match I tried sleeping tablets. I got the team doctor to give me a Valium tablet two or three times, but just found I was waking up feeling drowsy the next morning and generally felt rubbish for the rest of the day. So I quickly brushed that experiment.

That night I ended up getting Lor to come get me early. The next couple of months drove me up the wall. I couldn't get comfortable at bed time and during the day I pretty much had to sit there with the leg in a brace so it wouldn't bend and elevated to try to get the swelling down. I can't sit still even when I am feeling great. I mean, I struggle to get through a movie in one sitting. I read books in dribs and drabs – it takes me forever and I generally find at any one time I have about four or five books I have partially read. So being stuck with daytime TV for a couple of months felt like a punishment of epic proportions.

Thankfully I was back walking a few weeks prior to our wedding on October 27. I still had a pretty bad limp and the bridal waltz wouldn't have been well received on *Dancing with the Stars*, but it was still a sensational day. As wonderful as a lot of my experiences on the field have been, nothing compares to those really personal occasions. My wedding day and the birth of my son are, by far, the two greatest days of my life.

Two weeks after the Broncos' year had ended at the hands of eventual premiers Melbourne, I was back at the club working on my rehab. I was really impatient with it – a fact which came back to bite me the following season. I started on the stationary bike trying to get the flexibility and stability back in the joint. However, Dean Benton and Robbie Godbolt were both worried about the amount of muscle atrophy my quad and hamstring had suffered. I actually required three further 'clean-up' surgeries before the knee was right, though it will never again be 100 per cent. The scar tissue around it means I can't do a full squat movement in the gym without pain or grinding noises. Similarly, when stretching, I cannot get my heel to touch the back of my buttocks, damage which robbed me of a lot of my explosive speed off the mark. Down the track I will almost certainly require a knee replacement, though by such time I am hopeful there will be ways to simply replace the cartilage and prevent the decay caused by bone-on-bone movement.

Andrew Johns: The way Locky fought his way back after that knee reconstruction – for me, that cemented his status as one of the out-and-out champions our game has seen. It took him to a new level, because he was able to re-invent himself for probably the third or fourth time and within a year was as dominant as ever.

I mean, people forget how good a fullback he was there in those early years. He could hurt you on kick-return, but he did the most damage pushing up into the attack at first or second receiver. He had the ability to change the pace of the game because he had genuine explosive speed off the mark. I think people again forget or don't appreciate how quick he was. He was lightning in those first five or six seasons he played. Think Michael Jennings, Billy Slater, these blokes – that is how quick Locky was early on. He had this beautiful running technique too, where he just made it look effortless. The other thing he had was that ability to maintain his speed through a swerve or a veer. It wasn't just straight-line speed.

He could also read the play so well that when he was playing at fullback trying to find space with kicks was a nightmare. With Alf and Kevie there, he wasn't doing too much ball-playing, which allowed his athleticism to shine through. He was such a good ball-runner and he is as good a support player as has ever laced on a boot.

If you watch his game in the final match of the 2001 Origin series – the match when Alf came back . . . Everyone raves about Alfie, who was great – don't get me wrong. But Locky was head and shoulders the best player on the field that night. He was playing a different game to the other blokes out there. I was hurt and I just remember watching him set up these long-range tries and scoring himself. I remember thinking, 'Geez, this bloke is just at the peak of his physical powers.' He was poetry in motion.

There was another time in Origin a couple of years after that when one of our backrowers – and I won't say who – just got taken to school by Locky. He beat him once early, just using that skip step he had to get on the outside and then taking off. So Queensland went back there again and again and again. And each time they did, Locky would leave this poor bloke grabbing thin air. After the second try down that side, he just came over to me and said, 'Mate, we got to swap things around on the edge. I can't catch him, he's too f***ing fast. He is doing this move where he stops and skips to the outside and I can't stop him.'

I ended up telling him to piss off and I went and defended him. He had a blinder that night and Queensland won easy. I loved the challenge though – because I knew I was testing myself against the best.

After Alfie left, he took on the main playmaker duties even though he was still defending at the back. Then there was the move to five-eighth, which really tested him. Teams were finally able to get at him with him defending in the front line. It took him some time to get his defence up to the standards he sets himself, and that is what he did – to the point where he is a very competent and reliable defender.

Then the knee went and he had a really tough time coming back. A lot of people probably thought it was over and for a lesser bloke it most likely would have been. But Locky willed himself through that first year and got his leg back to a satisfactory level, though his days of beating opponents with pace and footwork were consigned to history.

So he changed things again. He started using his experience and his knowledge of the game to steer his side around. He still has that wonderful kicking game which he uses to put his side in ideal field position over and over. Slowly the pressure builds on the team bringing the ball off their line on every possession. He is so patient and disciplined these days and you cannot rattle him no matter the situation, so in a grinding battle he is close to unbeatable, as New South Wales has learned on numerous occasions since 2006.

It is ridiculous to think that after 17 years Locky still manages to find a way to impose himself on games and he will bow out of the game still one of the top three or four halves in the NRL.

You don't see him playing many shockers. His Test debut is probably the exception. But then again, Bradman got a duck, didn't he?

On the advice of Iki, I did a mountain of work in the pool in the initial stages of my rehabilitation, but it was slow going. One of the things I got into was some big walks. One route I ended up doing a lot of was the base of Mount Coot-tha to the top, which is where all of the TV networks in Brisbane are based. Once I got to the top, I would turn around and head back to the start. It is a really tough hike, particularly when you are on your own and feel like you are on one leg.

I will never forget that on about my third walk, without me saying anything and without so much as a hello, Wayne greeted me and walked the whole course by my side. He continued to do so for weeks afterwards – this at a time when he was scheduled to be on annual leave. It is the sort of thing Wayne does for all his players. Just little things that let you know that you are not on your own and that he cares.

While I wasn't meant to be running, I did stretch out on a few occasions when I was out of sight. I got out there for the opening round win over Penrith – Petero's return to Suncorp Stadium. I nursed the knee through six of the first 12 rounds before I was forced to undergo the second of the three arthroscopes. Having already missed the Centenary Test and the chance to fulfil a long-held desire to play at the fabled SCG, I was forced to rule myself out of the 2008 State of Origin series. I was in camp for a short time ahead of all three games and watched each match from the coach's box.

Mal got me to come down on the field after we won game three and while I was stoked we had beaten the Blues and was personally really happy for the boys, it just didn't feel the same. I hadn't contributed and as soon as I got onto the field I made the point of steering clear of the main celebrations. I didn't feel a part of the euphoria. Those moments straight after a game – they are the special few moments you share with your team-mates and the other guys involved, coaching staff and so on. I have always believed others should allow them to enjoy that time before joining the celebrations.

I can admit now that I returned to the field with the Broncos energised, largely because I had begun to think that this might be it for me. I didn't talk about it with too many people, but in my own mind I knew I wasn't the same player as the one who had been running around prior to the reconstruction. I didn't have the same zip and just didn't want to be someone who ruined his reputation by playing on when my body just couldn't do what I needed it to do.

A lot had changed or was changing. A lot of my peers and closest friends at the club had departed for one reason or another. Petero, Shaun Berrigan and Brent Tate had joined other clubs, Thorny was back in New Zealand playing rugby. Webbie had retired and Tunza was set to join him. There was also the small matter of Wayne leaving at season's end to take over at the Dragons. With the World Cup final to be played at Suncorp Stadium, even someone as jaded as me could see the romanticism of bowing out with a World Cup win on home soil.

It wasn't until a short time before Ricky brought the squad into camp that I shelved thoughts of retiring, simply based on the fact that slowly but surely I had started to find my old self out on the field. The first place I began to notice things getting back to somewhere near where they had been was with my long kicking game – which has been an area I have always considered one of my real strengths.

Johnathan Thurston: To me, that big left boot of his is the best in the game. Just in terms of the variety, accuracy and length – I think when you look at the overall package, he certainly has the best kicking game I have seen. Other guys might grubber better. There may be the odd bloke who can kick it further, though not necessarily with the same accuracy. But no one has the whole array of kicks that Locky does and it is really undersold. I can't tell you the number of times we have been under the pump playing for Queensland or Australia and Locky would just grab it and put it into orbit. And inevitably he would somehow manage to find the grass. He uses his kicking to control the pace of games and dominate field position and also to attack with his bombs and of course his drop goals . . .

Like I said, for me it's the best all-round kicking game I have seen. It was what he could always fall back on if all else failed.

Matt Johns: I remember a game at the back end of 1999. I was still at the Knights and we were going pretty well at the time. We travelled up to ANZ to play Brisbane and got spanked. My lasting memory from that day was just seeing Locky get the ball around the halfway line and just going whack! He was letting these monumental drop punts go and again and again they sailed over my head and over the head of our fullback and just sat down in the in-goal. Locky was probably the first bloke to master the drop punt in our game. He could kick sides to death.

I played in sides he did it to and I have watched him do it to plenty of others since retiring. It is some sort of weapon.

Of course, the end to the 2008 season was the furthest thing imaginable from a fairytale finish. Australia lost the World Cup final to a Kiwi outfit that played in a manner befitting a team which boasted Wayne as an assistant. As frustrating as the result was for me, in hindsight I am glad Wayne was able send a bit of a message to his doubters and critics, even if it came at my expense. I hope that in some small way it helped ease the pain I know he felt in departing from Brisbane in the circumstances he did.

There is no doubt that following revelations in late 2006 that he was negotiating a possible move to the Roosters, there seemed to be some instability surrounding Wayne and the club for the first time ever. That may not sound surprising under the circumstance, but for anyone who knew Wayne and the Broncos it was an enormous departure from the past.

In the wake of the 2006 premiership, Wayne had gone on public record, committing himself to the Broncos indefinitely. Given he had helped build the club from nothing into the NRL's most dominant franchise, collecting six premierships in his two decades at the helm, I would have thought that would have been music to the ears of any member of the Broncos' world. Tensions continued to simmer and seemingly grow by the day. It was like the ground had just suddenly started to move, and before we knew it Wayne was advising us that he was to leave his beloved Broncos.

The success Wayne has enjoyed in his time at the Dragons is a testament to his coaching philosophies and values. We had a great reign with Wayne at our helm, so it is with envy that every other club no doubt looks on and wonders 'what if' they had Wayne.

Of course, on the field, we failed to deliver the glorious exit that a tenure like Wayne's deserved. We had a grand final appearance there for the taking that season, but were knocked off in the dying seconds of our semi-final match with Melbourne. Greg Inglis scored out wide with 45 seconds left on the clock to snatch the win. Watching GI stroll over, I just couldn't believe it. A year's worth of frustration – culminating in our preparation for the Storm game, ranking amongst the very worst weeks I have been part of at the club – bubbled over and I screamed at the top of my lungs.

The week leading into that match had been thrown into turmoil when a big night out the Sunday before ended in disaster, with Karmichael Hunt, Sam Thaiday and Darius Boyd interviewed by police over an alleged sexual assault. No charges were ever laid against any of the three, but the damage done to their reputations and the Broncos brand was enormous. Wayne called us all in and the instruction was to batten down the hatches. No one was to talk to the media without the club's express permission beforehand. And that went doubly so for anything to do with the investigation into what might have happened at Alhambra Bar in the Valley.

The media coverage of that week opened my eyes to the commercial reality of news organisations in this day and age. That is, they are businesses and so are driven by sales and/or ratings; and the fact is the sensationalist, tabloid style of paper is what sells. I got caught up in the frenzy late in the week when ABC News got footage of me horsing around at a bar in Caxton Street and feigning to tackle one of the guys who was on the door. I confess to initially denying the grainy picture that first went to air was me, because for the life of me I have no recollection of that 'incident'. A second release, however, confirmed it was me on the video. I immediately put my hand up and apologised for any harm I may have caused. But that apology was one of those occasions when, as a club captain, you have to say some things you don't necessarily believe because it is in the best interests of the team that you do. Obviously the timing of the release of the footage and the profile of my position were what drove this story, as opposed to any real substantive news value.

I have never spoken to any of the three boys about what did or didn't happen that night – after they were cleared by the police it was none of my business. All three paid a heavy price, with the hammering they took in the papers and on talkback radio leaving their respective reputations in tatters.

Sammy seemed to be the one who moved on quickest and he hasn't put a foot wrong since. I know he did a lot of work in the community in the 12 months that followed and it is a credit to him that he has once again established himself as a fan favourite at the Broncos and seems to be particularly popular with the hordes of school kids that come down and watch us train at different times throughout the season. While the club has a number of options available to take over as Broncos captain in 2012 – and this should not be taken as an endorsement of one player over another – I will just say the player and leader Sam Thaiday has grown into over the past two years would not look out of place should his name carry a 'C' beside it in the years ahead.

K took things a little harder and it was months before he came to grips with his predicament. It had only been a couple of weeks prior to the night in question that K had been the toast of the town. In fact, he had really been lauded by all and sundry after he became the youngest player in the history of the NRL to reach the 100 first-grade appearances milestone. Wayne had anointed him the captain in waiting and he appeared to have the world at his feet.

I do wonder what role the affair had in his eventual departure at the end of the 2009 season, but what I will say is that he too managed to use a really tough period in his life as a catalyst for making some really positive changes. K has gone on record as saying the incident in the Valley in late 2008 was the culmination of a wild few months. I desperately wish he had remained here at the Broncos. Mature beyond his years, K and I are close friends, as are our partners, and I am in awe of the courage, confidence and talent he has shown since rocking Australia's sporting landscape with his decision to attempt to forge a career in the AFL, having already proven himself at the highest level in both rugby league and union.

As is his way, Darius internalised everything in the aftermath of the police investigation and interviews. Everyone knows he had a tough upbringing, with neither of his parents in the picture. Since his arrival into the first-grade squad at the start of 2006, there has always been a real intensity and wariness in his demeanour and in his public persona. Thankfully, though, Darius has managed to grow both as a person and as a player, thanks in no small way to the guidance and care Wayne has given him.

Coaches talk about wanting to create a relationship with a player akin to that of family. Rarely, though, does that happen. With Darius and Wayne, there is a bond which is as close to father and son as one could hope to get. I only hope Darius is smart enough to stick close to Wayne in the years ahead. Not just because it will inevitably mean he is playing in part of a handy football team, but also because Wayne is the perfect bloke to help Darius grow into a man who is confident and comfortable in his own skin and free of the baggage left by the past.

The Bennett and Boyd combination will, of course, take up residence at Newcastle in 2012, after Nathan Tinkler's big promises about his desire to build the Hunter region into a rugby league powerhouse helped lure Wayne to the Knights after three very successful years at St George Illawarra. Wayne's decision shocked many, with most pundits convinced the king was ready for a triumphant return to his home, to once again take the reins at the Broncos. I had spoken to him a couple of times in the weeks after Ivan Henjak was sacked and we also shared some time together during the week leading into the 2011 NRL All-Stars match, with Wayne coach of the NRL side I was captaining.

I have learned by experience the dangers of trying to 'read' Wayne, but by the time round one of the 2011 season arrived, I was firmly of the belief Wayne was coming back in 2012. As he loves to do, though, Wayne kept everyone hanging in suspense for some time before finally revealing his decision to take over at the Knights on a monster four-year deal.

I have to admit I was a little disappointed. It would have been nice to have him back here in the saddle at the Broncos. However, I had a chuckle listening to the stunned reaction of fans and media. Surely after 30 years they know Wayne marches to the beat of his own drum. It may sound a little odd at times but seven premierships suggest its timing is impeccable, just like that of its composer.

TWELVE

Reforming the Family

IVAN HENJAK WAS coaching the Broncos reserve-grade side when I arrived at the club in 1995. I only played a handful of matches in reserve grade, but for whatever reason really struggled at that level. The few reserve grade matches I played that season were undoubtedly the worst games I played that year, so Ivan probably didn't have real fond memories of his first encounters with me.

Ivan had joined the Broncos coaching staff a year earlier, having retired as a player at the end of the 1993 season. Over the course of his playing career, he amassed 185 first-grade appearances during stints with Wests, St George and Canberra in Australia and Hull in the English competition. A versatile utility-type who could play in the halves or centres, he was renowned as a feisty and fierce competitor with a great work ethic. He was also a devoted student of the game and absorbed the lessons on the fundamentals of the game taught to him by some of modern rugby league's best minds. Warren Ryan, Brian Smith, Wayne Bennett and Tim Sheens are some of the coaches under whom Ivan learned the game.

I quickly learned of Ivan's well-established reputation for being pretty fiery and delivering some decent sprays when he was upset with something he had seen from one of his players. There's no doubt over the years Ivan got on the wrong side of a few blokes who weren't able to deal with his intensity and rather authoritarian managerial style. There was no doubting his knowledge or understanding of the technical aspects of rugby league at the top level. Nor could anyone ever question his dedication to the role – he was a relentless worker. But while his single-minded approach worked well when he was helping teach developing talent the intricacies of the game, such an autocratic attitude doesn't work all the time when you are dealing with grown men at the top level.

I didn't have a great deal to do with Ivan after I was elevated to the Broncos first-grade squad at the back end of 1995. It would be almost a decade before we had any real interaction at a professional level.

Wayne Bennett: Locky came into an environment where there were some wonderful trainers. I can't put Alf or Steve Renouf in that category, but guys like Wendell, Darren Smith, Michael Hancock, the Walters boys . . . it reinforced for him what he already knew about reward for effort and having that ability to push yourself at training. But it wasn't long before he revealed himself as something above them again. As time went on, no one matched him and still to this day no one matches him. We had people coming to Broncos training from all over the world – coaches, administrators, other athletes – and a lot of them didn't know a thing about rugby league. Their first question was always, 'Who's that bloke?'

Locky just stood out – his athletic ability and fitness were just on another level and they could see it.

I could see – anyone could – that he was going to be a player, the trick for me was to find a place for him. The same thing happened with a number of other blokes. Kevie Walters, for example, should have been a halfback, but we had Alf so he learned to play five-eighth. It was actually a real dilemma for me initially. Here we are with this special playmaker, 18 years old, but it is 1995 and Alf and Kevie are at their peak.

So we are doing a drill one day, some work under the high ball. It was actually for our wingers, but a couple miscued and there was Locky just taking them easy as you like. So I got him to join in and he isn't catching them, he is up there plucking these balls out of the air.

The penny dropped. We'd been having some drama at the back. Julian O'Neill was gone and it was becoming an Achilles heel for us. I got them to keep peppering him with these kicks, because one of the criteria to play back there in first-grade teams is you have to be able to handle the high ball. I just thought if he could handle bombs like that, his five-eighth skills would just be a bonus. A couple of weeks after that, I just said to him, 'You are going to be our fullback.'

And how did he take to it? He made it his own. They talk about Clive Churchill in his era and what he did for fullback play. This guy did the same thing in his era. There was never any chance he was going to slip back into reserve grade or Colts. He didn't belong there . . . he never did.

Ricky Stuart: The hardest part about planning for Locky when he was playing fullback was actually finding him on the field and knowing where he was so we could structure our game accordingly. Locky had this ability to be on one side of the field during a play and yet would pop up right over the other side of the field the following play. Obviously his speed and fitness were just incredible through those early years. It complemented his ability to read the game – which I think he does as well, if not better than, anyone I have come across. Most guys are out there counting heads trying to spot an overlap. Not Darren. He didn't count. He knew when there was an overlap. It is something instinctive and requires a feel for the game that only the true greats enjoy.

There is no question in my mind that Darren Lockyer

changed the manner in which fullbacks are viewed within a team's attacking structure. He introduced a level of skill in his ball-playing no one had ever seen from a bloke wearing number one. That ability was what made him different from every other fullback in history, but you shouldn't forget the standards of excellence he set in relation to the more traditional fullback tasks.

I think this was where he made the biggest impact, because he just did everything better than even the other 'best' fullbacks in recent memory. Gary Jack was a wonderful player, rugged and tough as nails. He was a real handful with the ball. I also played a lot of football with Gary Belcher, who had that similarly effortless running style as Darren. Locky always looked like he was gliding across the field. His balance was so good when he moved that he could step and swerve at full speed. His hands were better. He read the game and opposition kickers better. He linked with his wingers on kick-return better and sits comfortably with Terry Lamb as the best support player in the modern era.

Billy Slater is the only player who has even come close to doing what Darren Lockyer did at fullback. His ball-playing has improved a lot over the past two or three seasons, but as good as he is becoming, you are comparing him against one of the great distributors of the football the game has seen. Lockyer had a natural feel for ball-playing. Billy doesn't, but in relation to their ball-running and athleticism Billy is right up there with what Locky could do during his time at fullback.

Ivan was in charge of the Broncos reserve-grade or Queensland Cup feeder team until 2000, when he stood down for personal and family reasons. He returned to the club in 2004, when he took a position in the football department helping Cyril in talent identification and recruitment. Following Kevin Walters' axing, Ivan was appointed as Wayne's first assistant, where he was specifically responsible for helping implement a new offensive gameplan. He also ran much of the video analysis work we did, particularly the week-to-week breakdown of opposition teams – their strengths and weaknesses, patterns of play and structures. It was a role in which Ivan excelled, particularly the 'counter-intelligence' analysis. In the video room, Ivan was in his element and his contribution to the Broncos' success in 2006 was enormous.

Not surprisingly, given his background working with developing players, Ivan is a big believer in doing plenty of specific core skills work at training. Our counterparts in rugby union dedicate an enormous percentage of their training to perfecting the different skills involved in their game, in contrast to the majority of clubs I know of in the NRL, who have gone away from the individual skill work. Generally it is incorporated within game-related drills and exercises, though I think there is room for far more core skills work in rugby league. The play-the-ball and scrums aren't areas we set aside time for at training these days. It's probably no surprise that they happen to be two of the real problem areas in the NRL. But even standing there and throwing spiral passes on both sides to a team-mate, practising flick passes, one-handed passes, all that sort of thing, these are skills which I think could benefit from some more work at training. You only have to look at the improvements made in goal-kicking over the past 20 years to see what can be achieved when professional players are given proper instruction and can put some hours into one area of their game.

Early on in 2006, Wayne was clearly still the dominant voice. But as the years rolled on, Ivan's input steadily increased to those final months of Wayne's tenure at the back end of 2008. I certainly am not a big fan of that sort of situation, because even if it is an amicable arrangement, it almost feels like a bit of a power struggle for players' focus and attention. Ironically, it was a similar situation which probably brought about Ivan's undoing a couple of years later, when he and Anthony Griffin were essentially both coaching the team.

When the Broncos began looking for a replacement for Wayne for the 2009 season and beyond, Ivan's was not the first name put forward. Craig Bellamy was the name on everyone's lips. Wayne's right-hand man in both the 1998 and 2000 premiership wins, Bellamy had long been touted as the heir apparent to Wayne's throne at the Broncos. Bellyache had more than proved his worth as an NRL head coach during his time in charge of the Melbourne Storm. He was coming off contract and still had family living in south-east Queensland. With Melbourne and Brisbane both owned by News Limited, everything appeared in place to make the move happen.

I didn't speak to anyone within the Broncos management while negotiations were taking place, because I didn't
feel the need. There were a number of candidates who
had been floated for the position – Kevie Walters, Daniel
Anderson, Neil Henry, Ivan Cleary and Ricky Stuart had all
been tossed up. But I assumed, given the club's status and
the fact Wayne clearly felt he was being pushed towards the
exit, that not only would they be looking for the best, they
would quite likely already have secured their signature.
And outside of Wayne, Craig was the best.

As we now know, the men in charge of the appointment
– managing director Bruno Cullen and chairman Darryl
Somerville – missed their man. To this day I am still not
sure where it all went wrong, because as I understood
things, the Bellyache to Brisbane deal was done. In early
April the word I was being told was that it was all over bar
the shouting and that Craig was just being careful with
managing his exit from Melbourne.

I am unsure what sparked the about-face which saw
him sign a five-year extension on April 17 to remain at the
Storm. I have heard Craig was upset with the way he was
spoken to by one Broncos official involved in the interview
process when he was reportedly being given an ultimatum
about how and when things would be announced. Now,
anyone who knows Bellyache knows he is not the sort of
bloke who will be pushed around by anyone. If you have
seen the footage during a game of his reactions in the coach's
box, you understand he has a short fuse and is certainly no
shrinking violet. He isn't the sort of bloke who would react

well to ultimatums or anything he felt resembled bullying tactics. And so it was that Bellyache stayed down south.

Neil Henry was option two, but he instead opted to accept the Cowboys post, where he had previously been an assistant to Graham Murray. Both these misses were widely reported, so Ivan was well aware he had been down the list of preferences when the job was offered to him just hours after Bellyache's change of heart was made public. He gladly accepted the highest-profile gig in the NRL. I was happy for Ivan to have been rewarded with the job.

Letting Wayne go was most unlike the Broncos. When a six-time premiership-winning coach is about to leave after more than 20 years at the helm, you would hope that the incumbent was well and truly in sight. While this may have been the case, unfortunately it did not quite pan out as expected and this was compounded by the whole affair being carried out in the public arena. Wayne's immediate success at the Dragons probably magnified the situation even more. That Ivan was replaced after just two years is indicative of not only how tough it is to be an NRL coach, but also that the level of success expected in succeeding Wayne Bennett is enormous.

That is the most disappointing part for me, because nothing that Ivan did during his time as head coach should have come as a shock or surprise to anyone at the club. Ivan had been part of the organisation for 10 years, working either on the coaching staff or in the recruitment and development department. I don't recall noticing any discernible changes to his persona after he took over from

Wayne. He was still meticulous and dedicated to his work. As was the case when he was coaching the lower grades, Ivan was particularly good at dissecting both our game and our opponent's. He could identify weaknesses to exploit and conversely weaknesses we needed to work on.

However, his obsessive nature and the intense media scrutiny on his performances as coach often led to him being on edge. It sometimes felt as though we were paddling upstream; it was an ever-present pressure-cooker environment. At times, even when we seemed to be performing okay, it became a habit to focus on the negatives. There were a couple of occasions I recall all too well when Ivan's eye for detail, coupled with his quick temper, resulted in him zeroing in on one player and being critical. Perhaps this was part of the overall Ivan plan, but I did see some of my team-mates respond negatively to this strategy. While this philosophy may not have affected me directly, some of the younger players found it very difficult.

There were occasions when Ivan and I would have scheduled post-game meetings. From time to time during these one-on-one meetings I could sense the pressure was on and Ivan was probably looking to vent at me. Generally, though, he maintained his composure, although the tension and negativity emanated from his body language. In the first couple of months of 2010, which was tough time for the club, Ivan suggested that I just focus on my job, rather than the rest of the team. While this may sound ludicrous, at the time there was some logic to his point as it may have helped me with my personal performance.

I very well might have been preoccupied with our young team and not paying attention to my own game. I always believed the most important thing I could do both at games and at training was to set the best example possible. From being punctual, to the intensity with which I trained, to the discipline I maintained both at the footy club and at home – I always felt young footballers tended to learn best through observation. Watching the blokes who had been there and done it all before, knowing they had been part of successful Broncos teams in years gone by, was how I learned about what was required to be successful in the NRL.

I had the fortune of being Kevin Walters' room-mate throughout my first few seasons at the Broncos, just prior to him assuming the captaincy from Alf in 1999. While Kevie is a little more boisterous than me, he wasn't one for inspirational speeches or thinking he needed to be constantly critiquing other blokes in the side. I can assure you, though, that he was one of the most passionate players I have played with. He enjoyed himself when he was out celebrating a win, but I can't remember him being involved in an incident which reflected poorly on the club. He was an outstanding trainer and has become a studious assistant coach. He was so important for us in that 2000 premiership season, despite not getting the accolades he deserved. The way in which he bought into the changes Wayne and Craig implemented that year was the key to our entire season and it was a real lesson to me.

Whether it was at club or representative level, I always made a point of giving my coaches the respect of doing everything I could to fit in with how they wanted the game to be played. In return, I can honestly say I have been able to learn something from each and every one of them – whether it was in the intricate detail which Tim Sheens, Ivan, Michael Hagan or Neil Henry put into their preparations, or Craig Bellamy showing me just how effective structured football can be in the NRL.

Craig and Ricky Stuart also reminded me that fire and passion can still be part of your make-up as a head coach – provided that the yin had a yang. Playing for those two guys, you knew they could deliver a frightful spray, but you also knew they would do anything to protect you as long as you wore their colours. Wayne's mastery of psychology and the value he put on discipline are what make him the coach he is, while Mal and Chris Anderson both excelled at rep level especially because they understood that when you have the talent at your disposal, creating a particular environment helped build the trust those types of players needed to go out there and do what they can do.

Wayne Bennett: He always wanted the captaincy, he enjoys the responsibility, but it is something he has had to work at. There have been critics, but it is dumb criticism from people who think he isn't in charge because he isn't out there ranting and raving at players, walking around pointing his finger and telling his team-mates off – things some people seem to think you have to do to be a leader. No Broncos captain has ever done that, it would never have been tolerated. Not by me and not by a lot of the other players at the club. That is the system Locky was brought up on – to lead from the front. Respect is earned – it isn't just handed out like chocolates – and you earn the respect of your team-mates with your actions. So when Locky was made captain, he knew what was expected of him at the Broncos, for Queensland and for Australia. If you can say a few words, that's a bonus and really, towards the end of his career, he has done that extremely well.

Phil Gould: Some blokes lead in very different ways. Lockyer's style is unique to him. It's one of inspiration and gets its strength from the players around him wanting to be around him and wanting to be respected by him. As an observer who hasn't seen him within a team environment – though I have had a lot of players I have coached tour with him – I think it has become an enormously powerful style of leadership. You see the meticulous way Darren Lockyer presents himself off the field and that attention to detail is reflected in how he goes about his football. He has standards and you aren't going to be with him or respected by him if you can't meet those standards.

Ricky Stuart: From the first field session I ran with the Test team, Locky was as easy a bloke to handle as you could wish for. So coachable . . .

He was totally team-driven, which is the very essence of leading. He'd do anything for the team and his team-mates know it because they have seen it. Players love playing with him. When I was coaching at the Roosters, the boys would come back from the tour – Luke Ricketson, Craig Fitzgibbon, Craig Wing, Anthony Minichiello – they'd be, 'Locky this, Locky that'.

It is maybe a little hard to explain, but when I got to work with him in the Australian team I saw how his humility was the key to it all. He never wanted any favours. He never wanted special treatment. In fact, he probably worked harder than anyone at training and around the team camp. As a player, you see those things. You see the bloke who is happy to take all the raps when times are good but goes into hiding when the knives come out. Locky has the respect of his peers because he works the other way. He's happy to wear criticism for the team, because it doesn't worry him, and he will always direct praise coming his way to the blokes around him.

That selflessness is why he is held up on a pedestal by his peers. And their opinion is the one worth valuing.

Taking over from Wayne at the Broncos was always going to be a difficult task, but the chances of Ivan enjoying a lengthy stay as head coach weren't helped by the fact that his appointment coincided with some significant changes in the way the different arms of the organisation functioned. The most obvious was the blurring of the very clear lines which had previously existed separating the front office administration and the football department. Wayne always insisted on having complete control of the football department. It was his domain and no one upstairs would dare look to intervene without first getting express permission from Wayne to do so.

Yet, when Ivan began his first year as a head coach, he was faced with the unenviable prospect of managing the biggest staff in the NRL. Amongst his high-profile support team were a staggering five assistant coaches, with club legends Allan Langer, Shane Webcke, Peter Ryan and Michael De Vere joined by the addition of former Queensland Origin halfback Paul Green.

I have heard Wayne say on more than one occasion that there is no place for democracy at a football club. For a club to be successful, it must be supremely efficient, flexible and agile – traits rarely associated with rule by committee. While smart leaders will always surround themselves with wise counsel, in the end those same leaders, alone, must make the final decision on a variety of important matters. At a football club, the head coach has to be the man responsible for making those important decisions ... the tough decisions. Not that Ivan wouldn't make tough decisions – far from it. He remains the only coach to have been able to get anywhere near the best out of that unique specimen by the name of Dave 'The Coaltrain' Taylor. In the second half of the 2009 season, Dave was the most dangerous attacking threat in the entire competition. As has been the way with Dave ever since his NRL debut for the Broncos back in

2007, size, strength, speed and skill weren't an issue at the start of 2009. His weight and fitness were.

Ivan spoke to Dean Benton – who had returned after two years in charge of performance programs with English rugby giants the Leicester Tigers – and it was decided Dave needed to get well under the 120 kilos he weighed to have any chance of reaching his undoubted potential in the modern game. Dave was told he would not be considered for selection until he got his weight under 117 kilos, a hardline stance applauded by a few but questioned by others.

That reaction probably reflected the public relations battle Ivan fought throughout his time as Broncos coach. He was never able to win the hearts and minds of the hordes of fans who so loved Wayne. That Ivan bore the brunt of the resentment stemming from the club's handling of Wayne's exit was unfair, but hardly unexpected. He became almost paranoid about any questions that went anywhere near Wayne's name. I know he was ropable when *The Courier-Mail* ran a photo of him with a painting of Wayne in the background. For me, that sort of approach is destined to disappoint given the magnitude of past successes. You have to deal with what is real and the reality was Ivan was following an icon – a man who helped build the club from nothing into the most dominant force in the competition across the two decades he spent in charge, filling the trophy cabinet with an array of trophies and awards, including six NRL premierships, a World Club Challenge and a World Club Championship. My philosophy is that you can only change what is in the present – not the past – so it is useless wasting energy on things that you cannot control.

With the guidelines in place, Dave went back and, I thought, over time, began to show the sort of improvements in his attitude and discipline Ivan was after. But the manner in which Ivan handled Dave through those few months he spent back in Queensland Cup was probably a snapshot of Ivan's stint as head coach of the Brisbane Broncos. Much of what he did with Dave that year was bang on the money. Calling in the club's very own GI Joe, Chris Haseman, to essentially become Dave's personal trainer worked a treat.

Hasey is probably the hardest man I have ever encountered. The bloke made his living fighting in cages in Japan and Russia long before anyone had heard of the Ultimate Fighting Championship. He also held down posts as a prison guard; as the hand-to-hand and munitions instructor for the Queensland Police Special Emergency Response Team; and as a contractor for the US Department of Defense working with the army and police in Iraq. Simply put, he is a bloke you want beside you when shit hits the fan.

So, with Chris cracking the whip, Dave got himself in shape and as I said earlier elevated his play to the very highest level more quickly than any other player I can remember seeing. One of the things about Dave, though, is his nature and demeanour belie his ridiculously big frame. Dave is the quintessential 'gentle giant' and, as he has demonstrated on more than one occasion, would much rather use that thing he likes to call a sidestep or perhaps even use the old chip and chase to get in behind the defensive line rather than simply splintering a defensive line with sheer force. Maybe, when you are that much bigger and stronger than everyone you have ever played against, it gets boring just steamrolling people. I wouldn't know, given I have never seen the needle on the scale sneak past 85 kilograms.

I should make the point here that, when people refer to Dave as being 'overweight', they are not talking about fat. If you have seen him without a shirt on, you'd realise there is a hell of a lot of muscle in his 126-kilo physique. But you simply cannot play a game of rugby league at the pace at which the NRL is played carrying that sort of weight around. Dave's problem is that he can build muscle at an abnormally fast rate and so must be extremely conscious about his diet and portion sizes – something Dave took some time to get his head around. I know when he was under Hasey's watch Dave was banned from lifting weights. All his strength work was done via plyometric training with Dean Benton and functional strength training with Chris, which incorporates a lot of traditional movements like push-ups, chin-ups, rope pulls, with some wrestling and core strength work, and relies on using your own bodyweight a lot of the time.

Everyone, including Ivan, wanted Dave back in the top side because he is one of only a very few players I have ever encountered who could single-handedly change the course of a match. He was a freak – a fact we were all reminded of at Red Hill one morning in early 2009. I am on record as saying Greg Inglis is probably the most naturally gifted footballer I have encountered in rugby league, but in terms of a combination of freakish power and speed I don't know whether any of the three major football codes in Australia have seen anything like Dave Taylor.

Dave had not lifted a single weight during the 2008 pre-season, nor through the early rounds of the season proper, during which time he was stuck playing with the Central Comets in the Queensland Cup, where his size and skill made him close to unstoppable.

Having farewelled Petero Civoniceva, Shane Webcke, Ben Hannant and Brad Thorn in the previous three seasons, we had a young but close-knit group of forwards including guys like Corey Parker, Sam Thaiday, Nick Kenny, Ashton Sims and Joel Clinton. On this day the forwards, led by the props, were doing their 1–3 rep max test on bench press – probably the most universal movement in the weights room. The Broncos have long been blessed to have on staff Dan Baker, who is renowned internationally as one of the best resistance coaches in sport. A former national powerlifter, Dan is constantly reminding us of the importance of tracking and recording the weights we are lifting. There is something to be said for being able to physically see how much you have improved or perhaps regressed after an injury.

Anyhow, Dave Taylor just so happened to be wandering past the gym as the lads went up with a wave of whooping and hollering. Nick Kenny had just rolled out a 175-kilogram press – it was a new record. Dave's almost sheepish persona makes him an easy target for when the stirrers in the group are looking for someone to wind up a bit. And so as the man-child – as we used to call him, given that he had arrived at the club straight out of school weighing a phenomenal 116 kilos – ambled past, the boys were into him, challenging him to see what he could do after such a lengthy stint away from weights.

It was all tongue-in-cheek stuff and everyone was having a bit of a chuckle until Dave just started to wander over to the bench. When he got there, he leaned over the rusted Olympic barbell which was still carrying Nick's impressive weight.

'How much did he do?' Dave asked.

'175 kilos, mate.'

Dave nodded and, without saying a word, slapped a 5-kilo plate on each side, took position under the bar without so much as a stretch, and pumped out three unassisted presses before dropping the bar back in its catch. Everyone was in a sort of stunned silence. Dave got up and smiled broadly. Then everyone just erupted again.

It was out of this world.

Now, I wasn't privy to what occurred in the meetings Dave and his management had with Ivan through the early part of the season. What I do know is what I saw as a result of them. Dave Taylor went from being a really likeable kid, with an untapped reservoir of talent as big as the Pacific and a desire to be at the Broncos for life, to being a player questioning his talent and worth to the point where some weeks he didn't even want to play or train. Dave and his management asked for a meeting with Ivan mid-year to ask what more he needed to do to get his chance.

Having been raised in rural Queensland, I am not averse to the idea of a bit of tough love. I think a coach needs to have in his arsenal the ability to deliver a spray once in a while. But if you keep telling young blokes they are not up to it, eventually they will start believing it and then what are you left with? Coaches need to have balance and the ability to understand the mindset of each individual on a personal level. They should offer some praise when a player has done something good, give some positive reinforcement, balanced with constructive criticism from time to time. Otherwise you run the risk of shattering their confidence beyond repair.

Although I have never asked Gordie (at the time the forwards coach with South Sydney) about it, I wouldn't have thought it took too much after that meeting to convince Dave his future lay elsewhere. The Rabbitohs snapped him up. I still shake my head in disbelief that we lost yet another prop forward – this one clearly the most talented prospect in the game.

The 2009 season was a strange one for the Broncos. Wayne's teams had always prided themselves on consistency of effort – never giving up. Very few teams coached by Wayne have been flogged. At the very least, they kept the scoreboard respectable. But in Ivan's first year we really struggled for consistency and were on the end of four 40+-point losses – a notion previously unheard of at the Broncos. A 56–0 drubbing at Canberra Stadium in round 21 was the low point of the year, though I was encouraged by the manner in which we were able to regroup and surge all the way through to the preliminary final, where Melbourne again proved to be our nemesis.

The following year, however, started badly and finished worse.

At his first pre-season training session, Justin Hodges ruptured his Achilles tendon and was ruled out for the year, leaving Israel Folau to carry an enormous load in attack as the only established strike weapon left in the team.

Ivan had overhauled his staff, with Alf and Anthony Griffin, who had been in charge of the under-20s squad previously, his only assistants. There had been some angst around the departures of Peter Ryan and Paul Green, and the dramas on the staff continued in the early stages of the year when Dean Benton resigned after clashes with some other staff over suggestions the team was not fit enough at the start of the year. An impromptu fitness test was held and a number of young blokes performed disgracefully, which conflicted with the data collected over the previous three or four years. Pre-season training had been different, with a lot more emphasis on game-related fitness. We didn't do a lot of really gruelling stuff, which I believe was at the heart of our 1–4 start to the year.

It wasn't anything to do with the fitness of the group, but rather we were mentally very soft. I think the one thing that is difficult to account for in all the sports science testing you can do is that mental toughness you need to compete in the NRL. Maybe this is an old-style approach, but I think that is built when you are taken out of your comfort zone and made to do things you don't want to do. There is a reason boxers get up and run at the crack of dawn, and it is not because they like to watch the sun rise. It is because on those cold mornings when everyone else is in their warm beds, they are out working. It is the same reason I make myself get up at 5.10 every morning, because discipline and routine build mental toughness.

I remember a drill we used to do with Kelvin Giles when I first arrived at the Broncos, where we would be split into three groups – A, B, C. Group A would run 400 metres, then group B, then group C, then the three groups together and you had to finish as a group. It was horrible and had very little application to a rugby league match, but you just felt like you were working hard.

Had it been the Broncos of 2007 doing the same pre-season training as in 2010, I would be willing to bet the results through the first five rounds would have been significantly different, because back then we had a roster littered with experienced, representative players who knew how to push themselves when things are a bit tough on game day. The efforts required to get across and help your team-mate late in the game are only partly to do with fitness. More than that, the efforts you learn are the type expected of you every time you go out onto the field wearing the Broncos jumper. If you want to keep wearing it, you push yourself to get there. In 2010, however, we had the youngest Broncos squad in history and when the going got tough they were, unfortunately, exposed.

Against Dean's advice, Ivan decided to have us come in on our days off for extra fitness work under Tony Guilfoyle, who had taken over from Dean. Gilly had a much more 'old-school' approach, which I felt we benefited from almost immediately. The effort that was required to get us to the desired fitness level and back into the competition took its toll at the back end of the season. We were putting the foot on the accelerator but there was no gas left in the tank, and we dropped our last four games of the year to miss the finals for the first time since 1991.

The run of losses coincided with my absence due to a rib cartilage injury suffered after being crunched by North Queensland backrower Luke O'Donnell. A lot was made of my attempt to get back on the field for the final-round match against the Raiders and the fact that Ivan made the decision to rule me out early in the week. I had been close to playing against the Warriors in the second-last round when I threw a pass that aggravated the ribs to the point where I could barely move. But as bad as the pain was, within 72 hours it was back to where it had been.

The doctor had told me that when you re-injure your cartilage it often comes back stronger thanks to the scar tissue build-up, and by the Monday ahead of the final round I wasn't feeling too bad. I managed to train with the team on Tuesday, although I didn't do any contact work, and was again starting to feel that I was an outside chance if I could get myself right by Friday.

I was sitting in the rooms after Tuesday's training session when Ivan came in and I could tell he looked a little stressed. He wandered around for a while and then asked me what I was going to do. In my mind I was probably hoping he would say I had till match day to get my fitness. I am not sure if it was the media's focus on my injury, but I could sense Ivan wanted to make a decision there and then. I was puzzled that I didn't get the chance to possibly get back by waiting until later in the week, but I guess I can see how Ivan would have wanted to end the speculation. Still, it didn't make me feel any better about having to sit on the sidelines unable to do anything as one of the great streaks in Australian sport ended with an 18–16 loss to Canberra.

At the board's insistence, GeeGee had been asked to conduct a complete review of the Broncos' football operations. What he found was a partly disillusioned playing group, some of whom had lost faith in the coach. I had met with GeeGee late in the season for a discussion about the direction the club was heading in and how I viewed the different roles and relationships of the people within the football department. I was as honest as I could be. This was about making decisions for the betterment of the club and not about individuals.

The family, as Wayne used to refer to the Broncos, had been splintered. The dissension amongst the playing group and the coaching staff, interference from the administration in football matters, the worrying turnover of players . . . Things needed to change.

In his final days as chief executive, I am sure the last thing Bruno Cullen wanted to do was to stand down the head coach – a bloke who had been a loyal servant to the club for a very long time. So the task fell to Paul White, who had only assumed the managing director's position in January. It was a gutsy call, but he has had a long association with Anthony Griffin and Paul assured us that he is the right man to start moving us forward again. I also spoke to Andrew Gee, who is one of the most honest, straight-shooting men I know and who loves the Broncos like few others. GeeGee backed Paul's assessment of Hook (as Griffin is known). Hopefully down the track, when I return for a family reunion, I will be able to look back and say I was there for the start of the Broncos' next great era.

THIRTEEN
Brave Sam

I HAVE BEEN asked countless times in the months following my retirement announcement to rank almost every conceivable aspect of my football career. Best player I have played against? Best I have played with? Hardest to tackle? Greatest match I played in? Biggest hit I have seen? Funniest insult? Worst piece of foul play? You name it, I have been asked it.

One of the most common is who I consider to be the toughest player or players I have played with or against. It is a difficult one to answer. Everyone who takes the field in the NRL is tough. Of that there can be absolutely no question. But there are certainly some guys who can just push through incredible pain barriers and force their bodies to do things which leave you shaking your head. Shane Webcke and Petero Civoniceva both played matches with broken arms. Dallas Johnson was knocked out cold in the first tackle of Origin III, 2007, yet not only managed to return to the field after two others players went down with injury but incredibly topped the tackle count as well. Kevin Campion was another bloke who was able to just push pain to one side for the duration of a match. I played only three years of footy with Kevin, but that was more than enough time to realise he was as hard as nails. I have never seen another player carry the ball into a defensive line like Karmichael Hunt would on his kick-returns and there were some frightening collisions as a result. But every time he got whacked, K just bounced straight back up. He seemed unbreakable. There were plenty of others – Gordie, Paul Gallen, Jeremy Smith, Luke O'Donnell . . . I could go on all day.

But if I was to be asked for the name of the toughest person I encountered in my time in the NRL, none of those blokes would even come close to Sam McCurley. For those of you racking your brains trying to place the name, let me save you the trouble and time of rummaging through any old NRL yearbooks, because you won't find him there. In fact, you won't find *him* anywhere, because *he* is in fact a *she* and, as I am writing this, Miss Samantha McCurley has only recently celebrated her 15th birthday – a night of celebrations of which I was thrilled to be a part.

It was a milestone worthy of celebration, too, given it had been almost eight years since we first crossed paths. That meeting came during the 2003 State of Origin series when Sam came into camp and spent the day with the Maroons.

It had been organised through the Make-a-Wish Foundation, an amazing organisation which tries to brighten the lives of children who are terminally ill. See, 12 months earlier, doctors discovered a tumour covering around a quarter of her brain. She was supposed to have only a matter of months to live. Outside of my family, I don't know that any one person has had a bigger impact on my life and my outlook on it than Sam. I feel blessed to have had her enter my life.

It is one of the special things my profile as an NRL player has afforded me – that is, the opportunity to bring just a little bit of joy to the lives of those in our community who most need it. I want to make it clear from the outset that I am no different from any number of NRL players with regard to giving up time for charities and hospital visits. As a body, NRL players do an amazing amount of this sort of work. This is one area in which no other sport or code in this country comes even close. But in staying with the honesty I have tried to maintain on these pages, I must admit initially the volunteer work, particularly the pretty regular visits the Broncos would make to children's hospitals, was not something that I looked forward to, or enjoyed doing. Not that Wayne or anyone else at the club for that matter was asking me in my early years with the first-grade squad. As a kid from the country, I found it pretty nerve-racking being around those kids and their families. I just didn't know what to say or what to do. I didn't know how I should be feeling or acting. It wasn't like anyone knew who I was back then anyhow, so what could I possibly offer?

Over time, however, as my profile started to grow a bit and as I became a little more worldly, I started to understand that even if it was only for an hour those visits could brighten the day of kids whose quality of life is so bad it is upsetting to even imagine. To see a child's face light up smiling or laughing – to be able to help to do that if even just for a little while – there is no more uplifting feeling in the world. Of course, there are difficult moments, especially with the parents. Children are so resilient and almost always seem to be coping with their particular circumstances better than Mum and Dad. With a little one of my own now, I completely understand. There isn't anything you wouldn't do for them.

I know now my initial insecurities were also preventing me from meeting some incredible people – people whose lives and attitudes are an inspiration and also a pointed reminder of how fortunate we are to be fit and healthy. Dean Clifford, for instance. Dean was 31 this year and just broke his personal best on the bench press at the Broncos – 120 kilograms, if you don't mind! It is a pretty fair effort from a guy born with a rare genetic condition called Epidermolysis bullosa, which doctors expected would claim his life before he turned three. Dean was particularly close with big Brad Thorn, who was his personal trainer at the Broncos gym, where Dean would come to lift weights a couple of times a week. While Thorny has moved on, Dean still comes in to pump some iron and he is one of the boys' favourites.

I am constantly amazed at how the sickest kids are so pragmatic with the battles they face, none more so than Sam.

Sam is far more concerned about how I am going and how the Broncos are travelling than she is about the daily challenges she has faced for the majority of her life. For her to be able to block out whatever she is going through so she can find out what is happening down at Red Hill ... it made me realise what these teams I play for mean to a lot of people out there in the community.

Along with all the children you meet in such awful predicaments, Sam has also been a wonderful reality check for me whenever I get a little wrapped up in the importance of what it is I do for a living. It really puts things in perspective when you have a loss or play poorly and are down on yourself and then you head up to see these kids walking around with tubes coming out of their faces and all sorts of illnesses. In those moments, I know I have felt more than a tinge of embarrassment at the way I have moped around because something didn't go my way in a game. These kids are up there fighting every day for things you and I don't even consider. The most important thing in life is life itself. Good health is something a lot of us take for granted, but these kids don't have that luxury.

I know on some of the days when I am getting really down on myself for one thing or another, more than once my mind has turned to those kids up in the Royal Children's Hospital wards and I realise that, you know what ... my life is pretty damn good.

Obviously, on the flip side to the wonderful moments these sick children provide, there is the devastating and harsh reality that a lot of them aren't getting better. There have been a number of times organised by either the Starlight or Make-a-Wish Foundations when we have had a youngster down to the Broncos. Asked what the one thing is they'd like to experience, the one dream they'd like fulfilled, all they want is to come down and meet the Broncos or perhaps lead the team out onto Suncorp Stadium. Then, a month or two later, the club will receive a letter from the parents. I have been in a lot of dressing-rooms and it isn't often that they are quiet. But whenever one of these letters comes through, you could hear a pin drop. They just wanted to let us know their child hadn't made it, while at the same time thanking us for the day because they had loved the experience. It is heart-wrenching stuff. Since becoming a dad myself, the enormity of what those families have to deal with has been rammed home. It is cruel what they endure.

Towards the end of Sam's visit back in 2003, her parents, Peter and Karen, came and spoke to me and told me I was her favourite player to the point where Sam would get quite upset at any commentator who spoke in an even remotely negative manner about me. Sam wouldn't stand for even the slightest criticism, always noting who said what for future reference. I told them I would like to stay in touch with them, just to see how she was doing.

At the time, Sam was booked in for what I believe was her third round of surgery and I just wanted to keep a bit of an eye on her progress. Peter and Karen explained that, while the doctors hadn't been overly optimistic, Sam never entertained the thought that she wouldn't come out the other side. Time and again she has been faced with the prospect of needing to fight off a tumour growing inside her head that is around the size of her little hand. Ten times now she has gone under the knife, ten times she has woken unfazed and a little dismissive of all the concern and emotion amongst the people around her.

The last few have been especially dicey operations and each time I have found myself just sitting somewhere staring at my phone, nervous at what news might come through. The relief when that news turns out to be that Sam has got through yet again is a godsend.

Sam has got to know all the people in my life – Loren and Sunny, most of my team-mates. Even Wayne has been up to see her a few times. In fact, Wayne was there just before her most recent surgery in late February. I had got the call from Peter a couple of days earlier.

'It's back,' was all he could get out.

Then, after a couple of moments, 'This time it's bad.'

I spoke to Sam as soon as I could, trying my best not to sound too worried. There is an open-door policy for the three of them to any game I am playing in, and so they headed down to Robina to watch the second NRL All-Stars match. If she is ever at a game, she knows I expect her to come down to the sheds afterwards to see me and so she did, once the formalities were wrapped up on the field.

When I saw her, I knew straightaway things were bad. She'll never tell you, but I could see she was in a lot of pain. The tumour was growing by the day, but the surgeons had to wait until Wednesday before opening her up once again. I'll never forget standing there with Wayne as they approached and just the terrified look in the eyes of both parents. You could see there and then that they weren't sure their precious little girl was going to survive this time. Wayne was despondent and I had this awful feeling in the pit of my stomach that this might be the last chance I would get to speak with Sam.

When my phone started to ring with Peter's caller ID showing up, I took the call praying for a miracle. With a bit of difficulty, Peter managed to get out the news that Sam had pulled through. A perfect 10!

I went up to see her the following day. Before I went into the room, Peter explained the size of the operation was such that she had been left without sight in her left eye. I went in to see her and she smiled straightaway and immediately asked how Sunny was and the Broncos? They were fine, I said as I gave her a hug.

'How are you feeling now?' I asked and she explained she was pretty good, though struggling to adjust to the change of perception now that she had the use of only one eye.

'I'm so sorry, Sam,' I said.

'It's okay, Darren,' she replied. 'I still have one good one.'

FOURTEEN
My Life

IN THE WEEKS after announcing my plan to retire at the conclusion of the 2011 season, I was asked both in private conversations and by those ever-inquisitive media folk whether I had struggled to contain my emotions at any stage during what was a hectic day.

Now, anyone who knows anything about me knows I am not big on public displays of emotion. I like to maintain my composure when in the public spotlight. Most of the moments of high emotion in my life are personal matters involving family or those closest to me. I have always attempted to keep at least some of my world private. I firmly believe not everything is for public consumption, no matter who you are. I understand that, as Broncos, Queensland and Australian captain, I am essentially 'on show' 24/7 representing the respective offices of all three titles and the

proud history of individual excellence and strong leadership they share. If I am being honest with myself, however,
it wasn't until the final four or five seasons in the game that
I even paused to consider the magnitude of so many of the
honours I am privileged to have received over the course of
my playing career.

My longevity in the game is certainly one of the major
talking points whenever my impending retirement is being
discussed publicly. While luck obviously plays a big part
in how many games your body can physically endure,
I maintain that the forward-thinking mindset Wayne
drilled into me when I first arrived at the Broncos has been
the key.

'You need to have a short memory if you are going to
make it in this game,' Wayne used to say.

That's Wayne-speak for not dwelling on things that have
already happened. The past is the past. It's done and there is
nothing you can do to change it. Whether you just scored
the Try of the Century or coughed up a ball coming off
your own tryline, 'Keep your eyes on the road ahead, don't
get caught staring into the rear-view mirror.' It is probably
an idea that appealed to the perfectionist in me and fed my
slightly obsessive nature, because at the heart of all these
little sayings is the idea that you can constantly improve.
There is always something you can do better or perhaps
need to do better. In either case, the only way to do that is
to keep trying whatever it may be you are looking to do.

I also like the aspect that this sort of approach will
oftentimes reward the humble amongst us. I am not

someone who can sit still for long periods of time, no matter the reason. It makes me a particularly annoying partner to go to a movie with, for example. Lor doesn't even really bother asking, because she knows I get itchy feet and just need to be doing something marginally constructive to stay put for any length of time. More broadly, though, applying the same 'short memory' attitude to all aspects of my football has helped enormously with maintaining my enthusiasm not just for playing but for training and doing the necessary extras I have always felt I needed to do.

If your eyes are up, you can always spot the next challenge or obstacle ahead. When heads start dropping on a sporting field, it is the beginning of the end.

I am a highly visible public figure and know only too well that there are eyes everywhere just waiting for me to put a foot wrong. But I have done my best to keep my family away from and out of the public eye, particularly Sunny. While there is no way to avoid the questions about his father and football he will undoubtedly endure while growing up in Brisbane, I can at least let him enjoy his first few years oblivious to the strange world in which his dad lives. Being on hand to watch my son grow into a little man is something I am looking forward to enormously and this certainly played a significant role in my decision to hang up the boots.

As for the emotions I may have been feeling as I declared my hand for 2011, I only found myself stumbling on my words once or twice during the big media call held in the Broncos club boardroom that day just after lunch. A couple of references to Cyril and talking about some of the players and staff who have played such big roles in my life for 17 years was very touching. But for the most part I was fine, which I think shows the timing was probably just right for me to call it a day.

I am totally at ease with things. I have loved every moment of my NRL career and am soaking up each and every day I have left. However, I am equally as excited about beginning the next stage of my life. I am convinced a lot of athletes announcing their retirement fear the trepidation they feel about what they will do next with their lives. I understand some people struggle with the adjustment to life after sport. While I am sure I will miss playing rugby league, I just don't think I will struggle with the adjustment. I am looking forward to packing the car and taking Lor and Sunny on family trips whenever we so desire. I am looking forward to having my brothers and their families over for weekend barbecues and I am also looking forward, I hope, to seeing my family expand in number. I think Sunny would love a little brother and sister he could show the ropes of life in Team Lockyer. But we'll wait and see about that.

I also feel as though I owe Lor a bit of a break from the life she has known since we first started dating.

Loren Lockyer: Darren and I had known each other for quite a while before we started seeing each other. We hung around in the same group of friends. I was especially close with Wendell and Tara and Phil Lee and his partner, Renee.

The first time I met him, we were introduced just within a group of friends and he literally sat there in the nightclub and did not say a word all night. I almost thought something was wrong, but it was just him. He is so, so quiet and I guess my initial impression was that he was really boring. Thankfully he got better, especially after he had a few vodkas and loosened up a little. Then you almost can't shut him up . . . he is a very entertaining drunk.

We were good mates, but it wasn't until early in 2004 that we started to bump into each other a little more often. Then the phone calls started and . . . well, you know . . . here we are today, one happy little family.

So we were both single at that stage. I was actually living with my sister in Fernberg Road at Rosalie, just up the road from Darren's place. He was only recently single and let's just say he was making the most of his freedom. Just like everything else in his life, when Darren puts his mind to it he can party with the best of them and is just hilarious to be around when he gets in the mood for a bit of a night out.

I have no idea how it started, but whenever he had been out and was making his way home in the wee hours of the morning, Darren would detour, dropping past my sister's place to leave a piece of pizza on the deck to . . . I don't know really. Maybe it was a memento to let us know he had visited. How I drew a line from him dropping food on my deck to thinking he maybe liked me is something I struggle to understand these days, but that is just what I did. This little thing went on for ages before the first move was made. Courted by cold pizza . . . it's not quite Romeo and Juliet is it? But it is us. We are a little quirky, I guess. So if the shoe fits . . .

Anyhow, I had actually moved in with my sister because I was heading over to England around that July–August period and needed somewhere to crash for the few months before I left.

But the landscape changed dramatically for me in those months. Darren had made the first move, but within a matter of weeks, I would say, things between us leapt from being a situation I was initially a little wary of to realising I really liked Darren . . . a lot. For those first few months we kept things pretty low key. He would come to my place for dinner or I might head over to his sometimes. But we rarely stepped out in public together.

It was a week or two before I was scheduled to fly out to London when Darren asked if I'd like to go out for dinner that night. Then it was: do you want to go out to a café? Do you want to do this and that . . .? I knew what he was doing. But I just felt like I needed to go through with my plans to travel and that's what I did.

I made it clear to Darren before I boarded my flight that I didn't consider us boyfriend and girlfriend. He wasn't bound by anything. He could do what he wanted – as could I. I didn't want him to feel like he owed me any sort of loyalty or commitment. I quickly came to realise what Darren wanted, courtesy of the five phone calls a day we averaged during the first three months of my time in London.

Then, before I knew it, he was in London with the Test team, wanting to meet up. I didn't meet him straightaway, but he won me over with how patient, though persistent, he was about catching up. We eventually caught up around Kensington and had a nice meal together.

It was actually during that week that Darren bought our current house. George Mimis bid on Darren's behalf and the deal was sealed during a conference call at 4 am London time the day of the Kangaroos Test match. The team moved to Leeds, but my work commitments meant I only had time to visit once before they again took off. They actually headed all round the place that tour – to France and all over England – and it wasn't until just before they were set to head home that we caught up again.

Darren asked me when I was planning to come home to Australia, and I told him I wasn't ready to just up and leave. He said he understood, then asked me to think about moving in with him when I was ready to head home. Within four months I was back in Brisbane and trying to add a woman's touch to Darren's place, which he was sharing with a friend of his.

Wayne Bennett: Darren is a bloke who needs people to make him laugh. He is an introvert. He is happy sitting back watching and observing. He enjoys just being in the background, letting others take the floor. In that way, we are a lot alike. But when you are as introverted as Locky is, you seek out your opposite. That's why he and Wendell are such good friends. It is the same with Lor. She is much more open and outgoing, which he needs just to balance his life out. I know a lot of my closest friends are completely different to me. When people ask about those relationships, I tell them I don't want to be like those people, but I absolutely love being around them. Darren is the same. Since the day I met her, Lor has been outspoken. She speaks her mind and tells it like it is, which I know is something Locky values. He's not one for bullshit, Locky.

Loren: Things just cruised along for the next 12 months. We ended up going away with Wendell and Tara, travelling around the States after the European leg of the Kangaroo tour was over. Darren had broken his foot, so getting around the icy sidewalks was a bit of a nightmare.

Before I met up with them, I had been at home in Brisbane and spent a lot of time thinking about where I was at with Darren and just where I thought things were heading. I actually came to the conclusion that I was going to break up with him when he was back in Australia. I thought it just wasn't where I wanted to be. It all felt a bit uncertain and I don't do pointless relationships.

But then he got back and it was like he had undergone some sort of awakening. From Christmas 2005 onwards, our lives have been driven by this new level of discipline and focus Darren seemed to find almost overnight. He had always been disciplined with his training and had that meticulously neat approach to most things he did. But during the 2006 pre-season he matured into this confident man whose life had real direction – professionally and personally. Even when things started a bit ordinarily, Darren never wavered. It took people a long time to realise how resilient and determined he is. When he puts his mind to something, he won't let himself fail. He has a will which I don't think can be broken. He showed that in the 2006 season. He just won everything.

He had made it clear he wanted to get married and start a family, but I never saw it coming. Two years to the day since I had arrived back in Brisbane and agreed to move in with him, Darren asked me to marry him.

February 13, 2007. I'll never forget it.

We went to The Lab at the Casino, which was my favourite restaurant. Darren was leaving the next day for the World Club Challenge, so I thought this was just a fairly standard night out together before he took off. Darren asked for a table with some privacy – which is not unusual for him – and nothing appeared out of the ordinary initially. At the time I was in a bit of a family tiff and was a bit upset, so I was actually in tears not long after we sat down.

When dessert comes around, Darren leans over the table and says, 'Listen, babe, I need to ask you something, but you need to keep it together, okay?'

So he pre-warns me, but before I knew what he was on about he just starts with, 'I love you very much and want to spend my life with you . . . blah, blah, blah.' Then he holds out this box and says:

'Lor, I am asking you to marry me. I want you to marry me.'

I was just like, 'Oh shit, oh my God.'

Then I saw the ring, which he designed himself. Apparently he had begun having it made almost 6 months earlier.

Anyhow, I saw the sparkle as the light caught the diamond and I just screamed . . . loud as anything.

I had always wanted a marquee wedding, so when our friends Rachel and Marty Spinks suggested we have it on their tennis court, which overlooked the city, I couldn't believe it. It was the perfect venue for just the perfect day.

We were married not far from our home, at the Ithaca Uniting Presbyterian Church, because that was the church I was brought up in. Darren had never been baptised – though he has been since, because he thought he should before we began having children. We had 130 guests and after the ceremony had some buses come and pick everyone up and take them back to the Spinks' one-acre property for canapés and drinks.

All three of the groomsmen spoke. Dell's speech was mainly about himself. Benny was fantastic and Phil, who is really quiet, spoke really nicely as well. Then we had a local music group called Phoenix, who were sensational, and everyone just danced the night away. It was magic.

We did our best to keep things private. I wasn't interested in parading in front of a bunch of cameras. This was a day for family and friends. When you spend your life in the public eye, you don't get all that many of them, so I was really pleased that everyone respected our privacy and our wish to keep things relatively low-key.

Ben Ikin, Phil Lee and Wendell were by my side. I have got to say that on the day I wasn't nervous at all. Lor looked amazing. Benny gave a brilliant speech and Dell got his shirt off on the dance floor. All in all, it was everything I could have hoped for and then some. It is funny looking back at the photos of the day. Wendell was in the middle of his little 'holiday' from football. Let's just say the big fella had enjoyed having the feet up for the first time in about 15 years, and his training program had clearly changed if his waist size was anything to go by. He was big, and I had lost so much weight that he looked even bigger. My gift to the boys was that I had bought them the suits they wore that day. Ben and Phil are still able to wear them, I'd have to stop eating for a month to slip into mine, and Dell could use his to parachute safely out of a plane at 30 000 feet.

He has said to us a number of times since, 'I was so big . . . why didn't anyone tell me?' I just say, 'Dell, everyone told you.' But after three or four visits to the bar he wasn't listening to any of us. After that point, he was 'the man', and we loved it.

Ben Ikin: The wedding was typical Locky. There were only a handful of team-mates past or present who were invited. Wayne was there, of course. But it certainly wasn't the celebrity wedding some people may have expected. I am sure some others might have expected there would have been blokes there that didn't get invited. I am just as sure Locky didn't worry about that for one moment. I was honoured to be there.

Wendell Sailor: It was such a good day, but I guess I took a little something more out of it, given what I was going through with my suspension at the time. I don't think Locky would have been thinking it when he asked me to be one of his groomsmen, but I just took it as somewhat of a show of solidarity. And I am not too big a man to admit that at the time I needed it. And you know we cut up the dance floor . . . it was good fun.

Sharon Lockyer: We have always kept our distance and let Darren be his own man, live his own life. But as a mum I definitely feel like there were a few years that I sort of missed in his development as he grew into a man. I always trusted Wayne would help him when he needed someone to go to for some advice and I will say one of my favourite memories of his wedding day was a conversation I had with Wayne. I so wish I had a tape because we sat there and spoke for 15 or 20 minutes. It may have been longer, I am not sure. But he spoke to us about what it meant to him to have been there to watch Darren grow up and become the man and the footballer he became. He said some lovely things – things that just make you feel proud as a parent. It was probably one of the only real lengthy conversations I have had with Wayne because, well, Wayne is Wayne. But for me it was one of the special moments on what was a fantastic day for the whole family.

As big an occasion as our wedding was, in real or practical terms our day-to-day lives didn't really change a great deal. By 2007, we had both moved past the phase in our lives when the prospect of heading to a jam-packed nightclub till the early hours of the morning had any great appeal. While there are definitely times when I have loved getting out and having a few drinks with my mates, I was 30 years old when I married Lor and had moved on to a different stage in my life. The two of us are home-bodies, which was just as well, because we spent a lot of time over the next few years renovating our home at Paddington.

Kids were on the agenda for both of us, but, as with many couples, things didn't happen for us straightaway. In fact, while the two of us would laugh off any questions about how things were progressing with the standard, 'We're just enjoying the practice at the moment', in actuality it became a bit of an ordeal and Lor especially got pretty upset and stressed out at different times. In August 2009, all those worries disappeared when Lor returned from seeing our GP. I was going to be a dad.

This was, as they say, a game-changer.

Sunny James Lockyer arrived into the world on the afternoon of 28 April 2010. Lor had actually gone into labour in the morning, but she was totally in control of things from start to finish. It was amazing to see how she managed the whole thing. And by whole thing, I mean from the morning sickness, to the belly bump, to the way everything in her life got turned upside down, yet she did not so much as stutter. Lor has always been someone who enjoyed staying fit and that didn't change throughout her pregnancy. She was one of those women who just revelled in the time she spent as a human incubator. I had never really known before what people meant when they referred to the glow some women have during pregnancy, but through the majority of that nine-month period, Lor was glowing and smiling and just as happy as I have seen her.

Obviously, it was a different experience for me. I was talking with a friend recently about this very topic and I asked him when he sort of felt it was all really happening.

He said it was the first time he held his hand on his wife's stomach and felt his son kick and it was absolutely the same for me with Sunny.

The day of his birth, I actually took Lor and her sister to the hospital after the contractions began to come every four or five minutes. I was keen to keep the media in the dark, just to avoid anything silly happening with a photographer or cameraman at the hospital. No one wanted that. So, after Lor got settled in I ducked back out and went to training at Red Hill. I clocked off early and tore straight through our dressing-room, out the back door and into my car. I am not usually much of a leadfoot behind the wheel, but on this occasion I will simply say I am glad I don't remember looking down at the speedo at any stage before pulling up in the hospital car park. My mind was elsewhere and really my only thought while driving was to get there ASAP.

Lor was amazing and nothing I have experienced has come close to matching the excitement and emotion of seeing my son delivered and having a nurse place him in my arms for the first time. I had goosebumps from the whole experience, and it is a moment in my life that I will never forget. Amazing!

Loren Lockyer: I was a little worried early on after Sunny was born, because Darren was just never home. He was born only a couple of weeks out from the start of the State of Origin series and with everything that was happening at the club, not to mention the early-season Anzac Test . . . the timing of it just worked out in a way which meant Darren was away for quite a chunk of the first couple of months. And as much as I missed him as well, I loved it when I heard and saw his frustration at missing out on time with his son.

I expected Darren to be a great dad, but he is above and beyond anything I imagined. He is just brilliant with Sunny, who loves every second he gets to spend with Dad. Especially as he got older and became mobile, Sunny would wait till his dad wasn't looking before setting his sights on the pots and pans drawer in the kitchen. I have wondered once or twice whether, if Sunny had been a girl, Darren would still be as hands-on all the time as he is with his boy, because it has definitely had a major impact on his very neat and orderly existence.

Sunny's birth also brought out a side of Darren I had never even glimpsed before fatherhood arrived. He is always hugging and kissing his son and, with Sunny having already turned one, he loves it when Darren calls him in for 'family hugs'. It's just beautiful to watch their relationship. While I get Darren talking a lot more than the general public sees or hears, the icy, stone-faced look with which we have become so familiar – that's not a put-on for show. I have seen that same stare and never known him to be the overly affectionate type. He is very well controlled in terms of managing his emotions.

David Lockyer: Sunny has done wonders for Darren, just in terms of settling him down. It's relaxed him a bit and given him a new focus in a lot of areas in his life, because Sunny is his number one focus. It has probably been good just in terms of his perspective and treating the trivial things we can get caught up in sometimes in the manner they deserve.

Sharon: The big one for me is just the way it's calmed him, because he was just getting too worked up there at different times. Lor was telling us he just can't sit down and often just walks around his house for ages – prowling the hallways 'like a caged lion', as she puts it.

But Darren is a very good father. He is enormously protective and is very well disciplined. He works hard and is a wonderful family man with his own brothers and us.

While the arrival of your first child is always going to be the start of a big change in the way your life runs, there is no question I underestimated just how much satisfaction I would draw from simply sitting on my couch holding my son for hours on end, just watching him slowly listen, learn and evolve. Whatever had gone on at work that day, I knew by the time I got home he'd be ready for a burping and would then just want to sit with Dad and watch the world pass by. It was the ideal way to clear my mind of the stresses elsewhere.

The Broncos' 2010 season had been a disappointment, with the team missing the finals for the first time since 1991. As a result, football operations manager, Andrew Gee, had begun his review of the football department and clearly there were to be some changes. Having always shared a really close bond with Wayne, it was obvious GeeGee was looking to install some of the stability that had been part of the club from day one. On a personal level, I too was concerned about our current and future direction, and I wanted to ensure that we could quickly turn around the disappointment of 2010 and re-establish ourselves as premiership contenders for 2011.

The frustration of all that was compounded when the Kiwis claimed another win when it counted against Australia in the Four Nations final – the sort of one–two punch to end another long year of footy that leaves you comtemplating what might have been for half the summer.

Well, that's what I would have been feeling in the same situation in any of the 16 preceding years.

Loren: I have never seen Darren as happy and relaxed as he was from start to finish of the Christmas holidays in the 2010–11 off-season. He was absolutely brilliant and I did think to myself how much I enjoyed seeing him in such a good frame of mind. I might have even said a little prayer asking that when he did retire he would be ready to live every day like he did that break away with Sunny.

We were at the Backpackers Hotel there in the middle of the main drag at Airlie Beach this one night shortly before Christmas and Darren was staring off somewhere into the distance, clearly mulling over something. So I asked if he was okay and he just looked at me and said, 'I'm thinking I might make this my final year.'

It was a bit of a shock at first, because Darren had been playing quite well and his body was feeling as good as it had at any time since his knee reconstruction. He'd even been giving some thought to pushing through to the 2013 World Cup and seeing if he could possibly gain some semblance of revenge. But I know Darren well enough to know he wouldn't have just said something like that out of the blue. It was obviously something he'd been thinking over for some time in his own mind. I played a bit of devil's advocate initially, but he was clear about what he wanted. Spending a weekend together sounded pretty good to me.

I have actually just kept an eye on Darren since he made the announcement, just checking to see if I could detect any hint that he may change his mind or that he was at all worried. It's been quite the opposite. It's been a great ride, his rugby league career – but where one door closes another opens, although with Darren it seems to be more like half a dozen doors at present. He has that many interests he is building towards, just making sure things are all in order for next year so he can throw himself into it straightaway. It is almost as though footy is getting in the way of all the other things he is doing at the moment, which I think is fantastic. When he is not at training at the Broncos, he is constantly in meetings.

I don't think Darren is going to be one of those players who struggles to make the adjustment from professional athlete to regular 9 am–5 pm working stiff. He is ready for the next chapter in his life and, knowing Darren as I do, I am at ease because he'll make a success of it. He's annoying like that.

It's not that I have lost the motivation for footy, but I am 100 per cent certain that the time is right for me for my main focus to move away from playing the game and into being a family man. Now, I know there will be plenty of people out there making the point that there are a lot of NRL players who are fathers. All I say is good luck to them. That is them. I have no doubt the heights I have reached during my career, the things I have been able to achieve, have come on the back of the fact that I work as hard as, if not harder than, anyone else. I could do that because I didn't have young lives dependent on me and as such could devote an enormous amount of time to my footy. Now I want to devote that same sort of time, dedication and commitment to the next phase of my life and the partnerships that I am able to be involved with.

Physically, I probably could go round for another year or two, but I don't want to play when I know my level of commitment is down on where I feel it needs to be to satisfy my own personal standards. I have also been very conscious of not being that player who goes around one year too long.

Wayne has always been firmly of the belief that you want to go out one year early, not one year late.

Or put another way, you want people asking, 'Why did he retire now?' You don't want them asking, 'Why on earth didn't he retire now?'

Ben Ikin: I have known Darren since back when we played age group footy against each other as kids and he dead set has not changed. He has never been someone who has been comfortable in big groups, particularly when he is surrounded by people he doesn't know well. When he does get comfortable, Locky is a different guy, though. He is very funny . . . well I think he is, anyhow. I think that is what connects Locky and me, we share the same slightly twisted, weird, off-beat sense of humour. We laugh at the same stupid stuff as one another. It is difficult to properly explain, but the best I can do is say that if you get the movie *Joe Dirt*, put it on and watch it about 80 times in a row and you are still laughing on the 80th replay, you share the same sense of humour as Darren Lockyer and me.

FIFTEEN

Rebuilding the Maroons Legend

As MUCH AS I treasure my time in the green and gold of Australia, there is no denying the fact that in modern rugby league in this country, your status in the game is linked directly to your performances in State of Origin football. In no way am I trying to denigrate the intensity of Test matches against Great Britain or New Zealand, but the magnitude of the build-up and ferocious intensity of each and every Origin fixture is unlike any other contest in rugby league. If I was to select the 10 toughest matches of my career I wouldn't need to look outside the 36 matches I played against the Blues.

State of Origin football was what made me love rugby league as a kid. You can't help but be drawn in by the ferocity of the contest. When the Blues and Maroons square off, every element of the game lifts a notch or two . . . sometimes three! The hits are harder and more frequent, but the breakneck speed of the contest is unrelenting. It examines your physical and mental limits equally – it separates the men from the boys. In the moments after being crunched by three defenders, you find out what you are made of. Your head is spinning, your lungs are screaming for oxygen and your arm is numb from the impact of the tackle ... but your team needs you to drag yourself up and keep moving. Do you have what it takes to push the pain aside and do what the team requires? Lying down is easy. Are you happy taking the easy option?

Because in Origin taking an easy option has a ripple effect. Every single ruck is a contest in itself, but the result of each extends well beyond that one play. When in possession, you fight for quick play-the-ball first and foremost to protect your team-mate. A fast play-the-ball means the next man up is charging at a defensive line in retreat, rather than one which has been able to properly set itself courtesy of a lacklustre effort by the bloke playing the ball. One or two seconds might not sound like much, but when you are heading towards a wall of defenders consisting of, let's say, Paul Gallen, Greg Bird and Anthony Watmough standing side-by-side and snarling, it can mean the difference between a solid hit-up and being stretchered from the field in a Medi-Cab.

My Origin career can be separated into two very distinct sections. The first runs from my debut in 1998 through to the end of the 2005 series, when Joey Johns came out of retirement to hand us our third straight series defeat. The second section began with Mal's arrival in 2006 and, while it would be nice to talk about only those years and the success we have enjoyed, I think much of what we have achieved had its roots in what happened from 2003 to 2005, when Queensland lost three series in a row.

Over the course of my first three series, I was exposed to the full spectrum of passion and emotion which so drive the concept of Origin football. The 1998 series in which I debuted was just an amazing experience, but looking back it probably eased me in a little too softly having Wayne as the coach and nine Broncos team-mates alongside me. Gordie and Webbie were outstanding in the middle of the field, giving Alf and Kevie all the room they needed to weave their magic.

Going head-to-head with Joey Johns, Alf was especially brilliant through those three games. I have heard Joey talk of the way Alf mesmerised the Blues defence and that no matter what they tried they just could not devise a defensive scheme to contain him. I once heard Warren Ryan talking about the difficulties of coaching against Alf, who he said gave him more headaches than any other footballer because he could not for the life of him figure out how he kept finding a way through the defence. He wasn't that fast, he didn't have a bullet-like pass, his kicking technique was unorthodox, yet week after week he would leave the game's best defenders looking foolish, sending them one way as he went the other.

After Wayne stood down as coach, the loss of Alf for the 1999 series was a huge blow for Queensland, who did well to keep the contests as tight as they were, given the way Laurie

Daley, Brad Fittler and Andrew Johns were playing behind what was an outstanding Blues pack. I missed the opening two games of the series – the first won 9–8 by Queensland with a Mat Rogers field goal before the Blues levelled things with a 12–8 win in game two, which happened to be the first Origin match to be played at Stadium Australia, Homebush. I was back for the decider and snared my first try at that level in a match which finished 10–10 at full-time.

I have to admit that, while some of the boys were celebrating, I felt a little hollow. I understand those who would argue against the introduction of 'Golden Point' extra-time in regular-season NRL fixtures, but in rugby league's three-game showpiece event, you need to have a winner and a loser. I say that despite feeling quite the opposite after game three in 2002, which finished 18–18 thanks to Dane Carlaw's famous last-gasp effort. He steamrolled Blues winger Jason Moodie, who had been caught defending out of position, before turning on the afterburners and racing 50 metres to score in the corner just seconds before full-time.

I suppose the different emotions I felt at the end of the respective matches show that players generally know in their hearts whether the result on the scoreboard was a true reflection of the contest that had transpired. In 1999, I thought we were pretty satisfied to have snared the draw in game three. In 2002, I think it is fair to say everyone in maroon believed we had earned the right to retain the shield for another 12 months.

I have never been one for bagging referees, and they now operate at a very professional level. They are a really important part of our game and I think more often than not they are an easy target for players and coaches who don't want to acknowledge their own failings. But to this day I don't know what more I could have done to score the try video referee Chris Ward denied me 12 minutes from full-time. We were up 14–12 at the time when a kick-through bounced in the Blues' in-goal. It looked certain to bounce dead in goal, but instead bounced much straighter than usual. I saw half a chance and just took the odds to it. I jumped and took the ball at the highest point I could and brought it down as fast as I could, driving the point of the ball into the turf a few inches inside the dead ball line. As soon as it touched the turf I released it, just before I hit the ground. While there are occasions when you don't know whether you have managed to get downward pressure on a ball; or whether you have managed to keep your body inside the field of play, this wasn't one of those times. I knew I had scored. You could see I scored. Most of the Queensland team had started to make their way back to their positions for the kick-off when the decision came down. I was stunned. I understand at some stage down the track Chris Ward admitted he had made an error. We all make mistakes and it is nice that he was big enough to concede he had made a blue. But I am baffled as to how that happens when you have time to watch a video replay five or six times before handing down a decision.

Wayne Bennett: Terrible . . . awful decision. It was one of the great Origin tries.

The 2002 series was the last Origin series I played under Wayne. He had taken over the year before after the debacle that was Queensland's 2000 Origin campaign. Former Maroons halfback and Melbourne Storm assistant Mark Murray was back in charge for a second series, but for whatever reason was just not able to find a way to bring the group together. The size and athleticism of the Blues forwards just allowed their halves pairing of Brad Fittler and Brett Kimmorley to run riot and I can only think of maybe one other occasion which left me feeling as shattered, embarrassed and even a touch ashamed as I did following the Blues' record-breaking 56–16 win in game three.

Wayne returned and put in place the structures – Emerging Origin camps, the creation of a pathway from under-14s through to the senior State of Origin side, all under the same Maroons banner, pre-season camps, and so on – which would eventually see Queensland wrest back control of the battle for interstate supremacy. A lot of people were disappointed when Wayne walked away at the end of 2002, but with the chance to look back now, I think Wayne knew he had done his job and that if Queensland were to move forward into another era of success, it was going to be under someone other than him.

I think a big part of what Wayne was doing with this pathway he had formed, which was run under the banner of the Queensland Academy of Sport and was backed by the State Government, was his way of attempting to break the Maroons' over-reliance on the Broncos. It's something that probably didn't occur to me until many years later, but there were certainly times when the environment was just too familiar. It just felt too much like another club game. It probably wasn't until my time under Mal Meninga that I really started to 'get' Origin football and the passion it engenders both amongst the participants and the general public either side of the Tweed – a passion which has earned the three-games series such a special place on Australia's sporting calendar.

To that end, I probably understand a little more now what some of the Queensland FOGS were alluding to when they suggested Wayne never really used the Queensland spirit as the focus of his coaching. Wayne has never really bought into the fire and brimstone approach to football. He is far more calculated and methodical, which goes to the heart of what makes him the best club coach in the game. You cannot ride on emotion for long, but Wayne has an uncanny ability to get a group of men to buy into his 'team-first' mentality and a commitment to a set of fundamentals he knows are what wins football games and eventually premierships. He believes, or I should say *knows*, that if you put yourself in the mix often enough eventually you are going to come out on top.

When it comes to Origin, you can be guaranteed that every player is at the peak of their powers. At times the slow-and-steady approach is called for, while at others you need to be able to lift when your opposition lifts. Motivation and team spirit are a part of what decide these games. The game plans and tactics are rudimentary, given you have a limited preparation with your team before the game comes around. While Wayne can certainly evoke the competitive spirit you always need, I think having Mal with a full-time focus on the Origin team has enabled him to find the ideal balance between ticking all the boxes in regard to our preparation on the training track and drawing on the passion and spirit upon which Queensland's State of Origin history is built. When Mal talks about Origin, everyone listens. He was there in game one. He was part of it all – part of those great Queensland teams of the 1980s. He is part of Origin folklore.

> **Phil Gould:** Queensland has had one 30-year-long Origin campaign. There is not much different about the way Queensland play their football in 2011 from what they did 30 years ago. I think it is a mentality and a style of play that is passed down from team to team, from generation to generation, from player to player. When you think Lockyer has played in more than a third of those games, obviously he has become an enormous part of that.

If you are in need of a textbook example of what I regard as a career-defining moment, you need look no further than the 2006 State of Origin series. It was the making of me as a captain and as a player – though the manner in which it has defined my career seemed little more than a pipe dream in the days that followed our one-point loss in the series opener.

> **Mal Meninga:** When I decided to take on the job as Queensland coach in 2006, I went and spoke to a

number of my old team-mates, guys I respected and guys I knew had a similar passion and connection to the Queensland jumper as I did.

The overwhelming opinion from a lot of former players was that the current players had just lost touch with the history behind that first game back in 1980 and what it meant to pull on that Maroon jumper. There was bickering and sniping at players in the team . . . We had just lost our way a bit. So I came in with a pretty clear idea about the style of football we should be playing, the types of players we should be picking and the way our camps should be running. And a lot of it was a bit of a change from what some of the more experienced guys in the group were accustomed to. So it was my job to make sure the leaders of the team understood what we were looking to achieve and that they bought into it. Top of that list was Darren.

I won't lie, it took a bit of work. He isn't easy to get much from when you are first getting to know him. It probably wasn't until the first team camp in February 2006 that we started to make some progress. That was where we addressed the history of Origin football. Arthur Beetson and Dick 'Tosser' Turner spoke to the boys about what this game meant to people in Queensland and seriously, there wasn't a dry eye in the room. They spoke about the belief of those early teams – that while we could never match New South Wales man-for-man, if we pulled together as a group, we became something much more powerful.

And we were able to pull together back then because of the years we had spent being belted by New South Wales, watching all our best players come back and help smash us. The game was on its knees before Origin football arrived. That is the legacy these current players needed to understand they had been given and needed to uphold.

Game one in 2006 was a struggle. We played terrible footy. But I took heart from the mental strength that kept the margin to a field goal in the final minute. The media and the experts mainly down south, but some up in Queensland too, they took aim at us after that performance and Locky probably wore the brunt of it, though Petero and Steve Price and myself – we all got a serve. What those people didn't realise was that things had changed. There was a new mentality in the team. The belief was building and if we could just improve our execution slightly we were going to be very difficult to beat.

Locky took the loss pretty hard and when we met I could tell he knew he hadn't played the way we needed him to play. I was pretty upfront about that. We had all spoken about the style of game we wanted to play and that required a five-eighth who would run better lines than Darren had in game one, and more importantly would go to and challenge the line and commit defenders. The Blues' defensive structure was too good out wide for him just to do what he was doing a lot of the time at the Broncos – essentially we needed him to play a more physical type of game. I said to him if he wasn't able to do that for us we needed to look at moving him to fullback and bringing in someone who would.

Now, I know Darren isn't very emotional but I thought if anything would get to him, challenging him like that would. And it did. He got his back up a bit and there were some words exchanged. I just kept at him, asking him if he was prepared to make the changes necessary. Eventually, he just said pretty plainly that he would do what was required and to pick him at five-eighth. He wasn't interested in entertaining the idea of a move, which was good because I didn't want to move him.

By the time we came into game two, Darren was a different person and he just tore them to pieces. They had no answers for him that night and that was all he needed to start really believing in this new message. By the decider, he had gone from being the Queensland captain to the leader of the Queensland team and there is a big difference. His belief was unshakable, even in the face of a lot of things that went against us. When the guys around him started to drop their heads, you could see him talking to them, telling them to hang tough, 'Be patient, be patient, our time will come.' And of course in the end it did come. The ball started to bounce our way and it was only fitting that in the end it was Darren there to jump on the loose ball that won the game.

Obviously that was a huge game, not just for Darren but for Queensland rugby league, so a lot of people talk about the try he scored that night. But the thing about Darren is, that is just one of many games he has been there, on the spot and able to come up with the right play when it matters. It isn't a fluke. It all stems from the belief he has in himself and his team-mates, which again comes from hard work. He works incredibly hard and pushes himself on the field and off it. His discipline sets the standards for all the other guys to meet.

Phil Gould: In his neat appearance, his controlled manner, Lockyer goes about his business. And he has made winning his business. He knows what works – what works in his own game, what works with others – and he doesn't stray too far from that. I would say he goes through the same routine every day, whether it is having a shave, doing his hair, brushing his teeth . . .

You can't do what he has done without having that almost robotic routine. And whenever he has been struggling I would be willing to bet that routine has been broken. He would know the minute he walks into a dressing-room when something isn't right. It would be the same with his warm-up or when the game starts. He would be like, 'Well, we have to keep going because we haven't done that yet and we haven't done that yet . . .' The game would just go through a process for him.

I have no doubt that the meticulous way he presents himself off the field is reflected in the way he plays and prepares for his football.

It was probably the time I spent working with Mal and Neil Henry, planning and strategising our Queensland's Origin campaigns, that gave me an understanding of the value of structured gameplans, particularly these days. Over time, my input into team strategies has increased and I have grown to really enjoy becoming a student of the game.

Wayne Bennett: When the legs have slowed down, Darren is one of the few players who has been able to maintain his place amongst the best in the game through the strength of his mind and his ability to apply himself to a gameplan. He loves drawing opposition teams into a test of willpower to see who will crack first. His patience and control in pressure situations . . . it is unmatched.

Mal Meninga: Darren's grounding with Wayne was as good as you can get and through Wayne's teachings – which haven't changed greatly over the past 40 years or so – Locky learned his philosophy of momentum and pressure in football and how to build each. Locky sticks to this religiously and can do it more effectively than anyone else I have seen in the game. There is no one like him in this area, in my opinion.

His leadership has advanced to the point where he can and does control training sessions. He isn't afraid to lay down the law now and again; he has just grown into the ideal team leader. He has the respect of every player that comes into the side, because he never asks any more from his team-mates than he is prepared to do himself.

Our relationship has grown well beyond the usual captain–coach routine, because from the first time we spoke I was looking to empower him probably more than he ever imagined possible. He warmed to the extra responsibility and as he has learned to push himself as a leader it has taken his game to another level.

I see Darren Lockyer's role in State of Origin football going well beyond his retirement as a player at the end of the 2011 series. He is one of the rare players I know these days who 'gets' what a legacy is and who knows the type of legacy he wants to leave behind. I have loved the opportunity to reconnect this current Maroons squad to those of the past. I was there for the first game back in 1980 and it has been important to have this generation of players learn the history behind the creation of State of Origin, because that is where this sense of passion and spirit we share for Queensland stems from.

But the time will come when a new generation of Queensland players will come through the ranks and need that guidance and assistance about what this thing they are doing is all about. I have long seen Darren

Lockyer as the man I want to fill that role. I have told him that – he is the guy I think can bridge that gap from the old blokes like me who were there in the beginning to the next generation of Origin players who will pull on the Maroon jersey. They'll need to know what Queensland teams are all about. Darren Lockyer is the perfect man for the job because he has seen Origin both ways. He now knows what works and he commands the respect of everyone. When he speaks, people listen.

Johnathan Thurston: I was a bit starstruck when I first came into the side in 2005. I was just hanging around the back watching Locky do his thing for the first couple of sessions. I barely touched the ball the entire time. At the end of the second session, he just pulled me to one side and said, 'Mate, you are here for a reason. Everyone knows you can play. We know what you are capable of out there, so get in and do it. I'll be there to back you up. Don't worry. We've all got your back.'

I have always remembered that because it just eased some of my nerves. I walked away feeling 10 foot tall – one of the greatest players ever to lace on a boot believed in me . . . It was the biggest shot of confidence I have ever received.

The thing with Locky that I have loved when we are playing alongside one another, but which I hate when I have to play against him, is just his ability to remain calm and give nothing to an opponent. I have tried to teach myself that sort of discipline, but I can't control my emotions out there. That's why Locky has been so good for me. No matter how bad the situation is, he doesn't lose focus on the task at hand.

That final game of the 2006 series is the perfect example. He had just been smashed by everyone after we lost game one. I was surprised how much of the criticism was directed his way, but he never once gave off the impression it was getting to him. And he responded by winning the man of the match in game two and scoring the winning try in game three. It was the perfect response. Since that night he has done the same thing over and over again and I think his stature in the game has grown with each victory Queensland and Australia have had under his watch.

Over the years that I have been a part of the Queensland side, it's been amazing to see the sort of player and captain he has grown into. He is like another coach at training and even during games and the great thing about him is the way he cuts through all the bullshit and can just deliver a message that is right on the money.

It is the same when he wants to deliver a personal message, which he did to me in no uncertain terms at the start of the 2010 series. In 2009 we won the first two games of the series and went to Suncorp Stadium for game three with the wrong attitude. A lot of the boys just saw it as a chance to party, given the series was over. We had made history by becoming the first team to win four Origin series in a row and a few of us thought that was worth celebrating. To say our preparation left a lot to be desired is a massive understatement and Locky was furious.

He didn't say anything when we got into the sheds after New South Wales thumped us 28–16. I just remember the glare he gave me when he came back from the media conference. Before the start of the 2010 series, he pulled me aside and let me have it. It is as angry as I have seen Locky. He told me I had let myself and every one of my team-mates down and that it was something I could never undo. He said I needed to take every chance I had from that point on to make things right, which I have tried to do. I felt that low after the conversation . . . He has that effect because he doesn't get upset often. So when he does it means you have really f***ed up.

But for the most part, while he is the skipper, he is one of the boys you want to be around. He is very funny to be around. He has a great memory for movie lines he likes to trot out – particularly Will Ferrell movies. He just drops them occasionally and cracks everyone up. *Step Brothers* was one of his favourites and there is a line where someone says, 'This wedding's horseshit.' Every time someone starts rambling on too much in a team meeting, you'll just hear him yell that out from the back.

And we all love being around him when he has a few drinks and gets dancing. It's good fun, though it has its dangers.

Cameron Smith: Look, I am going to tell this story because I know Locky won't. I know most of the public see Locky as this very controlled, dry, cold sort of figure, but seriously behind closed doors he can cut loose with the best of them. He loves wearing wigs and just doing random, peculiar things that you just can't help laughing at. I have heard the stories about him finding some bloke in a bar – usually the worst-dressed there – and convincing this bloke to swap their entire outfits for no particular reason whatsoever.

His dancing is the thing we have all got to know and love, and I think this book is the appropriate place to address one particular accident he had while he was lighting up the dance floor. Or in this case the top of the bar, where the skipper was well into the one night Mal will generally put aside at the start of most camps for the entire squad to go and have a few drinks together.

Now, Locky rocked up the following day to training sporting a wound over his eye which required quite a few stitches. 'Slipped in the bathroom' I believe was the public explanation at the time. Well, let me clarify that, because that's not quite accurate. The injury was sustained after the shirt came off and was swung around his head in a move that appeared to come straight from *The Full Monty*. Unfortunately for the skipper, he failed to see the ceiling fan that was on just a little way along. His shirt was caught by one of the blades and pulled him hard enough that he lost his balance and came crashing down, cracking his head on the metal footrest which ran around the bar. After realising he was okay, we all fell into hysterics.

Origin camp has become like a second home away from the Broncos, such is the familiarity I have now with a lot of the guys who have been part of this amazing run of wins Queensland has enjoyed since Mal took the reins. It has been such a significant and enjoyable part of my football career, and I am fortunate that I was able to progress from our lean years through to the string of unprecedented Queensland successes.

While I will take a break from football in 2012, I intend to offer Mal any assistance he needs. It is the least I can do for him.

SIXTEEN

What Tomorrow May Bring

As EXCITED AS I am about moving into the next phase of my life, I don't know that I possess the words to properly convey how fortunate and blessed I feel to have been able to spend the past 17 years playing the game I love and getting well paid to do so. That is fantasyland stuff. Reality in the big, bad world we live in is supposed to be far grimmer. When you are living in the world of a professional athlete, it is very easy to lose your perspective. Occasionally, it is important that we take the chance to step back from the little world we inhabit to see the bigger picture and the role we play within wider society. We are entertainers for the fans out there who turn over their hard-earned cash buying memberships and season tickets year after year. Without fans, we don't get to do what we do. Without fans, what is the point? There is no excuse for any NRL player ever to forget how indebted we are to the fans and sponsors who allow us the chance to work in what has to be the best job in the world.

As AFL legend Leigh Matthews said, we are all getting well paid to do something that is essentially a hobby. When you stop and think about it, we all loved these games we play so much as kids that our parents paid money to let us take part.

Over my time in the NRL, I have seen the code go through a huge number of issues and implement some significant changes – most for the betterment of the game, but some that had me scratching my head. On the positive side of the ledger, the on-field product is outstanding. The growing use of dangerous wrestling and jiu jitsu techniques in tackles led to the introduction of the two-referee system and there is no doubt the ruck area is much cleaner in 2011 than it has been for the past few years.

In fact, the game in general is as clean as it has ever been. The work here by referees and the NRL judiciary should be applauded. The public image of the NRL has made marked improvements, particularly over the last few years.

I look at the stringent alcohol policy the Brisbane Broncos have in place as part of the club's strict code of conduct and the public scrutiny that goes with that, and think back to how it would have been received by, say, the Broncos' 1998 team. Alfie, Kevie, Gorden Tallis, Shane Webcke, Wendell, Peter Ryan and Andrew Gee were all players who enjoyed a few social beers after a match. I think about the light-hearted antics they used to get up to as the nights wore on and can't help but reflect on how far the game has come when you consider the two young Broncos, Andrew McCullough and Ben Hunt, who were stood down for one match. Their crime – they were refused entry at a couple of nightclubs, which led to them being approached by police who issued both of the boys an on-the-spot fine. I shudder to think what might have happened had some of the mischief that players got up to back in the mid to late 1990s ever made its way into the public spotlight. Times have changed for all sports people.

The professionalism and overall demeanour and behaviour of the young blokes coming into first-grade these days is well ahead of what was the norm back when I moved into the first-grade ranks. In fact, I think the behaviour of NRL players stacks up fairly favourably compared to many sections in society. Sometimes I just feel some of the coverage fails to acknowledge the fact that the NRL is made up of more than 400 young men aged from 18 to 34. While we must always strive for perfection, there are always going to be some blokes who make mistakes from time to time. I am happy that the league has taken a strong stance with regard to penalties for those who stray from the standards expected of players within the NRL.

All I would ask of those who pass judgement on these players, especially those within the media, is to balance the reporting of those incidents with the endless list of wonderful things NRL clubs and players are doing on a daily basis within their respective communities. From the celebration of Indigenous culture during All-Stars week, to the incredible pink-laden Women in League round which raises funds for the McGrath Foundation, to the more personal hospital visits players make – many off their own bat and without any desire for publicity or attention. As a code, we need to be better at showing off the amazing work of so many of our players.

The intensity of the media and public scrutiny of NRL players today is quite remarkable. I have found it tough enough dealing with the traditional television, radio and print media dissecting me on a weekly basis. But to have to deal with the explosion of social media even when you are on your own time is not a development I would have coped with all that well, reinforcing just how right I was to call it a day when I have. Truth be told, some of the external pressures associated with being the Broncos, Queensland and Australian rugby league team captain absolutely played a part in my decision to walk away from the game at the end of 2011.

I love our fans – and by our fans I am referring to all rugby league fans, not just those who support the teams in which I play. They are the lifeblood of our sport – without them the NRL would not exist and I would probably be working a nine-to-five job as a tradesman. Having done just a little time on the tools, let me tell you I know which life I would prefer. As is so often the case in life, however, you always have a few who want to ruin things for the overwhelming majority of fans and players who interact in a really positive manner.

Over the years some little things have started to wear me

down. While I am always happy to sign autographs and be in a photo with kids who approach me, I have been surprised at the number of times middle-aged men will interrupt me during a meal with friends or family to have me sign things. The one that really got under my skin, though, happened during a visit to one of my favourite holiday retreats at Pottsville on the north coast of New South Wales.

We travelled down there for a few days over the 2010–11 Christmas–New Year break, looking forward to spending some time in the sun and the sand with our rapidly developing little man. On two different occasions, I had blokes come and knock on the front door of our house to ask if they could have photos and autographs. To say I was startled having someone on my doorstep is an understatement. One of them had brought a number of items for me sign, but I just said, 'I am in the middle of dinner right now, perhaps another time.' While that situation took things to another level from anything I had experienced previously, the fact I was starting to get a bit frustrated at those situations and the relentless focus that you have on your every move was another marker in my mind when I was working towards making the decision to retire.

It seems extraordinary to me that it has been seven years since Gorden Tallis drew a curtain on his remarkable career and handed me the club captaincy at Brisbane. I had long held ambitions to see my name on that exclusive list in the Captain's Room inside the Broncos leagues club: Wally Lewis, Gene Miles, Allan Langer, Kevin Walters, Gorden Tallis.

It's a fair legacy to inherit and I only hope whoever takes over from me in 2012 has seen enough from me to understand what is expected of the man charged with leading the NRL's highest profile team and its most successful franchise of the past quarter-century. Brisbane has long been the NRL's flagship in the way it has run its business off the field. It is the game's most visible brand and most profitable organisation, consistently posting seven-figure profits annually. The corporate support the Broncos enjoy is unrivalled, which has its benefits for the playing group, with the Broncos' facilities and support structures second to none in the game.

However, those putting their cash on the table under-standably expect certain things in return and more often than not it falls to the players to keep the clients happy. Attending corporate luncheons, golf days and dinners, speaking to staff members at different companies on everything from our favourite footy anecdotes to health and nutrition, shooting commercials for magazines, TV and radio, using our profile to help promote a major event – these are the jobs that help fill a player's week when he isn't at the club preparing for the upcoming weekend's fixture. And while I always understood and accepted that side of things as simply being part of my job, there is no doubt over the past two or three years it has started to take its toll.

I don't think I have been helped by the circumstances at our club. The rebuilding phase which began in 2008 robbed the top 25 of many of its most familiar names, meaning for the best part of two years Israel Folau, Justin Hodges, Sam

Thaiday, Corey Parker and myself shouldered the load for pretty much the entire squad, simply because we were the names people knew, so we were the ones who were always requested.

The sponsors' commitments, corporate functions and club promotions that you are required to attend, on top of the fairly significant media load you are expected to carry as skipper of the Broncos, started to become an issue for me in 2010. That's when I realised I needed to really think about where my career was heading and, more importantly, how and where I saw it ending. I have had so much pleasure from my career that I wanted to make sure I continued to enjoy all of the aspects that being a professional footballer requires. I knew how lucky I was to be playing the game I love for a living and getting well paid for it.

Wayne Bennett: I held Locky back from the captaincy for as long as I could. In reality, he was ready to take over when Kevie left in 2001, but I didn't want to burden him with that much responsibility at such a young age. And I didn't have to because we had a wonderful captaincy option in Gorden Tallis, who obviously had the respect of everyone not just at our club but right around the league because of the way he went about his football. I had seen captaincy wear great players out. It wore Alf out, it wore Wally Lewis out – I had seen it with my own eyes the way things eventually started to wear on them after they had been in the captaincy role at a big club for a number of years. To be captain of a club like Brisbane in Queensland . . . It is a huge role with a lot of different aspects that require your attention. You need to be experienced to handle it.

So the right play was to just wait a few years before loading him up with too much responsibility off the field.

The question I have been asked more than any other since I made my retirement decision public is just how I am planning to fill my time. And the answer, initially anyhow, is with a break. I am going to take some time off after I get home from the Kangaroos tour of England, and I am going to enjoy having a holiday. I am fortunate that I have had a number of future opportunities presented to me that flow from having been a part of the game for so many years.

Beyond that, people seem to have got really excited about this notion that I will move into some sort of assistant coaching role at Brisbane. Let me tell you right now, I will be taking some time away from any direct involvement with coaching the game in 2012 – maybe even enjoy a weekend or two just relaxing with some friends and family having a quiet beer and possibly watching Sunday afternoon footy on the box. Mal has raised the prospect of getting me to help in some capacity with the Maroons' preparations for State of Origin, and of course I will always be there for Queensland.

I will probably also expand my involvement with regard to some more work in the media, looking at the game I love from a different perspective.

I have had the benefit of learning the game from some of its finest teachers – Wayne Bennett, Tim Sheens, Neil Henry, Mal Meninga, Craig Bellamy, Ricky Stuart, Michael Hagan, to name a few. This has equipped me with a knowledge of the game that I can apply to my involvement in the media or perhaps to some coaching role, if that is a path I decide to take.

Andrew Johns: I actually use footage of Locky going to the line when I am trying to explain to some of the young blokes I work with the importance of having attention to detail. The main thing I like to show them is how Locky will carry the ball in two hands as he is coming to the defence, but as he draws nearer he drops his hands so the ball is waist height or lower and his fingers are pointing towards the ground. A lot of ball-players these days, they come at the line holding the ball out in front, but it is often up around chest height and their fingers are pointing out or up. By dropping his hands and having the fingers pointing down, it opens more passing options and also just softens his touch. I doubt it is something he has been taught – I am sure it is just something he has taught himself over the years and it is a very small adjustment but in practice makes life so much easier.

Matthew Johns: The thing I tell any of the young halves I get to work with is that the key to Locky's effectiveness is the fact he challenges defensive lines with his feet. I think the time at fullback ended up proving extremely beneficial for Locky when he moved back to five-eighth, because he had terrorised kick–chase teams for that long, they were immediately wary of the danger he posed running the ball. The thing Locky did at fullback better than anyone else who has played that position is the way he brought his wingers into play. He always seemed to be able to isolate a defender to create a two on one for Lote or Wendell or Brent Tate or whoever was out wide for Brisbane at the time. He moved so well in those early years.

He has lost a few yards of pace and doesn't have that jet acceleration he possessed in his 20s, but even now Locky will challenge defenders running the football. He has other tricks he can use to get him through games, but really when he was a fullback playing in the frontline through the late 1990s and early 2000s into the first few years he spent at number six, he changed the way ball-players operated through his ability to beat blokes with his speed. It was predominantly Darren Lockyer who could, as a ball-player, get at a defensive line and beat a quality defender with that amazing burst of explosive power he had.

Now it is the first thing I look for in a young half. I will take them to the park and set out a few drills and look for that one-step speed, the acceleration off the mark that you need to be effective against these complex defensive structures. Gone are the days when a half could play his football before the line; Darren Lockyer is one of probably two or three guys who helped take the game away from that.

Wayne Bennett: Locky has got to be careful with any move into coaching he looks at, because while he doesn't have a big ego, he still has an ego. He has to leave that at the door and step back from his status as one of the greatest players the game has seen. His wonderful record as a player needs to be left in the past and Locky will need to go and do his time and learn the trade. I have no doubts he can. I haven't coached many footballers I would consider more attuned to the specific demands of coaching than Darren, but he can't come in and expect to start at the top. He needs to learn and get his head around the fact that you have to do the hard yards early.

Of course I say all this not knowing if coaching is even a path Darren will end up going down. I think he has all the traits necessary to make a fine coach, but I think he is still some way off making that decision and, knowing Darren, he will have plenty of things to keep him busy next year.

Loren Lockyer: As much as it will hurt him not having footy as part of his life next year, I just see how excited he is about some of the things he is wanting to do and I don't know that the adjustment will be all that difficult. He is ready to retire. Physically, he could probably keep going. He is still the fittest at the Broncos, but he knows his mind is ready for something else.

He is starting to spend some time now focusing on planning and preparing the various projects he intends to undertake early next year.

Ricky Stuart: Everything Locky has done he has done with class. He arrived in the game as an impressive young man. He rose to the very peak of our game and has remained there for more than a decade and now he is ready to stand aside. There was no fanfare, no bells and whistles, no tears. It was just classy.

Andrew Johns: I think Locky just seems to be in a really good space and is at a really good time in his life since the birth of his son. I understand they are just about ready to go again as well, so you don't have to be Einstein to figure out Locky is moving into a stage of his life where he wants to be home and around his kids as they start to grow up. I think he can see the end coming and he is driving the Broncos home. But whatever happens from now on, Locky's place in the game is secure. I spoke to him not long after he made the announcement and he just looked so relaxed and comfortable.

It is a big trip you go on over the course of your football career and it takes up an enormous chunk of your life. But after seeing him and speaking with him I just know he is one of those guys who is going to love his retirement. It probably helps that he has done pretty much everything you can possibly do in the game. Still, he is clearly settled and happy and I couldn't be happier for him.

I only hope the game ensures it doesn't lose him. He has so much to offer and, as crazy as it sounds, given all that he has achieved and all the records he holds, his biggest contribution to the game might be yet to come.

Mal Meninga: The great thing about Locky is that he has spent the last five years preparing for this retirement. He has worked to leave the game in a better state than it was in when he arrived and he has done everything within his power to ensure that was the case.

In my mind, he is a future leader of our game. Whether he goes into coaching, I am not sure. I think there is an administrative role there just waiting for him. I would love to see him go into administration because we need people like Darren Lockyer steering the ship. I only hope the game recognises what they've got in Darren Lockyer. He could be an enormously influential figure in the future of the code here in Australia, provided he is given the appropriate platform. That might mean some longstanding people have to move on, but we have to start getting these decisions right now. They can't let Darren Lockyer just sail off with the breeze.

Johnathan Thurston: The more intense the pressure, the bigger the gap is from Locky to the rest of the players who have laced on a boot. That is where he comes into his own and I think that is really the legacy he has left the guys in the Queensland team – the benefits of being able to maintain your composure and keep a cool head when everyone else around you is starting to panic. People talk about 2006, but he did the same thing again the following year. He has done it over and over again for the Broncos and Australia as well. He knows where to be in the crucial moment because he sees things on the field ahead of time.

Then there are just the standards he set for everyone in the way he carried himself. He is the highest profile, most popular guy in the game, but he is so humble. He speaks to everyone politely, he is really accessible, and he is always willing to help. I know I have phoned him a couple of times when I have been struggling. He always has good advice.

Ben Ikin: I have read a bit about the history of the game and across multiple generations there seem to be one or two guys every 10 years or so who elevate themselves beyond the other great players. They are something else again and Darren Lockyer fits that bill. It is near to impossible to compare across eras, because you are comparing apples and oranges. The game has changed and evolved over time. They moved the defensive line back from 5 metres to

10 metres; they introduced the six-tackle rule; there were different rules for catching the ball in your in-goal . . . it is a different game today.

Locky certainly ticks a lot of boxes when you are talking about the elements that lift players into that most rarefied air. Durability, loyalty to one club, calm under pressure, ability to deliver in big matches, ability to deliver at the death of the game, intelligent, tough, humble, well-liked, selfless, great leadership . . .

So he falls into that generational player category. How he compares to the other greats? Well, I reckon the defining feature of Locky is the completeness of the man. If you lined the other 10 or 12 greatest players in the game's history up against Darren Lockyer and had 100 different boxes with all the different attributes champion players should bring to the table, I think he might tick more of those boxes than anyone else.

Phil Gould: He'll be great at whatever he does. I have no doubt Darren Lockyer now sees how influential he is in the game and probably feels a little frustrated he didn't stand up for certain things more along the way, but his time will come with that.

He will become a spokesman for the game and I would like to bet his opinion will be sought.

Everyone has been saying he will make a great coach, and I have no doubt he would. But in all honesty I see bigger things than coaching football teams for Darren Lockyer. I think the development of worldwide rugby league, the development of player rights . . . the entire administration and management of rugby league is screaming out for someone with his background and experience.

Of course he would be a good coach. But I think he has more to offer than that.

SEVENTEEN
What a Journey

I SHUDDER TO imagine how I would be feeling if Mal Meninga and Tim Sheens had simply let me have my way and not forced me to reconsider my decision to retire quietly from representative football at the start of my final season. The regret and frustration of having to sit and watch Queensland (and Australia) play while knowing I was still capable of contributing to the team is something which would have eaten away at me for years. Thankfully, however, I am writing these words with the memory of Queensland's famous victory in the 2011 State of Origin series still fresh in my mind.

I will never forget what I experienced at Suncorp Stadium on the evening of Wednesday 6 July 2011. Game three – The Decider. My final appearance for my beloved state. The last chance I would have to pull on the Maroons jersey I treasure so much. For one of the few occasions in my career, I was struggling with nerves. And I couldn't shake the awful thought of what it would be like to finish my time with Queensland with a loss. But history will show the night played out like a fairytale. I couldn't have scripted it better if I had written it myself.

My team-mates delivered one of rugby league's most remarkable displays of skill, precision and patience through what has been described as the greatest opening to a match in the game's history. With seven minutes still to play in the first half, the game was as good as over. Four tries, 24–0 ... we were never going to be run down from there. The elation I felt at full-time was the equal of anything I have experienced. The smile still hasn't left my face.

To have missed the chance to be a part of not just game three, but the entire series – not to have shared in all the incredible hype and excitement that surrounded each clash – would have been disappointing. But the fact is, when I returned for the start of pre-season training following the Christmas–New Year break, I was pretty set on the idea of spending the final 12 months of my career focused solely on my job at the Broncos. I had seen Shane Webcke, Brad Fittler and Andrew Johns do the same thing and their games had benefited enormously from the reduction in workload and the removal of the mental drain that comes with being involved in representative football, where everything is much more intense.

I sat down with Mal in the first week of February to let him know I would be relinquishing the Maroons captaincy and was about to let the ARL know I would be standing down from representative football and would not be available for the 2011 State of Origin series. We met at one of our regular meeting venues. He knew something wasn't right, because he is usually the one to initiate our little rendezvous. On this occasion, however, I had taken the step of asking him to meet me – 'Need to chat about a few things.'

When we sat down, he asked me straight out, 'What's up, mate?'

I had been preparing my response for a while: 'Look, I have decided this is going to be my last year. I am going to retire at the end of the season and I think it might be best if I step down from representative football so I can pour all my energy into finishing on a good note at the Broncos.'

Mal took it all in and nodded. After a bit of a break, he told me he respected where I was coming from in regard to wanting to dedicate all my energy towards the Broncos' 2011 campaign – particularly given the disappointment of our 2010 season.

'But,' he added with some emphasis, 'you need to understand . . . you're a very long time retired and you're never going to be in this position again. You have the chance to do something no other Queensland captain has done.'

He went on to point out that I was in the very fortunate position of being in control of the end of my playing career. With the constraints of the salary cap, the never-ending stream of young talent pouring into the NRL, and of course the ever-present threat of injury, there are very few NRL players who get to end things on their own terms. Mal explained that he had been one of the lucky few to depart the game at his own choice of time when he hung up the boots in 1994. He committed to exiting the game as strongly as possible and making the most of every opportunity.

While Queensland fell short in the Origin series that year, at club level Mal captained the Raiders to a grand final win and capped things off by steering the Kangaroos through an unbeaten tour of Great Britain. Mal said he considered those moments to be amongst his most treasured memories. He told me he wanted me to play, but would respect my final call. When I got Tim Sheens on the phone, he reinforced Mal's sentiment that I should play the rep season.

The 2011 series elevated Origin into a new stratosphere in terms of public interest and media focus. In Australian sport, nothing comes near its drawing power, with the TV audience for game three peaking at well in excess of four million nationally. Host broadcaster Channel Nine also reported record-breaking numbers in almost every individual demographic and grouping. I have never seen anything even remotely like the immense build-up for game three – thanks largely to the fact it was a decider and Queenslanders were genuinely concerned about the challenge to the Maroons' five-year reign, and rightly so.

The young and enormously talented Blues squad, which had been brilliantly marshalled by Ricky Stuart, in fact entered the final match of the series as favourites with experts and bookies south of the Tweed, despite the fact that it was being played at 'The Cauldron' – the spiritual home of Queensland Rugby League. Desperate for some success, Blues fans started to rediscover their swagger and arrogance, encouraged by what they had seen from their team at ANZ Stadium in game two. The previous five years of Maroons dominance was seemingly dismissed as irrelevant, as was all that led to Billy Slater's match-winning try at the death in game one.

All anyone in New South Wales wanted to talk about was game two, when the series was levelled on the back of a performance which was undoubtedly the best by a Blues side since they last won a series back in 2005. Led by skipper Paul Gallen, the undersized Blues forwards used their superior leg speed to work over our big boys in the middle of the park. Petero Civoniceva, Matt Scott, Ben Hannant and even the likes of Sam Thaiday and Nate Myles found themselves almost constantly backpedalling and scrambling in defence. Gallen, Anthony Watmough, Luke Lewis, Greg Bird and dummy-half runners Kurt Gidley and Michael Ennis kept the tempo of the match at a level we struggled to contain.

Oddly, our preparation for game two in Sydney was noticeably down on what I have come to expect from this group of players, the majority of whom have played alongside one another in Origin for five or six years. While it's always difficult to replicate the intensity of preparation for game one or a third game decider in a Series, I could tell from the first ballwork session that something was awry. When you are dealing with the game's elite, enthusiasm and intensity on the training track rises to a whole new level, with one feeding off the other. But during this camp the usual spark

322

and energy was missing. The coaching staff sensed it and tried a few different things to snap us back into action, but unfortunately their continued efforts probably resulted in us overtraining.

While the Blues were magnificent in front of what was the first sell-out crowd in Sydney for a long time, our execution was off our normal standard and we were guilty of turning over too much ball. It was never going to be good enough against a New South Wales side which dropped the ball just once in the first 40 minutes and finished the match with a staggering 94 per cent completion rate.

Cameron Smith: The reaction to that result was crazy – it was as if the series was over. Everyone seemed to forget there was a third game still to play and it was being played back on our turf. It isn't the first time it has happened, but it did feel like the media down south took it to another level this year. It was the same stuff we have heard again and again over the past five years. Apparently they had found the formula and found the players who could take care of Queensland. The coach is great . . . the players were getting rapped up like nothing else.

I think there were a few eyebrows raised, but within our camp we just tipped our hat to the Blues for the way they played in game two. They were too good on the night. The whole time they have been in charge, Mal and Locky have been big on showing New South Wales plenty of respect and making sure we remained humble. We did that after the loss in Sydney, but we certainly weren't thinking they had suddenly become unbeatable.

It gets a bit annoying when they trot out the same blokes year after year to declare us dead in the water – that they can't be beaten. But at the end of the day we have learned to take it for what it is. You still shake your head sometimes, but then we just get on with things.

Petero Civoniceva: We actually created quite a few chances in game two, but we just seemed to be a step off the pace the whole contest and weren't able to capitalise on those opportunities. It was probably a reflection of the whole build-up to that game, actually. We lacked that sharpness you need in Origin. The games are so fast and so physical that if you are even half a step off the pace you will get exposed.

Gallen was huge for them. His effort in game two was as good as I have seen from a forward at that level. I know he plays in tight in the middle of the field most weeks, but it is still unbelievable that he was able to move and fill a traditional front-rower's spot in defence and maintain his usual workrate with the ball for the entire 80 minutes.

It's unheard of at Origin level and all credit to him, but some of the reaction was way over the top. If you listened to or read certain sections of the media, it was as if big front-rowers had suddenly become obsolete.

On the evidence of one match, they wanted to forget about more than 100 years of conventional rugby league wisdom regarding the role of prop forwards. A good prop is the foundation stone for his side and Matty Scott and I definitely felt we needed to make a bit of a statement in game three. We owed it to the front-rowers' union!

But as much as we didn't talk about it at all, making sure we sent Locky out a winner was what was really important to everyone. I suppose we have known each other and been friends and team-mates for so long that it is only natural I felt a bit more of a responsibility than the rest of the team in relation to sending Locky out properly. Having to leave Brisbane the way I did robbed me of the chance to be a part of his final season in the NRL and with creaky old joints like Locky and I have these days, pinning my hopes to the end-of-season Kangaroo tour is risky at best.

That left the Origin series for me to repay just a little of what I owe him. I mean, he plays it down, but the fact is a lot of the guys in the current squad feel indebted to Locky for what he did to start this incredible run back in 2006. I am not overstating it when I say Locky saved my Origin career with his performance in game three in that '06 series. The selectors had made it clear to me that if we lost the series I was gone, as was Steve Price.

Locky's effort of sweeping through in front of two Blues to snatch a bobbling ball and then brush past

Luke Bailey to score the match-winning try with just a few minutes left on the clock put us in front for the first time all match with less than five minutes to play. I have never wanted to hug another man so much in my life.

Mal Meninga: I guess it is a bit ironic that, since we were able to turn the tide in our favour in 2006 by gutsing out a series win against the odds, we ended up facing a similar scenario six years on in what we all knew was Darren's farewell to Origin. Probably the difference between the two was how we dealt with the different external pressure you encounter during the build-up for Origin.

The pasting we received after losing game one in 2006 was harsh, given a field goal right on full-time was all that separated the two teams. Had the leaders in our team, particularly Darren, lost faith we would have crumbled. But we believed we were on the right path and were putting the right systems in place to make the results eventually start falling our way.

This year, we knew we were heading in the right direction. We knew the systems in place would give us the best chance at success, so it was relatively easy for me, as a coach, to keep everyone on track. No one wavered. No one flinched, no matter what challenges were put in our way.

All those little obstacles were pretty trivial, though. Locky and I had spoken early in the year and we knew then that the biggest threat we faced was from Ricky. I have known Ricky half my life. He is as driven and competitive as anyone I have ever met. Importantly, though, Ricky knows how to win. He knows what it takes in terms of preparation and the sacrifices you need to make. More than that, he knows what it takes to win at Origin level. He has been there and done it as a player on numerous occasions, and as a coach.

Ricky Stuart: After the sell-out at Homebush in game two, I didn't think things could get any bigger. But I was wrong, because the build-up to game three in Brisbane was like nothing I have ever experienced. We got a lot of things right down here this year and made up a lot of ground on Queensland. Top of that list was getting the right bloke captaining the Blues. Paul Gallen is the person to lead New South Wales forward. It is one of the first areas I identified as a problem when I took over the job, because the contrast between the two teams was so glaring. No one in New South Wales had put his hand up and declared himself the guy who was going to lead his state.

At the same time, Queensland has Darren Lockyer – one of the finest leaders our game has seen. He is universally respected, but I could see in everything the Maroons players did in the lead-up to and during games that he was their leader and they would do anything for him. He has Petero there as well and you can see the way guys like Cameron Smith, Billy Slater,

Johnathan Thurston and Cooper Cronk have grown as players and leaders simply by watching how Locky goes about things.

There was also the small issue we had to address of trying to stop the most talented Queensland team in history. Something like 11 of the 13 starting spots in the Anzac Test this year went to Queenslanders.

It was the combination of their playmakers – Slater, Thurston, Smith and Locky – that was always my biggest worry. Slater, Smith and Thurston are already considered greats of the game in their respective positions and then you have Locky steering the ship – one of the best players to have laced on a boot.

Over the course of the first two games, I thought we handled them well for really all but one set of six there late in game one. We had got our noses in front and had the momentum. We made one small error with a kick and that was it. Billy took the ball on the full and got them on the front foot and, if you watch the set of six I am talking about, you will see Locky actually jumps into dummy-half a couple of times. Slater does once as well. Cam is at first receiver once. The four of them just lifted the pace of the game and marched their side 90 metres in five plays without even taking a risk. Then, on the last play, the ball goes Smith to Thurston to Lockyer to Slater – try. Queensland wins.

They executed the play with absolute precision. Their real skill lies in the way they make things look so easy; but the reason Darren was able to pull our defenders apart before he turned the ball back to Slater was because neither he nor JT broke stride, because the passes were delivered perfectly.

I could go on and on about all the little things Lockyer did to allow Slater to score and how much skill and poise it takes, but I would just be repeating myself. It is what Darren Lockyer does when big games are in the balance.

I knew heading into the final game that we faced a monumental task, given how determined Queensland would be to send Locky out a winner, but I was convinced we had a side capable of spoiling the party. Not that I wanted to be the one to do that to Darren. He is a mate and for what he has done for the game he deserves every accolade he receives. But my job was to help New South Wales restore some pride in the jumper.

Still, I had a mutual friend send Locky a message on my behalf a couple of days out from the game wishing him all the best. It was the best way I could think of to do that and still avoid anything being misconstrued by Locky or anyone else. After all, while I love the rivalry and passion of Origin as much as anyone, it is still just a game of football.

Paul Gallen: Aside from doing some homework on the best way to deal with his kicking game, we never addressed Locky or the fact that he was playing his final series at all. Some of the other boys might have been a little surprised, but I knew that would be the case because when Ricky left the Sharks he sat down with me and said he would never use against me things he learned while he was my coach. He said he had too much respect for me and the work we had done together ever to do that and he actually said to me that he was the same way with Locky.

He had too much respect for him as a player and as a mate to target him with any crap and he wouldn't have tolerated any of his players doing it either. All we spoke about was trying to contain him on the fifth tackle, because his kicking game is one of the parts of his game that doesn't get the credit it deserves. It is somewhat deflating when you work hard to trap a side down their end for five tackles, only to see Locky step in and just cream a ball down the park so you are having to bring it back off your line anyhow.

I want to say I consider it an enormous honour to have been given the chance, first to captain my state, but secondly, to have had the chance to captain against one of the greatest, if not the greatest, captain the game has seen in his last Origin series. It didn't ease the pain of the final result, but it is something I know I will look back on when I retire and just think 'that was pretty cool'.

I almost rang him when I got appointed as New South Wales captain. He is someone I respect enormously and playing under him, I just loved the way he leads without grandstanding and commands the respect of his team-mates just by going about his business. I thought he'd be able to give me a few tips, but in the end I thought he might not like that, being such a proud Queenslander.

I knew the week leading into the match was going to be pretty full-on, so I sat down with Mal at the start of our camp, which was again based at Coolum on the Sunshine Coast. Where we normally have the newspapers waiting for us on the tables of the team's private dining hall at breakfast, we decided to put a ban on having the newspapers around at all in the week leading into game three. Mal had planned a pretty tightly run program with regard to media commitments and public appearances and, while that obviously gets some noses out of joint, I have to say I thought the benefits of bunkering down showed in the quality of our preparation. Every player, every session, was just bang on. The intensity was back and there was real purpose in the work we did at training. Petero Civoniceva and Greg Inglis were the two guys who really stood out to me. Both blokes are normally pretty happy-go-lucky, laid-back types, but this time around there weren't too many laughs or jokes. They were extremely focused.

Cameron Smith: You could see in the way he was around camp that week how much this match meant to Petero. He was just a bit more withdrawn and subdued. I remember watching him a few times around camp and at the meal room. You could tell he was preparing himself for something big and something that meant a lot to him.

What he delivered from the kick-off was as good a showing from a prop forward as I have seen. We followed him for those first 25 minutes and he was just relentless.

When he went to the interchange for a well-deserved breather, you could hear the crowd lift to acknowledge what they had seen from him in that opening period. He made a bit of a statement to his critics about what role he can fill in the modern game and at the same time laid the platform for the rest of the team to send his good mate out as he wanted.

Locky was his usual self. He never gives too much away and this occasion was no different. That is, until just before we went to get on the team bus to head to the ground. I can't recall him ever giving a pre-game speech in all the time we have played together, but he got up when all the boys were together in a room and it was as fired up as I have seen him. He just said we had done all the hard work and the prize was there waiting for us. He said New South Wales were standing in our way and basically, 'Let's get out there and f***ing give it to them.'

I thought, 'Geez, the skipper is fired up.' I looked around the room and some of the boys were nodding their heads. No one said a word. I knew then they were ready to go.

I am firmly of the belief that Origin matches are won and lost in the week leading into the match. With such a limited time to work on things, the team which is able to handle all the attention and hype so as to allow them to best get their game in order will inevitably get the result.

To that end, we couldn't have done any more. It was the best preparation, in terms of the quality of our execution at training, that I have ever been involved with. That is a tribute to Mal and his staff. To think this group is continuing to set new standards after six years shows the strength of character that exists amongst them.

I steered clear of all the craziness that I understand was swirling around outside our camp. All my energy and attention was on the task in front of me. I have become pretty adept at not getting stressed thinking which way a result might go, because I know there are a whole lot of things I have to take care of before we get to that. The steps or process I need to follow are what I occupied my mind with in the final few days.

I was confident about how the team looked, but I wanted to reiterate the point that this game wasn't about me. It was about something far bigger and more important and I wanted to deliver the message with a bit of venom and aggression because I wanted them to know I had that aggressive mindset. I wanted them to take that mindset with them. By chance, there was a picture of me holding the shield up. I just finished by pointing to it and saying, 'There is another one of those up for grabs tonight. Let's go and get it.'

Paul Gallen: We prepared well, but that opening half-hour from Queensland was as good as it gets. Petero and Matty Scott just pounded the ball forward again and again and Locky had the ball on a string, dropping it in our in-goal area. It was just ridiculous. The couple of times we got the ball, we were exhausted from all the defence and coughed it up early in the tackle count. I remember walking back for I think the third drop-out we were forced to take inside the first 15 minutes. We were out on our feet and I looked up and saw Glenn Stewart just sucking in the deep breaths and I just smiled at him.

We kept saying, 'Just one more set, just one more set', but it became too much eventually. It felt like we were doing a pre-season fitness drill out there – six tackles for a 40-metre sprint. As a captain, some of the boys were looking to me and I just didn't know what to do or what to say. I was absolutely gassed.

We held them out as long as we could, but you can't hold back a side like that forever. Once we broke, they just went bang, bang, bang and all of a sudden we are down 24–0. It was too much to peg back. They were too good on the night and they deserve credit for that performance in game three. We just had no answers to that first half-hour.

With about 15 minutes to play, it started to hit me that we were going to win the game and the series. Despite having all that time to prepare for it, though, the moment when the siren sounded was pretty overwhelming. Within a matter of seconds, I was swamped by my 16 team-mates. I was so humbled by the way they all came to me in those moments straight after the game ended. My contribution had been no greater than any of theirs, but I guess the selfless reaction of the group reflected the bond that exists in that team. The same response will be given to every one of those guys should it be known they won't be around in future. It is what Mal has instilled in the group. We want to do it for each other.

From the time the siren sounded through to a little after one o'clock the following morning, I was surrounded by a steady stream of people – friends, media, sponsors and team-mates. I wish I had a dollar for every hand I shook that night – it would have made for a hell of a retirement nest-egg. The official post-match function was still in full swing when I sneaked out a side door and made my way up to my room on the second floor of the Royal on the Park Hotel. I just wanted a few moments to myself, a bit of quiet time to soak in everything that had happened over the course of the Origin series. It had been a hectic couple of months.

My room looked out over the Botanical Gardens, and I reflected as I slumped into a chair. I cracked open a bottle of red wine and poured myself a glass. Over the course of a couple of glasses, I thought back over the game, the series and my entire Origin career. Looking over the gardens, I thought about how the people in different areas would react to the result when they rose that morning. I remember what it was like out in the small country towns around the region where I grew up; when Queensland won the State of Origin, everyone in the town walked a little taller the following day.

I thought about all the hardships Queenslanders had endured through the floods and cyclones which had threatened to bring the state to its knees. That we might have been able to cheer up some of those who were worst affected.

I thought about all the young kids coming to school tomorrow with their footballs, wanting to be the next Greg Inglis or Billy Slater. I remembered how I did the same thing when I was in primary school out at Wandoan. All those years ago I genuinely dreamed about wearing the Queensland number six jersey one day.

That was the last thing that crossed my mind before I drifted off to sleep.

What a journey.

EIGHTEEN
The End

'He is a Bronco – through and through. It was fitting that he finished up there and finished the way he did. If you want it all summed up in a few words . . . well . . . I'd just say as good as it gets.'

Wayne Bennett

My mind ran over almost every minute of the previous three days. I replayed the major events over and over again. It was almost as if I was reinforcing to myself the reality of what was an almost unreal set of circumstances. I could feel the frustration inside me building. After everything . . . to be so close to playing in the major semi-final, only to see it torn down by an injury over which I had no control. I could not believe it. I was so proud of our young team to have come this far that I desperately wanted to be with them in the next game. Having had an injury-free run in the 2011 season, my luck had run out.

From the 16 teams which lined up in round one of the 2011 NRL season, just four remained – New Zealand, Manly, the Storm and the Broncos. What was really exciting for me, however, was the manner in which the confidence and belief of the young Brisbane side I was leading had begun to develop into some genuine momentum on the field. As we headed into the preliminary final match-up with Manly everything was as it needed to be . . . well, almost everything. Written off at the start of the season, the Broncos had finished the 2011 regular season with a run of six straight wins before trouncing the Warriors at Suncorp in the opening week of the finals series. While the boys from over the ditch were clearly a little off their game, we looked sharp – especially in attack. The 40–16 scoreline, in fact, could have been even bigger had the Warriors dropped their bundle and not really forced us to work hard for the points we got.

We followed that effort with a gutsy golden point win over the reigning premiers, the St George–Illawarra Dragons, in a contest several of the game's most prominent and experienced commentators labelled the match of the season. We now know the match was, in fact, my 355th and final NRL fixture – the last time I would ever wear the Broncos jersey I dreamt of pulling on just once when I was a kid running around on the outskirts of Wandoan with my two brothers all those years ago. The benefit of hindsight now allows me the realisation that, that night, in front of a packed Suncorp Stadium crowd, against an old rival – and of course the familiar face occupying the visitors' coach's box – was, in fact, the perfect exit.

Wayne had already announced he would be moving on to a new challenge in 2012, having agreed to terms with Newcastle early in the year. As he said at the time, his move to the Dragons was never going to be long-term. He was there to do a job, and that job was to deliver the premiership the fans of the famous Red V had craved for three long decades. Two minor premierships, an NRL title and a major semi-final appearance – it was a pretty solid three-year stint by anyone's measure.

Locky's lament: Wayne should never have left

by Dan Koch
17 September 2011
The Australian

DARREN Lockyer grins as he picks up his ringing iPhone and sees the name flashing on caller ID.

'So I hear you're getting your own plane now, hey?' Lockyer says with a laugh.

On the other end of the line, Wayne Bennett chuckles before quizzing his former charge and close friend on just what he has heard. The conversation continues, lasting no more than three minutes. Having moved away to speak, Lockyer returns to his seat at the tiny coffee house in Paddington, a short stroll down Latrobe Terrace from Suncorp Stadium.

'I was just geeing him up,' Lockyer says as he resumes his seat.

'He just wanted to let me know he'd made up his mind. He's going to Newcastle – it's about to get announced publicly – think they are having a media conference or something in a couple of hours.'

That call on the morning of April 12 was the first time the pair had spoken in a couple of weeks. With a tinge of disappointment in his voice, Lockyer admitted part of him had hoped Bennett would return to the Broncos – the club he had helped build from the ground up and guided to six premierships in a 21-year reign.

'He should never have left,' Lockyer said, recalling that tumultuous period in Brisbane's history when Bennett left at the end of the 2008 season after a fallout with the administration.

'They'll love him down there (in Newcastle). If he wins a title there he'll be the first to win at three clubs, won't he?'

When Lockyer's enquiry was met with an affirmative response another grin broke out. 'He'd like that,' he says as he sips his coffee and moves the conversation back to where it had been pre-call.

Believe it or not the pair has only spoken a couple of times since that morning in April.

'I don't like to bother him, he's a busy man,' Bennett says. 'I sent him a couple of texts during Origin and before he broke the (NRL games) record up in Townsville. But we'll catch up when it's all over.

'He doesn't need a phone call. He knows how I feel about him.'

And how is that exactly? 'Well, we were side-by-side there for more than 300 games across club, Test and Origin footy, so we have a pretty special bond,' Bennett says. 'I know I slept a hell of a lot better the night before a game knowing Darren Lockyer was going to be there for me the next day doing his best. That's the thing with Locky. He never set out trying to be better than some other bloke.

'He never went out there trying to be better than the other great players in our game. He always wanted to be the best he could be, and he was relentless in pursing that goal.

'I was only watching vision of him the other day and here he was still barking out orders, telling these young kids at the Broncos where they need to be and what they need to be doing. Even at his age, with all the accolades, all the records, everything he has done, all his focus and determination was on that play. He is the ultimate competitor.'

This year's NRL season will forever be linked to Lockyer, who revealed in March that his 17th year in first grade would be his last. Each week thereafter, it seems, has marked another milestone – and another record. Lockyer now holds the record for most club games, Origin appearances and Test caps. There have been fond farewells from the Origin arena following Queensland's historic sixth consecutive series win, at various grounds around the country and of course the incredible scenes when 40,000 fans streamed on to Suncorp Stadium for his official Broncos farewell.

Barring injury he will sign off on the tour of Britain – a fitting finale, says NSW and former Test coach Ricky Stuart.

'He got handed the Test captaincy very young,' Stuart said. 'But he has never shirked the responsibility. In my time with him, I have never seen a player more aware of the influence he can have, not just on the other players in the team but on all the young kids watching at home on TV.

'Locky helped make that Kangaroos jumper mean something again, and every bloke that pulls on that jersey in the future owes him something for having done that because before he came along it had lost a lot of its standing.'

Before he gets to that, there is the premiership bid to finish.

Since Origin III the farewell tour has gathered momentum but will tonight climax as he leads the Broncos on to Suncorp Stadium for the final time in their semi-final with none other than Bennett's Dragons.

The pair has not spoken during what has been a huge build-up.

'It's still weird for me to coach against him,' Bennett mused recently.

'I just try to block him out. I am sure he does the same ... When I coach against Darren Lockyer I never relax because I know that with every fibre of his being he will be trying to get his team home. It's not personal with either of us, but that is who he is.

'Coaching against him like that, well . . . that's one thing that scares me.'

Wayne Bennett: He'd already got us once that year. When we had come up to Suncorp early in the season – it was through that Origin period – Locky did what Locky does. We had a hell of a lot of blokes backing up from the game on Wednesday; we were pretty busted that night. Brisbane had got the jump on us but we managed to work our way back into the match. Then, really against the run of play because we had taken the momentum at that stage, Locky grabbed the ball and hit a 40–20. It gave them the field position he was looking for and he gives the last pass for the try and finished us off with a field goal.

To me, that was just footy. The game was in the balance for the best part of 75 minutes. I have been at this for a while and when you are up against great players you learn that sometimes that sort of thing is going to happen and there isn't a great deal you can do about it. You just get on with life.

That last one, though . . . The feeling at the end of that game is one of the rarest feelings you get in footy. It was potentially the last game of the year and the end of my time at the Dragons – it was do or die. We came up and played a hell of a game of football. Up against anyone else that night we win – I have no doubt about that. We played tough for the full 80 minutes and then some. We couldn't have done much more than we did. We hung in the match when Brisbane was all over us for long periods and, really, they were the form side of the competition heading in.

In the end we were beaten on the last play of the game by a drop goal in extra time from the champion of champion players. The moment was made for something special from Locky. No one should have been surprised. I know I wasn't.

I didn't have any problem getting to sleep that night.

I can live with that.

The 2011 season was a triumph for the reformation of the Broncos 'family', and for that Paul White and Anthony Griffin deserve a tonne of credit. Old friends and what we at the Broncos like to refer to as the Rockhampton Mafia, Paul and 'Hook', along with Andrew Gee, are the perfect men to take the Broncos into a new era of sustained success.

As you need to do if you are going to achieve meaningful success, they have built from the ground up. Of the 2012 squad only Peter Wallace and Scott Anderson were not part of the club's development program, which was redesigned back in 2007 by Wayne, Dean Benton and Dan Baker. This young group they have put together have the opportunity to do something very special over a number of years. There is a bond between the group and their coach not unlike the one I was introduced to when I arrived at the Broncos way back in the mid-1990s.

And crucially, after 2011, they possess the sort of quality big-game experience necessary to make the most of the opportunities their wealth of talent will provide. As I have mentioned throughout this book, I have always believed in the power of positive thinking and the idea that if you want something badly enough and are prepared to make the sacrifices required any goal is attainable – coupled with a good club culture that revolves around all of the people in the organisation from the coach to the trainers and everyone in between. Obviously, however, when it comes to life in the NRL – or any number of other professional sports – there is a certain amount of natural physical ability or God-given talent required if a youngster's dream of playing in the toughest rugby league competition in the world has any hope of becoming a reality. What I am saying is that for all the fantastic work done by the performance and/or coaching staff at an NRL club, all their knowledge and effort will count for naught if their playing group doesn't have the capacity to take advantage of what they are offering. I have heard Wayne make the same point on numerous occasions over the years when he has been asked either about the secret to his coaching success or what he considered to be the most important ingredient in building a winning team. In his blunt, typically succinct manner, he would say, 'Good players helps.'

Wayne Bennett: I have had people ask me a lot over the years about whether footballers are born or made.

At the end of the day it is a combination of the two. They need that commitment and work ethic to cut it in the NRL these days. But the fact is to even get noticed by NRL clubs, you need to be able to play.

I was asked once about what quality I look for in a young player – what I thought was the most important asset. Well, they might be the best kid you have ever met, but being a good person won't help you much out on the field if you can't play. There isn't a bloke playing in the NRL today that hasn't got plenty of talent.

I can tell you no coach has ever won a premiership with a team of bad players. Talent alone won't win you a title. But you certainly can't win one without it.

Having witnessed first-hand the development of this young Broncos squad, I say without hesitation that the sky is the limit for the current group. They may not yet have the credentials to match some of the great Broncos teams of the past, but for pure natural skill they are every bit the equal of the premiership teams of which I was a part. What 2011 provided them with was a concentrated dose of big-game experience – the final essential ingredient in any champion team. It is something which is impossible to teach and impossible to replicate.

However, the hysteria – and I use that as a term of endearment when describing the manner in which I was farewelled – which accompanied the team throughout the season before really ramping up at the back end of the regular season and into the finals probably allowed the younger blokes to be a part of almost a half dozen 'big' games. It was unlike anything I have witnessed, and while I am sure there were times it grated on and overwhelmed all the youngsters around the place, one thing I can promise them as sure as I am here today: they will be better for it. The extra attention and saturation coverage from the media, the increased interest fans have in every minute of your preparation, the hype and excitement that takes over as the game draws close and the intensity and pressure of playing in front of a big crowd are all things which can overwhelm players and distract them before and during such games. How a player deals with those different facets varies enormously from one bloke to the next and knowing what works for you as an individual is critical.

The success of the current Queensland State of Origin squad is a perfect example. Cameron Smith, Johnathan Thurston, Petero Civoniceva, Justin Hodges and Billy Slater were the guys with whom I shared the team's leadership responsibilities during our incredible six-year run as owners of the Origin shield. All six of us had been part of at least one series loss prior to the watershed series victory in 2006. We had seen Fittler and Johns take wins away from us through their superior handling of the critical moments in games. Those guys could identify the crucial moments of the contest ahead of time; they also knew what they needed to do when the moment arrived. Most importantly, they delivered the goods at that moment. You only have to see the number of times Cam, JT, Hodgo or Billy has been responsible for pulling Queensland out of a precarious situation during the past years to know they learned from their experience of seeing how great players handle pressure situations.

Which takes us back to where this chapter started. In the end, Anthony Grifffin was the man who delivered the news, which is as it should be. Those sorts of major decisions at a football club have to be made clearly and decisively by the bloke who runs the show – the head coach.

I knew the moment Gerard Beale collected me that I had done some real damage. My jawline was all out of place, but when Springer (trainer Tony Spencer) came out to have a look, I just bit down hard on my mouthguard to feel if my teeth were in place and did the best I could to tell him I was okay to go on. The match was still in the balance, but the Dragons were coming home strong and I just couldn't let it end like that. I felt that, even if I couldn't do too much, I could steer the boys around for the final 10 minutes and make sure we didn't deviate from the plans we had been working from up to that point.

The cheekbone and eye socket began swelling almost immediately, but I found the pain wasn't too bad as long as I kept biting down into my mouthguard. It seemed to absorb a lot of the shuddering you get when you try to run with that sort of injury. Clenching my teeth together stabilised things enough for me to believe I could deal with the discomfort. There was no way I was leaving the game at that point. The idea that my final game on the hallowed Lang Park turf could end with me sitting on the interchange bench licking my wounds wasn't one I was ever going to entertain.

Not that I was able to stop the Dragons from seizing control in the final 10 minutes of the match. Both teams had locked into the 'arm wrestle' from minute one. It was tough, unrelenting, high-pressure rugby league, played at a ferocious pace. It is the sort of contest that sorts the men out from the boys – and on this night all 34 players stepped up to the mark. Having hung in the contest, the Dragons charged in the dying stages with Darius stunning the sell-out crowd by crossing for a try in the 79th minute to leave his side trailing 12–10 with their conversion to come. I didn't even bother waiting for Jamie Soward to kick the ball – I knew he was going to make it – and so we headed into golden point extra time.

When it comes to the coin toss for golden point, it is generally accepted the winner of the toss will choose the direction his team will run for the first period of extra time, which in turn means he will be receiving from the kick-off and will get first use of the ball. Metres tend to be much easier to find. Fatigue has usually set in, slowing the speed of the defensive line enormously and widening the gaps between tiring defenders.

Having lost the toss, with all that in mind, I took a bit of a gamble and really launched into the kick-off. If a gust of wind had pushed it even a little, the consequences would have been disastrous. As it was, the night was as still as Wally's statue and the ball did exactly what I had hoped, sailing high and to the deep right corner of the in-goal.

Hornby caught the ball a metre or so shy of the dead ball line. But as every coach from under-13s through to the NRL will tell you – a kick is only as good as its chase, and Josh McGuire led the charge, screaming downfield so quickly his first contact with Adam Cuthbertson on his kick-off return came inside the Dragons' own 10-metre area.

That one effort meant that for tackles two and three we were able to set ourselves and push forward off the defensive line. That is how you build pressure on an opponent – and pressure does funny things to people. Certainly I think Jamie Soward would like the chance to revisit his decision to kick early in the tackle count, with his side trapped inside their 30-metre zone. His kick was collected on the full by Gerard Beale, who did the right thing by charging as quickly as he could at the Dragons' chasers, grabbing every centimetre on offer. As he got up to play the ball just 15 metres shy of halfway, I started to prepare for tackles four and five and my chance to put us into a preliminary final.

While often players will take his drop goal attempts from a position deep behind the play-the-ball, on this occasion I took a different tack. Being a left-footer, I positioned myself about 2–3 metres to the left of the dummy-half, almost in line with him. A quick pass from that distance would reduce the amount of time the defence would have to get to me.

While I didn't strike the ball perfectly, it was enough to sneak over the crossbar, just inside the right-hand upright. I have always had a bit of a slice or fade with my drop kicks – a fact which I was praying would hold true this time also. There was an incredible roar from the crowd that hit a deafening crescendo. There was a fantastic euphoria amongst the team as we celebrated the moment. After such a surreal ending to the game, I soon realised that my career was over at the ground I love.

I must admit that while I shared the excitement of my team-mates and appreciated enormously the well-wishes from the fans who stuck around for my final victory lap and exit from the NRL playing arena, the mixed emotions I was having thinking about the injury probably didn't allow me to embrace that moment the way I would have liked. By the time we got inside, the pain was starting to set in. I couldn't sing the team song, and it took Dr Peter Myers all of 10 seconds to deliver confirmation I had fractured my cheekbone.

Wayne Bennett: If Locky stays healthy, Brisbane win that competiton. That was such a high-quality game, whichever side came out the winner was going to carry an enormous amount of momentum and confidence into the preliminary final. I can tell you we were coming good. Things were starting to feel right and fall into place for us, but the Broncos . . . they were primed. The tragedy for them was the collision there at the end of the game when Darren got hurt. That was the moment their premiership hopes ended.

I have been around long enough and know enough about winning premierships to know when a side is on to win a title and, mark my words, Brisbane were 'on' for all money. As the season draws on, there are little things that start to emerge that are key indicators for me about which teams are getting it right at the right time. Brisbane was going to take a lot of beating largely because of what he was doing in leading that group. He was playing as well as he has played for a number of years, which helped, but it was just his presence and the confidence and security he gave to the other guys in the team that stood out to me. They didn't want to let him down. In fact, I will go further than that – they would not have him being let down.

The frustrating thing for Locky was that he knew just as well as I did: it was their premiership to lose. He knew the team was doing the right things – I could see it in his demeanour on and off the field. I think he knew it a few weeks before the finals even began, though I am certain he never hinted as much to his team-mates or anyone else. He just knew that everything was on song there at Red Hill. He's been part of enough champion teams to know how it works . . . and it was on.

Anyhow, I went into the dressing-room after the game. He was sitting there on his own. His team-mates knew he needed to be left alone. I knew as soon as I saw him there was some real damage to the cheekbone; I knew he was done. He didn't want to hear that, though – and that is understandable. I have spoken a lot about this bloke's mental toughness and there is no question that if the decision about him playing against Manly had been left up to him, Darren

Lockyer would have played. If he didn't have other people around him, other people there at the Broncos looking out for him, I'm telling you, he plays. He would have willed himself into the game. How he would have gone and what impact it might have had on the final result that night, who knows? But he would have been there had it been left to him.

That said, it would have been the wrong decision. After all the fuss, the right decision was made.

We didn't say too much – he couldn't really speak – but I just congratulated him and said I hoped he could play. I knew he couldn't, but I also knew he was in no mood to hear that.

It might not have been the fairytale finish he'd been thinking of, but to me his whole season was a bit of a fairytale. It was more like something you read about . . . We were all privileged to be part of it. He went out on top – as he should have. I know there are people out there wondering if he could have gone around again. There'll be times through this year when he will probably think the same thing. The answer is he absolutely could have – probably could have played two or three more seasons if he had wanted to do that.

But this was the right time. If he went around again he would have compromised so much of the magic of the year he had. You look at it: Queensland wins the Origin; he wins his last two Tests in Australia; wins the Four Nations; his club comes within a whisker of winning the title. A bit of bad luck was the only thing that stopped them. But he has the incredible memories of those final weeks when the entire rugby league community came out to say thanks. His last touch of the ball is a drop goal that wins his side a semi-final at Suncorp Stadium. So he gets to share his last lap with his fans and his team-mates chair him off the ground.

That sounds like a fairytale finish to me.

While I now look at my final days with Brisbane in a similarly positive light, such sentiments were a long way from my thoughts following the decisive meeting with Hook [coach Anthony Griffin] on the Wednesday morning.

Anthony Griffin: It is hard to quantify how important Locky was for both me and for the club after the drama and upheaval at the start of 2011. Through those really awkward first few days and then into the first few rounds of the season, Locky just took control of the dressing-room and made sure the players remained firmly focused on their respective jobs. That gave me the chance to do mine.

Locky was the first bloke I spoke to about taking over from Ivan. He came to the club at about 6.30 am, and what I remember most from that meeting was the fact he didn't once ask about any of the messy details. His only concern was about the impact any sort of instability could have on the young squad he was leading.

From a coaching perspective, he is a dream – zero maintenance. His willingness to listen and work – second to none. His commitment to the team-first ideal – second to none. I consider it an enormous privilege to have had the chance to work with him. I still pinch myself a bit to think I was part of his final year in the game. I mean, I am still very much a footy tragic at heart. I love the game. I love its history, and Darren Lockyer has a very special place in that history.

To see the response from the public – it was just incredible – but Locky just took it all in his stride. It was a really good learning experience for a lot of the younger guys, just to see how to manage the different facets of life as an NRL player. It was an eye-opener for me as well.

I remember sitting up the front of the bus on the way to Dairy Farmers Stadium in Townsville. It was the match which gave him the all-time record for NRL games and the locals lined the streets heading out of the hotel. Seriously, it was out of this world. Anyway, I am sitting there looking out at the crowd and one of my mates sends me a text just saying, 'Good luck. It's the big show tonight. It's here. I can't wait for the game.' Then it just sort of hit me that this was a really big deal. I turned around and Locky is sitting in the seat beside me listening to his iPod. I just had a bit of a chuckle and thought, 'What the hell am I doing here?'

The whole year had been an incredible ride. Everything seemed to be following the script until the collision with Bealey. Locky was busted but he was absolutely set on playing and initially I was of the opinion that it was his decision – that if anyone had earned the right to make the call on whether he was fit enough to take his spot and do what he had to do in his role, then D. Lockyer had earned that right.

I suppose there was an element of hoping he would be right. But as the week dragged on, particularly after we arrived in Sydney, something just wasn't right and I knew that it shouldn't happen. Still I kept second-guessing myself, because of the situation he was in regarding the end of his career. It was really difficult, but I remember sitting there on the Tuesday night after Locky had flown down in the helicopter and I knew something was wrong. I went back to my room and called a couple of people I trust and bounced it off them.

On Wednesday morning I got up early and went for a walk. I just wanted to get things straight in my own head before I had the conversation with Locky. I called him and asked him to come to my room. I knew he'd have the shits – and he did. But even so I wanted to do what I could to ensure he was actually part of the final decision. I didn't want to just come down heavy and tell him he was out. I just said that I didn't think he should play, that I didn't think it was in either his or the team's best interests to have him out there when the risk of further damage was substantial.

Typically, he didn't give me too much, but I knew

he was disappointed. He said if I thought it was in the team's best interests he was okay with that. He asked if he could do a fitness test – so we did all that. He didn't talk to me for a couple of days but in the end he not only accepted the decision, he acknowledged it was the right thing to do. I don't regret making the call I did. I'd do the same again tomorrow.

On Thursday afternoon, we sat down for a coffee and I knew then he had accepted it. He asked if he could address the boys pre-match, which I was all for. I was just disappointed we couldn't get him that final match he so desperately wanted.

For me, I guess I just loved the chance to watch a champion at work. And that's what Locky is. He is a champion.

You know, he actually still brought his boots and playing kit to the ground with him on Friday . . . He said it was just in case one of the boys went down in the warm-up.

I took the chance to let my hair down at the end-of-season drinks the club and its sponsors put on at the team hotel following our loss to Manly – the eventual premiers. There was plenty for me to celebrate. For 17 years I'd lived out my childhood fantasy of being a professional rugby league player. I was so enormously humbled by the fanfare made for me wherever I went. I never set out to break records or be recognised. I wanted to be a professional rugby league player because I loved the game.

I still do. It has provided me with the most incredible opportunities to see the world, to make a life for both me and my family, to make friends I'll have for a lifetime, and to meet and learn from some truly great people.

While it was a memorable night for many reasons, it would have been nice had Wayne Bennett been able to attend.

All the people in that room owed him a debt of gratitude for helping to build the Broncos and what remains one of the strongest and most iconic sporting brands in the country. He personally helped mould the lives of hundreds of young men during his incredible 21-year stint as head coach. The acrimony surrounding his departure hurt both parties. Wayne felt somewhat unwelcome at a place he'd helped build, while the desire to move on from Wayne became an issue around the club. Whether in the front office or the football department, Wayne's shadow looms large and always will. Trying to change anything which bears his fingerprints at its foundation is simply unnecessary.

Times change and football clubs evolve. The Broncos squad in 2012 goes about things very differently to the way the class of '92 did. But in Andrew Gee, Allan Langer, Anthony Griffin and Paul White, you have people in key positions at the club who know and understand the values and philosophies upon which the club laid its foundations.

The final training run before my 'official' farewell against the Sea Eagles had drawn an enormous crowd. Training was nearly over when I saw a familiar face – or figure more likely – amongst the crowd. It had been a lot of years since Big Jus (Justin Bennett) had graced us with his presence, but there he was. It wasn't long before he made his way out onto the field to practise his kicking for goal.

It was a few minutes before I managed to spot Wayne. He was standing towards the back of the crowd, typically doing his level best to remain inconspicuous. It didn't take long before other people around the place realised he was there. Paul White, who has known Wayne since his days in the Queensland Police Force, went across and greeted him warmly. After Paul it was like a steady procession – with players, staff, media and even a number of the fans who had stuck around – making their way over to him, all of them welcoming him back. It was lovely to watch and was almost enough to get a smile out of him!

Having Wayne there that day meant an enormous amount to me. It was the first time he had been down to the facility he formerly ruled since leaving for the Dragons back in 2009.

'It's a pretty important day . . . thought I should be here,' he said.

We chatted briefly and he wished me luck and then spent the next hour mingling with old friends.

Wayne Bennett: He is right. It was him that brought me back. There were some bridges that needed mending.

He is certainly astute . . . always has been. Even as a teenager.

It was great. I felt for the first time that I was coming back to the club I knew . . . It's the club that I love.

I'll always be a Bronco. It's part of who I am.

It's funny how the wheel turns.

I owe much of the wonderful life I have today to the fact that 17 years ago Wayne gave me the chance to be a Bronco. He gave me the chance to build a future.

Now I have provided the opportunity for him to be reunited with the club.

It was Monday, 5 December 2011. At 5.30 am my alarm rang as it had done at that time for the best part of a decade. I rolled out of bed and wandered out to the front door of our family home high in the hills of Paddington. After 17 years testing my body in one of the most unforgiving sports, there were a few more creaks and cracks than most would consider healthy – but all things considered I wasn't feeling too bad. I gave my knee a rub. The doctors tell me it will probably need to be replaced at some stage down the track. I reached up, stretching as high as I can. My right shoulder takes a little while to warm up. I carried the injury for most of the 2011 season and will need to get an operation on it at some stage – but I'm certainly not thinking about going under the knife in the near future. The typical heat of summertime in Brisbane had well and truly taken hold. Even at this early hour, the sun was shooting through the cracks in the blinds on our windows and you could feel the thickness of the humidity sitting in the air.

I took my iPod off the charge and put the earphones in, hitting the pre-recorded playlist as I rolled outside for my morning jog. I wasn't 20 metres away from home before I recognised the song list. I hadn't changed it since the final week of the Four Nations tour in England, and for the first time since touching down in Australia I allowed myself to wind back the clock and think about not just where I was but where I had been. It was over now – my professional career was done – but as I started to stride out it was almost as if the music took me back to those incredible final couple of months of my time in rugby league, which I spent with the Kangaroos. In my mind, it was the perfect way to finish.

The squad headed off to the United Kingdom to try to win back the Four Nations Trophy we'd lost to the Kiwis on home soil 12 months earlier. I had the opportunity to play a farewell Test on home soil at the recently renovated Newcastle Stadium. Fans don't come much more passionate than those in the Hunter region, and the Novocastrians turned out in force and gave me a rousing send-off, for which I will be forever grateful and will certainly never forget.

I did come within a whisker of having very little memory of the entire day, however, thanks to a misdirected elbow from Kiwi giant Russell Packer. Russell is a ferocious-looking character at the best of times, but the shot of his heavily inked elbow collecting me flush in the melon in the opening minute of the game was ugly. Thankfully, it was one of those cases where the incident looked far worse than it felt, though. I'm not saying it tickled. Given I was playing my first game since fracturing my cheekbone against the Dragons, the incident got a lot of attention. I have to admit, even though I am convinced there was no intent to target my injury, I was a little surprised he escaped with only one match on the sidelines.

It was pretty similar to the incident which saw then Cronulla prop Ben Ross not only suspended for seven weeks for flattening Melbourne halfback Cooper Cronk, but also saw the big Queenslander absolutely laid out by a big, straight right from Storm enforcer Brett White.

Whenever you line up in a Test match – be it in the green and gold of Australia, or the famous black strip of New Zealand, or even with the red cross of England adorning the front of your jersey – you know the rules are a little different. It is the same in Origin. With officials from the two sides deciding whether incidents are punishable, inevitably conversations are along the lines of: 'You blokes got anything to report?' 'Na, mate, you?' 'Na, we're sweet. See you next time.'

In those arenas, it's still very much the age-old rule of what happens on the field stays there. Within reason, of course. But given Big Moz [English hard man Adrian Morley] didn't get suspended for famously icing Robbie Kearns with a brutal stiff-arm in the first tackle of an Ashes game back in 2003 – a shot which saw him sent from the field – it is clearly difficult to find yourself missing matches in the international arena.

I had been even more confident than usual heading into the Test and, save for the early scare I had from Packer, we were never really threatened. The thing that really struck me in that match, however, was the change in tactics from the Kiwis. For a side that was rightly being hailed as the best in the world after the 2010 Four Nations win, they appeared to take a strange, and I believe costly, diversion away from their strengths and instead resorted to a lot of misguided focus in and around the play-the-ball.

I think that, with this change of focus to the ruck, a number of the New Zealanders, including Issac Luke, Jeremy Smith, Jared Waerea-Hargreaves, Sika Manu and Adam Blair got really caught up and possibly distracted from their natural games that had brought them their recent successes.

All the guys I just mentioned are exceptional players in their own right, when they are concentrating on doing what they do best. In the end, the change of focus cost their own side badly because, by the end of the 2011 Four Nations, the Kiwis were out of contention and playing like an incredibly frustrated unit, largely because penalties and suspensions had robbed them of any real chance to challenge either Australia or England.

We played the Kiwis a couple of weeks later in the opening match of the Four Nations and again really controlled the match from go to whoa. The match marked Tony Williams's arrival on the international scene and, mark my words, he and Dave Taylor are the two physical specimens I believe could transform how the game of rugby league is played. Tony is a bit taller, but the pair of them are 120 kilograms plus. Just how much that plus is worth depends on how honest they are being and even what time of the day you get them. Dave probably has a few more weapons – the bloke is the only front-rower in the NRL with a legitimate short-kicking game – where the big T-Rex is probably a touch quicker over 100 metres. Still, both can foot it with the outside backs but lift extreme weights in the gym. When you are talking 175-kilogram-plus bench presses, you are moving a serious amount of iron.

With 14 Queenslanders on tour and veteran blokes from New South Wales like Paul Gallen, Luke Lewis and Anthony Watmough, the Kangaroos squad gelled pretty quickly. There is a good bond that exists among the group and not much is going to change with my moving on. Cooper Cronk will move into the halves, JT will move into the six jumper, and things will keep going as they have done for the past few years.

The one major change from 2010 to 2011 was the squad's adjustment to Tim Sheens' leadership and coaching style and structure. Tim is a professor of rugby league. His brain is wired in alignment with the game like no other person I have ever come across. While that allows him to develop some incredible and on occasions game-changing ideas, when you are at the helm of the Kangaroos and have a limited preparation time, but are working with the best players going around, the old KISS (keep it simple stupid) methodology is all that is needed. Give players like Cameron Smith, JT, Greg Inglis, Darius Boyd and Cooper Cronk a framework to work within and they'll take care of the rest.

While I think the Kiwis probably needed to take stock and make some changes, 2011 was a watershed series for the Poms, who were outstanding. Under Steve McNamara, they appear to have finally addressed the playmaking issues which have been their Achilles heel for as long as I can remember. With the likes of Nathan Brown, Terry Matterson and Michael Maguire enjoying successful coaching stints over in the English Super League, I think they finally accepted the need to employ greater structure in their play, starting with numbers nine, seven and six, who can play direct and organise. Gareth Widdop has learned his game under Craig Bellamy and is going to be a superstar. Rangi Chase learned his trade from Browny over here while young halfback Sam Tomkins benefited enormously from the time he spent with Maguire during his stint at the helm of English Super League heavyweights Wigan.

Around those three blokes, England can build a pretty formidable line-up because they have wonderful big men in the likes of Gareth Ellis, the Burgess brothers, James Graham and Chris Heighington and some equally exciting outside backs in Bronco Jack Reed, Ryan Hall, Leroy Cudjoe and Danny McGuire. If they continue to develop at the rate they are going – and can get and keep Sammy Burgess on the field – then there is absolutely no reason they can't challenge both the Australian and the Kiwi sides for the 2013 World Cup.

With their big pack dominant, and veteran utility Kevin Sinfield outstanding in England's final-round match against New Zealand, they ended up running away 28–6 winners to seal a spot in the final against us.

With the big local media contingent right behind them, the England side looked and sounded extremely confident heading into the final at Leeds. Two weeks earlier we had run away with our pool match against them to the tune of 36–20. In the process, however, we lost Billy Slater for the tournament with a badly broken collarbone, which he suffered trying to pull off one of his trademark try-saving tackles. Things got even worse in the build-up to the final. I still don't know how we got away without seeing it plastered all over the media, but JT and Matt Scott both failed to finish the second-last session.

The one with JT was the big concern. The incident itself was really nondescript. We were just working through some of our plays – not even at full pace. The ball went to JT – thankfully not from me – and I just thought it was a bad pass that he'd tried to stretch out for but couldn't quite pull in. Then, as quiet as you like, he just spun around on his heel and walked off the track with Kangaroos trainer Alex Corvo. The Channel 7 camera was right there. None of the media there seemed to pick up that he had strained his adductor muscle and was considered long odds to line up at Elland Road in less than 48 hours' time.

The Cowboys co-captains both missed the final session because they were off getting scans, but being a closed session we were able to keep it under wraps. Things went from bad to worse over the course of the final 24 hours, though, with Keith Galloway and Greg Inglis both picking up a nasty gastro bug, and Chris Lawrence aggravating the shoulder injury he had sustained against Wales in the pool match.

Mum and Dad arrived – and typically helped put my mind at ease. I was really thrilled to be able to fly them over for the match. We had spoken about it earlier in the year but Mum, being Mum, was worried about 'taking too much time off work'. She was back at it the Monday after the game.

We blew a lot of chances in the first half, so my message at the break was really clear. Patience was the key again. Even with JT's injury, he was the dominant force out there. Cam was . . . well, Cam was Cam. We needed JT to be JT. And in the second 40 minutes, he was.

It was nice to get the final try. As for the conversion attempt – well, the less said about that the better.

By Steve Mascord
23 December 2011
http://www.rugbyleagueworld.net/BLOG

This writer's final image of Darren Lockyer won't be the same as yours.

It won't be his 79th-minute try in the Four Nations final, when his own kick ricocheted off the goalpost pads and back into his arms as if propelled by an ancient, invisible force.

It certainly won't be his hilarious attempt at conversion or even the standing ovation the 34-year-old received as he walked out of the media suite at Elland Road after his last media conference.

My voice recorder shows it was 10.10 pm – ten minutes after the Australians had been officially evicted by stadium management – that I encountered

Lockyer in the corridor outside the green-and-gold dressing-room.

He was still in his shorts. And he was being interviewed by a young radio reporter he had never met before, carefully considering each question before giving detailed, informative answers.

It was the Australian media manager who had earlier said Lockyer was not giving one-on-one interviews. Turning down such requests had never been the Roma boy's style – and it wasn't on the very last night of his career, either.

Lockyer's omnipresence in the rugby league media presents a unique challenge to the writer of this, perhaps – only *perhaps* – the final tribute to one of the greatest careers in our game's 116-year history.

Sure, I have many memories from Lockyer's time in the spotlight – from his disastrous Test debut to him being afforded a guard of honour at the end of his record-breaking club game in Townsville only to be greeted at the end of the tunnel on live television by a very scruffy looking . . . me.

But it's all been written, hasn't it? He's answered every question, delved into every area of his life, canvassed every strength and weakness in detail.

Thank you and goodnight

This is the very last interview Darren Lockyer did as a rugby league player.

Steve Mascord: Two things . . . talk us through the goal and how worried you were about all the guys being crook before the game and injured.

Darren Lockyer: I wouldn't say I was worried about the guys being injured and crook. It was more . . . I think we were always determined, no matter what happened, we had everything covered. It was a good thing that JT and Matt Scott got through their fitness tests this morning and GI was right. I guess that boosted the confidence of the team but at the same time, if they weren't going to be there, we were ready for that.

SM: And the goal . . .

DL: Yeah, mate, I haven't done any goal-kicking practice for a while and it told. I've kicked plenty of goals over my years, but that one just didn't work.

SM: One memory from tonight and I'll leave you in peace.

DL: One memory? It's hard to pinpoint one but I think . . . I remember when we ran out and the national anthems for both countries were being sung, I've never seen that many England flags just waving, you know? I've played here a few times and that's probably the best atmosphere I've experienced here at Elland Road. So it was a great, great night.

The master's apprentice

An innate ability to be in the right place at the right time . . . It was on show in the final game of Darren

Lockyer's club career, when he kicked the winning field goal for Brisbane against St George Illawarra.

And it was there again on November 19 when he was there to regather his own kick off the right upright at Elland Road and dive over.

'He epitomises patience on the football field,' said the man who will replace him as skipper, Australia hooker Cameron Smith.

'He's just got the smarts to know where to be on the field. He came up with some big plays to get us back on top in the match. It's just his composure and his ability to turn up at the right time when a team needs it.

'That's what makes a great leader. It doesn't matter what the situation is in the game . . . he comes up with the right play every time. That's what's made him the player he is, a champion of our game.

'I think he knows how we feel about him and what he's done for all of us and everyone back home.

'He was my hero. Growing up in Brissy as a kid, he was one of my idols. I wanted to be like Darren Lockyer and now I've played in a Four Nations final in his last match ever. It's a very proud moment for me. I'm sure all the other boys feel privileged to be part of his last game and hopefully it's a lasting memory for him.'

Lockyer did his best to make the 30–8 win over England about everyone but himself.

'We didn't speak about [his farewell] all week until

[before kick-off] when we watched a bit of vision of him playing for Australia when he was a bit younger and had a bit of hair and you could actually hear him when he spoke,' laughed Smith.

'Everyone knew what this occasion meant to him and what it meant to us to be playing in his last game, and I'm just so happy for him that he gets to finish as a winner.

'If I'm given the job, I'd be delighted with that. There's a lot of guys in there who could fill the role of captain of this team. I'd be very proud to have the "C" next to my name. If I can do the job as well as Darren, I'd be very happy with that.'

My 5.30 ritual came to a contemplative end as my home appeared in the distance. The street signs, the shop fronts, the parks and even some of the faces I passed morning after morning during my jogs around Leeds on those cold mornings faded from my mind.

Suddenly the playlist ended. I opened the front door to be greeted by Sunny bounding towards me at full pace.

Back to reality.

Time to be Dad.

NINETEEN
Rugby League Legend

To conclude, we spoke to some of rugby league's biggest names and canvassed their opinion on the same question: is Darren Lockyer the greatest rugby league player of all time? It is a conversation with no real answer but certainly one that some of the game's greatest minds believe is a subject worthy of discussion.

Andrew Gee: It is a question you get asked a bit and for the best part of 20 years or so I have said without hesitation that Alf was the best player I ever played with or against. I suppose having played most of my career alongside him I saw first-hand how often Alf was the difference between two sides. He did it week in, week out, year after year. He was incredible.

But when you step back for a second and just start looking at Locky's career game by game – the sheer weight of numbers is unbelievable. Then you throw in his athleticism, his leadership, the way he made the transition from fullback to five-eighth . . . when you start going over it all it's undeniable.

He is the greatest player of his generation and quite possibly the best the game has ever seen.

It is always difficult to compare champions. But the thing that gives Locky an edge even when you are talking about the best of the best is the longevity and the consistency of his brilliance. I think he set new standards for the quality of athlete and the professionalism of players in the NRL.

Ricky Stuart: I had the opportunity to play alongside Mal Meninga for a number of years down at Canberra. I have never seen another player who could single-handedly change the course of a match like Mal. His presence on the field – he could just impose himself on an opposition side like no one else. I only played against Wally towards the end of his career, but his dominance at Origin level was incredible. You'd have to include Joey and Alf in there . . .

Darren Lockyer sits very comfortably in the company of those four guys. In fact, I'd go as far as to say you cannot have a discussion about who the greatest player of all time is without Darren featuring very prominently. The thing about him for me is – and

I have said this before – Darren is at his best when the stakes are at their highest. His poise and calm at the back end of matches is amazing. The number of times he orchestrated a match-winning play for Brisbane, Queensland or Australia in the final few minutes of the contest . . . he did it so often you almost started to expect it from him every time.

Is he the best ever? I don't know and I am probably not really equipped to answer that question with too much authority. All I will say is that if we ever do see a better player than Darren Lockyer – shit, I hope I'm coaching him . . . I hope he is on my team.

Cameron Smith: He is certainly the best player I have played with or against and, personally, I think he is the best the game has seen. Obviously there are plenty of wonderful players in past eras I haven't seen play, so all I can go on is what I read about them or what other people I respect tell me about what they were like.

But Locky's record at every level of the game is out on its own. There's no one even close when you start putting all the numbers together. Then there is the fact that he was the best player in the world in two positions – fullback and five-eighth – which again is unprecedented in more than 100 years of rugby league. He just had it all. He had the physical attributes – he was an amazing athlete and was blessed with incredible natural skills.

When you add into the mix the fact that most would

consider Locky to be the mentally toughest player in the modern era and you start to understand who he is, what makes him tick. His work ethic and professionalism in every single aspect of his preparation raised the bar for NRL players across the board.

Paul Gallen: He's definitely the best player I have played against. Just the way he can control a match without even touching the ball sometimes. He always seemed to have the game being played at the tempo he wants. Joey is probably the only other bloke I have seen who has that sort of influence over the other 25 blokes out on the field with him.

I felt so privileged to play alongside him for the Kangaroos a few times – it was an eye-opening experience to watch the way he prepares himself. It reinforced something I have always believed in strongly and that is the fact that there is no shortcut to the top. By the time I was in the Test squad he had been captain for six or seven years – he held all sorts of records, won everything there is to win. Some of them he'd won a couple of times.

But without fail Locky was the first man on the training track and *always* the last bloke off. He stayed behind every single session doing extra work on his kicking or passing, or running through some defensive drills with one of the forwards. I made a point of volunteering to wear the pads and I couldn't get over his attention to detail. Close enough wasn't good enough for Locky. Even the slightest of errors upset him and he would make the correction immediately then re-drill the same thing again and again and again.

He was still doing the same thing in his final year. It's an important lesson for young blokes, because it is what kept Locky at the top of the food chain for so long. If it is good enough for one of the greatest players of all time to be doing extras when he is 34 years old and in his last year in the game – well, it is good enough for anyone.

Phil Gould: I don't know the process or if there are any rules about when blokes are eligible to be anointed as an Immortal, but really, how long do they need?

He's got to be on that list. The longevity is the proof. The longevity of quality. The longevity of toughness. You just cannot deny it. At the end of his career, when it's all said and done, he'll have done it all at the highest levels of the game and he'll have done it more than anyone who has ever graced a rugby league dressing-room.

Now for this bloke to do what he has done . . . out of all the players who have played the game over 100 years, how is it possible? How does he do what he has done at a time when the game is meant to be bigger, faster and tougher than ever? How do you even quantify those numbers?

How does one man stand so far out from the pack?

I don't know. That is, unless he is very, very special. Unlike anyone else we have seen.

Lockyer has a clarity of thinking and a self-confidence that sets him apart. He knows he can deliver when he has to because he has done it so many times before. It's not that he keeps coming up with new things. There were no great tricks to Darren Lockyer. In those early years he certainly had unique talent. Unique athleticism. But there are things that Billy Slater can do, and Johnathan Thurston can do, that Darren Lockyer can't do. There are things Andrew Johns or Brad Fittler could do, that Darren Lockyer can't do.

But none of those blokes could do it nearly as often as Darren Lockyer did it when IT was absolutely necessary. When the clock is into the 79th minute and the game is still in the balance, he is the bloke you want with the ball in his hands 100 times out of 100. He won't win it for you every time . . . but geez . . . for every miss, I reckon he'd find a way to get you home 10 times over.

When you are that deep into a contest, it isn't physical. It is a mental strength – an emotional control which allows him to make the right decisions again and again, and it is what sets him apart.

Ben Ikin: He is as good as there has ever been. He is a generational player. Where that puts him in the overall standings – well, that is pretty tough. I suppose over the 100 or so years of the game you get a couple of blokes who come along through any generation who transcend the sport in their time. I have actually done a bit of research on the wonderful history of our game and as far back as Dally Messenger rugby league had stars who have elevated the game to the point it finds itself today. Locky is one of those blokes.

The thing I will say is that Locky ticks a lot of the boxes which you want your great players to show. There is his durability, loyalty to one club, ability to perform on the big stage in big games, selflessness, great leadership . . . and I suppose if I was to sum Locky's career up and try to define it, the thing that sticks out is the sheer breadth of his impact and influence.

I reckon if you wrote out a list of characteristics and traits you feel make up a generational player Locky would probably tick more boxes than anyone else in the game's history. He was the complete player – the prototype for modern-day footballers.

Wayne Bennett: You couldn't wish for a better end to what was simply a career of one of the all-time greats of our game.

You couldn't have scripted it any better and the wonderful thing for me to see was just the manner in which he was received by everyone – players, officials, coaches, fans – you name it . . . they all bought into it and it was incredible to see. I have never seen an outpouring of gratitude and thanks from the rugby league community anything like what we saw in the final few weeks of the NRL season with Darren. And it is all credit to him because it was recognition of the way in which he had carried himself over the course of his career. It was recognition for the sort of bloke that he was and is, and it was recognition from the people who for so long had got so much enjoyment out of watching him play rugby league.

The magnitude of it. I mean it was everyone . . . it's unparalleled in my lifetime.

From a personal point of view I was just so happy to be part of it. To have been part of seeing that young 17-year-old kid from Roma who arrived at the Broncos grow into this figure whose standing in the game and in the community saw him honoured like that.

You don't like to think too much – well, I don't anyhow – about the influence I may or may not have had on different individual players over the years. But I know for a fact the Broncos – the club – had a huge influence on Darren. It is one of the things I was most pleased about in his case – and for so many other young men – that he finished his career where he started it. He is a Bronco, through and through. It was fitting that he finished up there and finished the way he did.

I guess to finish up I am just proud. I am proud of who Darren Lockyer is and what he has done for the game of rugby league and the way in which he has always represented himself. I am more proud of the fact that he is and will always be a Bronco.

If you want it all summed up in a few words, well, I'd just say as good as it gets.

The career. The man himself. The player. The finish. The whole thing . . . as good as it gets.

POSTSCRIPT
Bulla is Back

At the time of writing, we are only about a month into the 2012 NRL season, yet the number of fascinating stories which have already emerged as well as those which appear to be slowly developing into something more significant would require another book to tell – and I don't have the time to do another one of these just yet.

It is incredible to see how much the landscape has changed in the few months since my playing days ended. Certainly the appointment of the NRL's inaugural Independent Commission and the subsequent handover of power to them by the game's former stakeholders, News Limited and the Australian Rugby League, has the potential to be the most important in the code's history. Finally the game can streamline its governance, which will immediately reduce overhead expenditure, but more importantly will eliminate much of the red tape and boardroom bickering which has stymied the progress of the game over the past 15 years. John Grant is a strong appointment as Chairman, bringing both outstanding business acumen and a strong rugby league background to the table. While I am all for the inclusion of business and industry leaders on the Commission, there must always be a strong rugby league presence as well, to ensure the integrity and history of the game is protected at all costs.

One thing I believe must be considered is the appointment of a Rugby League Players' Association (RLPA) representative on the Commission. Petero Civoniceva's commitment and desire to galvanise the entire body of NRL players behind the RLPA is starting to gain some traction, but it's still a long, long way from where it needs to be as an organisation.

The RLPA needs more funds, and I am convinced there are a number of avenues they can go down to secure the revenue streams it needs. A player's right to be compensated for the use of his image is one area. Income from betting agencies is another. I cannot tell you the number of times I have seen 'Limited Edition' posters, prints or cards featuring the Broncos or Queensland Origin teams being sold in memorabilia stores or online for considerable amounts of money. The sale of these 'unofficial' memorabilia items is misleading for the buyer, because, being unofficial, they simply don't hold the same value over time and, given they are unapproved, none of the money generated from the pieces goes back to the game or the players.

The league will no doubt push for a better return from the agencies who collect millions from the vast array of betting markets framed on individual NRL fixtures and the competition as a whole. Whether it is through government lobbying or in tandem with other codes that are in a similar predicament, the NRL will continue to protect itself and its assets staunchly and demand that those parties using our sport to make money put some of that money back into helping the game grow.

Of course, those are relatively minor income areas in comparison to the new broadcast rights deal the NRL is currently negotiating. The negotiations are, in my opinion, the key to the future of the NRL as a national sporting code as it is the single biggest source of income for the game. With the A-League slowly establishing itself and the AFL pushing hard into league heartlands on the Gold Coast and Western Sydney thanks to the $1.25 billion deal it secured in 2012, the NRL simply cannot afford to come away from these discussions with the commercial and pay television networks with a figure that isn't relective of the best value for our great game. The NRL has proven to be the lifeblood of Foxtel and Fox Sports in Australia for many years now. It is unbelievable to think that of the 100 highest-rating programs on Foxtel in 2011, NRL games filled 74 spots.

Wisely, the NRL is contemplating packaging the NRL regular season, the finals series, the State of Origin series, and Test football separately. Even the break-up of the NRL rounds is open for discussion, with commercial stations no doubt interested in the huge numbers generated by

Monday Night Football. I understand there will be plenty of competition for the rights to the Origin series – though it is hardly a surprise given it traditionally fills the top three spots on the year's ratings in both Queensland and New South Wales.

I believe there is also room to investigate the creation of a pre-season competition in future seasons. The current system of playing trials in regional centres is a wonderful way to ensure we keep in touch with the fans in those areas. It is generally agreed those matches are a necessary evil, with all players needing to get some game time before round one gets under way. However, I cannot see the logic behind having millions of dollars of talent on show without any return whatsoever. Again, it is at least worth a look and a discussion.

Around the NRL itself, things have been typically chaotic as well. Manly's premiership win and subsequent implosion was something to behold. I certainly haven't seen anything like it in my time. The end result saw Des Hasler move to the Bulldogs, with his long-time assistant and club legend Geoff Toovey stepping into the top job at the Sea Eagles. The speculation about which of his former charges might follow Des to Belmore has been relentless, and while none has yet committed, it appears certain the Sea Eagles premiership squad will farewell a number of big names at the end of 2012.

Not that big names are always the answer in the NRL. The Titans, Tigers and Eels have plenty, yet have struggled in the early rounds, with the woes on the Gold Coast especially concerning. It seems incredible that a club could find itself in such a predicament, with debts stemming from the Centre of Excellence facility blowing out to almost $30 million. Without the board of directors to govern the club and its finances, it is the kind of perilous state we can ill afford a new club to be found in within the extremely competitive sports market.

Todd Carney's move to the Sharks has been a major hit, with the 2010 Dally M Medal winner the attacking weapon Cronulla has so desperately needed to capitalise on the work of their inspirational skipper Paul Gallen. The new head coaches in charge at Penrith (Ivan Cleary), Newcastle (Wayne Bennett), Souths (Michael Maguire), the Dragons (Steve Price) and the Bulldogs (Des Hasler) have all made an impression, though the Broncos and Storm have established themselves as the benchmark in the early rounds. The Broncos' depth and strength on the edges has caught the eye, while the Storm just keep on keeping on – Billy, Cam and Cooper Cronk seem to only keep getting better.

Still, for me, the stories of the pre-season – actually I think they are the feel-good stories of the 2012 NRL season – are the returns of champion clubmen Petero Civoniceva to the Broncos and Danny Buderus to the Newcastle Knights. When Wayne took control at Newcastle he inherited a club which had lost its way in the post-Andrew Johns era. According to Matty Johns, it was a club with a 'losing culture', with too many players happy with being treated like stars in the rugby league – mad town, no matter the result.

I don't know if that was the case, but certainly Wayne made significant changes to the playing roster, coaching staff and the structure and direction of Newcastle's recruitment and development department. I heard Wayne say he wanted to ensure the local fans still felt the connection they have always had with the Knights, and what better way to do that than to bring back one of their all-time favourites for the final year or two of his career?

As well as being a great footballer and inspirational leader, Bedsy would be a grand finalist in rugby league's best bloke award. He is still super-fit and his competitive instincts are as strong as ever. Wayne isn't one to rap up a player without reason, so when he lauded Bedsy as the glue which had kept the group together through a tough run with injury and then called on Blues selectors to look at recalling him for this year's Origin series, I am sure Ricky Stuart was all ears.

Petero was still undecided about his representative future at the time I sat to finish this project, but I was impressed with Anthony Griffin's handling of the question whenever it was put to him.

'Petero has earned the right to make that decision himself – I am not going to be putting any pressure on him to retire from rep footy,' Hook stated. 'Petero knows what our expectations of him are and he knows his body and the demands of an NRL season well enough to know whether he wants to make himself available again.'

For a bloke who has never worked with Big Bulla before, I just felt it was a real show of respect for everything Petero has done in the game, particularly given Pet was facing six months of rehabilitation after undergoing knee and pectoral surgery prior to moving back home.

Petero's homecoming has, as I alluded to earlier, righted one of the great wrongs in the Broncos' relatively short, though proud, history. Since moving to the Panthers and assuming the club captaincy, Petero's status and presence as a leading voice for all NRL players had grown enormously. The Penrith community and the playing group loved having him around – but after a promising 2010, the 2011 season didn't go to plan for the Panthers and by mid-year coach Matt Elliott was informed his contract would not be renewed at season's end.

Soon after, Phil Gould, who had taken Penrith to their only title back in 1991, was appointed as General Manager of Football – a newly created role, which essentially gave him carte blanche to implement whatever changes he believed were necessary to reinvigorate the organisation on and off the field. Within a few weeks Elliott deemed his position to be untenable and tendered a resignation which was accepted by Gus. Steve Georgallis, a long-serving and well-liked assistant to Elliott, was appointed as interim coach and was told he had the next couple of months at the helm to prove his worth. Just a fortnight later, however, Georgallis's audition became moot, with news Gus had lured then-Warriors coach Ivan Cleary back to Australia to take up the head coach post at the Panthers.

This all went down while Petero was in camp with the Queensland squad ahead of the State of Origin decider and only learned of the surprise appointment when fronted by some members of the media. As club captain, he was understandably upset at the lack of consultation and was equally as aggrieved the promise made to Georgallis had not been honoured. He didn't say too much, but I could tell Petero was left a little disillusioned, not necessarily by the decisions themselves but the manner in which they were handled. Keen to be closer to family, Petero's wife, Bonnie, and their four children had already planned to return to Queensland at the end of 2011, so when I learned of Pet's frustration at how things were being managed at the foot of the Blue Mountains, I wondered whether a move north might prove just the tonic.

It was only a few days since Queensland's historic series-clinching win and I was in the locker room back at Broncos HQ when Andrew Gee casually strolled over to me and very quietly said, 'Mate, I have got some news for you.'

'Petero?' I replied quickly. GG looked shocked and asked how I knew.

'Just kind of worked it out,' I said.

GG told me the club had signed him on a one-year deal for 2012. Whatever the deal is worth, I say with confidence that it will be some of the best money the new administration will ever spend. With Petero back, Sammy Thaiday has the perfect mentor and sounding board in his first year as club captain. More broadly, the young guys in the squad will have the chance to play beside and learn from a genuine legend of, not only the Broncos, but of Australian sport. And it should not be forgotten that, even at 36, he is still rightly considered one of the premier big men in the game. The young forwards at the Broncos like Matt Gillett and Josh McGuire will get to see first-hand the legacy they will inherit – doubly so for the young Polynesian boys like Alex Glenn, David Hala and Ben Te'o.

I hope Petero enjoys his remaining years in the game back 'home' where he belongs. As I have said before, his return has righted one of the great wrongs in the history of the Broncos. Petero embodies everything I think is great about rugby league. I am proud to call him my friend and can't wait to share a beer with him on the day he does decide to hang up those big size-15 boots of his.

Full of himself, isn't he?

Acknowledgements

Wayne Bennett: without question the single biggest influence on my career. Some of the lessons he taught be about how to play rugby league continue to shape my life to this day, even away from football.

Mal Meninga: a great leader and coach. He helped me learn and understand what it is to be a true Queenslander. He was influential in my Origin career, and I am proud to be able to say I now consider him a good friend.

Craig Bellamy: to see Melbourne back atop the NRL less than a year after the salary cap scandal that rocked the club confirms his status as the prototype upon which the ideal modern-day coach should be based.

Cameron Smith: since arriving on the scene at just 19, Cam's composure and poise have impressed me most. He will almost certainly take over as Queensland and Australian skipper next year.

Johnathan Thurston: a champion player from a young age and a guy I always loved playing alongside. I admire his competitiveness and respect. It has been a pleasure to see him grow and mature.

Steve Renouf: I loved playing alongside Pearl in my early days at the Broncos. His speed, skill and class are unparalleled. He could make something very hard look very easy.

Petero Civoniceva: one of the finest men I have ever met and perhaps the most respected player in the modern era. A selfless individual who would never let anyone down.

Wendell Sailor: behind the Dell humour and confidence is one of the most loyal, big-hearted and generous blokes I know. He is terrific company and a great mate.

Ben Ikin: we became friends when we were team-mates in the Queensland under-16s side and have remained so ever since. We have similar personalities and enjoy each other's company.

Billy Slater: a freakish athlete. We seemed to strike up an uncanny combination from almost the first match we played together. He will go down in history as one of the game's greatest fullbacks.

Ricky Stuart: he taught me the value of being passionate about the Kangaroo jersey you wear and all that it represents. I won't forget the class he showed in quietly passing on his congratulations a couple days after my final Origin victory.

Paul Gallen: a highly respected opponent. He is so physical and confrontational on the field, with an extremely high work-rate. He is a guy I enjoyed playing alongside in the green and gold.

Andrew Johns: the most skilful and complete footballer I ever played with or against. A likeable larrikin whose friendship I value.

Matthew Johns: another likeable larrikin! He also possesses one of the sharpest rugby league minds in the game.

Phil Gould: he has an unrivalled knowledge and understanding of the game. He provides an insightful commentary from which I have learned many aspects of the game over the years.

George Gregan: I have always respected the class with which he conducted himself as Wallabies captain – a terrific role model on and off the field.

Michael Voss: a champion player and an inspirational captain. He was handed the captaincy at a young age and persisted through a period of poor results before coming out the other side to lead the Lions to four successive Grand Final appearances.

Dean Benton: he is a leader in his field and is a guy I learned a lot from despite the fact we only worked together for a relatively short period of time. His role in the 2006 Premiership should not be undersold.

Dan Baker: a favourite of mine around the club. Dan is part of the furniture. His enthusiasm and dedication to his job is inspiring. His expertise has improved an enormous number of careers, and he is without peer in his field.

Thanks to Dan Koch for working with me to capture the full scope of my story. We've produced a book I'm very proud of.

And last but certainly not least, my wife, Loren. She has undoubtedly helped me in so many ways but particularly in providing the stability for the longevity of my career. She has given me a greater appreciation of the importance of family and expanded my values and understanding with her outgoing and affectionate way. She has been my greatest supporter and has been there when I needed her most.

Statistics

Career Overview

	Games	Trs	Gls	F/G	Pts
CLUB CAREER 1995–2011					
Brisbane Broncos 1995–2011					
Premiership Games 1995–2011	355	123	341	21	1,195
World Club Challenge 2001, 2007	2	–	–	–	0
Super League World Club Challenge 1997	9	4	35	–	86
TOTAL	**366**	**127**	**376**	**21**	**1,281**
REPRESENTATIVE CAREER 1997–2011					
QUEENSLAND 1997–2011					
State of Origin 1998–2011	36	9	22	2	82
Super League Tri–series 1997	2	–	1	–	2
TOTAL	**38**	**9**	**23**	**2**	**84**
AUSTRALIA 1997–2011					
Tests and World Cup 1998–2011	55	34	32	2	200
Super League Tests 1997	4	2	2	1	13
Tour matches 2003–04	3	2	5	–	18
TOTAL	**62**	**38**	**39**	**3**	**231**
OTHER REPRESENTATIVE 2010–11					
NRL All Stars v Indigenous All–Stars 2010–11	2	–	–	–	0
GRAND TOTAL					
All senior matches	**468**	**174**	**438**	**26**	**1,596**

SEASON BY SEASON – Brisbane Broncos

	Games	Tries	Goals	F/Goals	Points	P	W	L	D	Position
1995	11	3	4	1	21	24	17	7	–	Semi-finalists
1996	20	7	13	–	54	23	17	6	–	Semi-finalists
1997 SL	20	7	70	–	168	20	16	3	1	Premiers
1998	26	19	98	–	272	28	21	6	1	Premiers
1999	22	6	17	2	60	25	13	10	2	Quarter finalists
2000	25	11	5	–	54	29	21	6	2	Premiers
2001	27	7	16	2	62	29	15	13	1	Prelim. finalists
2002	24	15	1	–	62	26	17	8	1	Prelim. finalists
2003	20	9	2	1	41	25	12	13	–	Quarter finalists
2004	19	2	21	1	51	26	16	9	1	Semi-finalists
2005	21	8	52	1	137	26	15	11	–	Semi-finalists
2006	26	13	19	5	95	28	17	11	–	Premiers
2007	14	2	23	3	57	25	11	14	–	Quarter finalists
2008	17	2	–	1	9	26	15	10	1	Semi-finalists
2009	23	4	–	–	16	27	16	11	–	Prelim. finalists
2010	18	4	–	–	16	24	11	13	–	10th
2011	22	3	–	4	16	24	18	4	–	Semi-finalists
TOTAL	**355**	**123**	**341**	**21**	**1,195**					

DARREN LOCKYER

Junior Football: Roma Cities

Premiership Debut: Brisbane v. Parramatta at Parramatta Stadium, 25/6/1995 (Rd 13)

Premierships: 1997 (Super League), 1998, 2000, 2006

Finals series: 1995, 1996, 1997 (Super League), 1998, 1999, 2000, 2001, 2002, 2003, 2004, 2005, 2006, 2007, 2008, 2009

Captaincy: 154 games (2001–11); 95 wins, 59 losses

Coaches: Wayne Bennett (1998–2008), Ivan Henjak (2009–10), Anthony Griffin (2011)

Awards:
Clive Churchill Medal 2000
Dally M Fullback of the Year 1998, 2001, 2002
Dally M Five-Eighth of the Year 2004, 2006, 2007
Paul Morgan Medal (Broncos Player of the Year) 2002, 2003
Provan-Summons Medal 2004
Golden Boot Award 2003, 2006

Records:
Most appearances for the Broncos (346)
Most points for the Broncos (1,186)
Most points in a season for the Broncos (272 in 1998)

STATE OF ORIGIN 1998-2011

No.	Date	Venue	Game	Tries	Goals	F/G	Points	Result	Score
1	22/05/1998	SFS	1	–	4	–	8	Won	24–23
2	05/06/1998	Suncorp Stadium	2	–	1	–	2	Lost	10–26
3	19/06/1998	SFS	3	–	2	–	4	Won	19–4
4	23/06/1999	Suncorp Stadium	3	1	1	–	6	Drew	10–10
5	10/05/2000	Stadium Australia	1	–	1	–	2	Lost	16–20
6	24/05/2000	Suncorp Stadium	2	–	–	–	0	Lost	10–28
7	07/06/2000	Stadium Australia	3	–	–	–	0	Lost	16–56
8	06/05/2001	Suncorp Stadium	1	1	5	–	14	Won	34–16
9	10/06/2001*	Stadium Australia	2	–	2	–	4	Lost	8–26
10	01/07/2001*	ANZ, Brisbane	3	2	4	–	16	Won	40–14
11	22/05/2002	Stadium Australia	1	–	–	–	0	Lost	4–32
12	05/06/2002	ANZ, Brisbane	2	–	–	–	0	Won	26–18
13	26/06/2002	Stadium Australia	3	–	–	–	0	Drew	18–18
14	11/06/2003	Suncorp Stadium	1	1	2	–	8	Lost	12–25
15	25/06/2003	Telstra Stadium	2	–	–	–	0	Lost	4–27
16	10/07/2003	Suncorp Stadium	3	–	–	–	0	Won	36–6
17	16/06/2004*	Suncorp Stadium	2	–	–	–	0	Won	22–18

18	07/07/2004*	Telstra Stadium	3	–	–	–	0	Lost	14–36
19	25/05/2005*	Suncorp Stadium	1	–	–	1	1	Won	24–20
20	22/06/2005*	Telstra Stadium	2	–	–	–	0	Lost	22–32
21	06/07/2005*	Suncorp Stadium	3	–	–	–	0	Lost	10–32
22	24/05/2006*	Telstra Stadium	1	–	–	–	0	Lost	16–17
23	14/06/2006*	Suncorp Stadium	2	1	–	–	4	Won	30–6
24	05/07/2006*	Telstra Dome	3	1	–	–	4	Won	16–14
25	23/05/2007*	Suncorp Stadium	1	–	–	–	0	Won	25–18
26	13/06/2007*	Telstra Stadium	2	–	–	–	0	Won	10–6
27	04/07/2007*	Suncorp Stadium	3	–	–	–	0	Lost	4–18
28	03/06/2009*	Etihad Stadium	1	–	–	–	0	Won	28–18
29	24/06/2009*	ANZ, Sydney	2	1	–	–	4	Won	24–14
30	15/07/2009*	Suncorp Stadium	3	–	–	–	0	Lost	16–28
31	26/05/2010*	ANZ, Sydney	1	1	–	–	4	Won	28–24
32	16/06/2010*	Suncorp Stadium	2	–	–	–	0	Won	34–6
33	07/07/2010*	Suncorp Stadium	3	–	–	1	1	Won	23–18
34	25/05/2011*	Suncorp Stadium	1	–	–	–	0	Won	16–12
35	15/06/2011*	Suncorp Stadium	2	–	–	–	0	Lost	8–18
36	06/07/2011*	Suncorp Stadium	3	–	–	–	0	Won	34–24

Statistics

Notes on Venues:
SFS refers to Sydney Football Stadium; Sydney's Olympic Stadium at Homebush has been known as Stadium Australia, Telstra Stadium and ANZ Stadium Sydney; ANZ Brisbane is also known as QEII Stadium; Melbourne's Docklands Stadium has been known as Telstra Dome and Etihad Stadium; Suncorp Stadium was formerly known as Lang Park

Injury: Missed the first two games of the 1999 series with a fractured cheekbone; missed the opening game of the 2004 series with a rib injury; missed the 2008 series with complications arising from a knee reconstruction

Position: Fullback 1998–2003; five-eighth 2004–2011

Coaches: Wayne Bennett 1998, 2001-03; Mark Murray 1999-2000; Michael Hagan 2004-05; Mal Meninga 2006-11

Summary of matches: 36 games, nine tries, 22 goals, two field goals, 82 points. Won 19, lost 15, drew 2.

Captaincy (matches denoted by asterisk): 22 games, 14 wins, 8 losses. Winning percentage: 63.6.

Man of the Match Awards: Game 3, 2001; Game 2, 2006; Game 2, 2010.

Other Awards: Dally M Representative Player of the Year 2001, 2006; Wally Lewis Medal 2006; Ron McAuliffe Medal 2006

Records: Most State of Origin appearances (36)

TEST CAREER 1998-2011

No.	Date	Opponent	Venue	Status	T	G	FG	Pts	Result	Score
1	24/04/1998	New Zealand	North Harbour Stadium, Auckland	Anzac Test	–	–	–	0	Lost	16–22
2	09/10/1998	New Zealand	Suncorp Stadium, Brisbane	1st Test	1	4	–	12	Won	30–12
3	16/10/1998	New Zealand	North Harbour Stadium, Auckland	2nd Test	1	3	–	10	Won	36–16
4	23/04/1999	New Zealand	Stadium Australia, Sydney	Anzac Test	–	–	–	0	Won	20–14
5	15/10/1999	New Zealand	Ericsson Stadium, Auckland	Tri-N	–	–	–	0	Lost	22–24
6	22/10/1999	Great Britain	Suncorp Stadium, Brisbane	Tri-N	2	–	–	8	Won	42–6
7	05/11/1999	New Zealand	Ericsson Stadium, Auckland	Tri-N Final	–	–	–	0	Won	22–20
8	21/04/2000	New Zealand	Stadium Australia, Sydney	Anzac Test	–	–	–	0	Won	52–0
9	07/10/2000	Papua New Guinea	Dairy Farmers Stadium, Townsville	Test	2	–	–	8	Won	82–0
10	28/10/2000	England	Twickenham, London	WC	–	–	–	0	Won	22–2
11	01/11/2000	Fiji	Gateshead International Stadium	WC	–	–	–	0	Won	66–8
12	11/11/2000	Samoa	Vicarage Road, Watford	WC	–	–	–	0	Won	66–10
13	19/11/2000	Wales	McAlpine Stadium, Huddersfield	WC	2	4	–	16	Won	46–22
14	25/11/2000	New Zealand	Old Trafford, Manchester	WC Final	1	–	–	4	Won	40–12
15	13/07/2001	New Zealand	Westpac Trust Stadium, Wellington	Test	1	–	–	4	Won	28–10
16	07/10/2001	Papua New Guinea	Lloyd Robson Oval, Port Moresby	Test	1	4	–	12	Won	54–12
17	11/11/2001	Great Britain	McAlpine Stadium, Huddersfield	Ashes	–	–	–	0	Lost	12–20

Statistics

No.	Date	Opponent	Venue	Status	T	G	FG	Pts	Result	Score
18	17/11/2001	Great Britain	Reebok Stadium, Bolton	Ashes	1	–	–	4	Won	40–12
19	24/11/2001	Great Britain	JJB Stadium, Wigan	Ashes	1	–	–	4	Won	28–8
20	12/07/2002	Great Britain	Aussie Stadium, Sydney	Test	2	–	–	8	Won	64–10
21	12/10/2002	New Zealand	Westpac Trust Stadium, Wellington	Test	–	–	–	0	Won	32–24
22	18/10/2003*	New Zealand	North Harbour Stadium, Auckland	Test	–	–	–	0	Lost	16–30
23	08/11/2003*	Great Britain	JJB Stadium, Wigan	Ashes	1	–	–	4	Won	22–18
24	15/11/2003*	Great Britain	Kingston Communications Stadium, Hull	Ashes	1	–	–	4	Won	23–20
25	22/11/2003*	Great Britain	McAlpine Stadium, Huddersfield	Ashes	–	–	–	0	Won	18–12
26	23/04/2004*	New Zealand	EnergyAustralia Stadium, Newcastle	Anzac Test	1	–	1	5	Won	37–10
27	16/10/2004*	New Zealand	North Harbour Stadium, Auckland	Tri-N	–	2	–	4	Drew	16–16
28	23/10/2004*	New Zealand	Loftus Road Stadium, London	Tri-N	1	2	–	8	Won	32–12
29	21/11/2004*	France	Stade Ernest Wallon, Toulouse	Test	1	4	–	12	Won	52–30
30	27/11/2004*	Great Britain	Elland Road, Leeds	Tri-N Final	1	6	–	16	Won	44–4
31	22/04/2005*	New Zealand	Suncorp Stadium, Brisbane	Anzac Test	1	–	–	4	Won	32–16
32	15/10/2005*	New Zealand	Telstra Stadium, Sydney	Tri-N	–	–	–	0	Lost	28–38
33	21/10/2005*	New Zealand	Ericsson Stadium, Auckland	Tri-N	2	–	–	8	Won	28–26
34	05/11/2005*	Great Britain	JJB Stadium, Wigan	Tri-N Final	–	–	–	0	Won	20–6
35	05/05/2006*	New Zealand	Suncorp Stadium, Brisbane	Test	2	–	–	8	Won	50–12
36	14/10/2006*	New Zealand	Mt Smart Stadium, Auckland	Tri-N	–	–	–	0	Won	30–18
37	21/10/2006*	New Zealand	Telstra Dome, Melbourne	Tri-N	–	–	–	0	Won	20–15

DARREN LOCKYER

No.	Date	Opponent	Venue	Status	T	G	FG	Pts	Result	Score
38	04/11/2006*	Great Britain	Aussie Stadium, Sydney	Tri-N	1	2	–	8	Lost	12–23
39	18/11/2006*	Great Britain	Suncorp Stadium, Brisbane	Tri-N	1	–	1	5	Won	33–10
40	25/11/2006*	New Zealand	Aussie Stadium, Sydney	Tri-N Final	1	–	–	4	Won	16–12
41	20/04/2007*	New Zealand	Suncorp Stadium, Brisbane	Test	1	–	–	4	Won	30–6
42	26/10/2008*	New Zealand	Sydney Football Stadium	WC	–	–	–	0	Won	30–6
43	02/11/2008*	England	Telstra Dome, Melbourne	WC	–	–	–	0	Won	52–4
44	16/11/2008*	Fiji	Sydney Football Stadium	WC	–	–	–	0	Won	52–0
45	22/11/2008*	New Zealand	Suncorp Stadium, Brisbane	WC Final	2	–	–	8	Lost	20–34
46	08/05/2009*	New Zealand	Suncorp Stadium, Brisbane	Test	–	–	–	0	Won	38–10
47	24/10/2009*	New Zealand	Twickenham Stoop, London	Four N	–	–	–	0	Drew	20–20
48	31/10/2009*	England	DW Stadium, Wigan	Four N	1	–	–	4	Won	26–16
49	07/11/2009*	France	Charlety Stadium, Paris	Four N	–	–	–	0	Won	42–4
50	14/11/2009*	England	Elland Road, Leeds	FN Final	–	–	–	0	Won	46–16
51	07/05/2010*	New Zealand	AAMI Park, Melbourne	Test	–	–	–	0	Won	12–8
52	24/10/2010*	Papua New Guinea	Parramatta Stadium	Four N	1	–	–	4	Won	42–0
53	31/10/2010*	England	AAMI Park, Melbourne	Four N	–	–	–	0	Won	34–14
54	13/11/2010*	New Zealand	Suncorp Stadium, Brisbane	FN Final	–	–	–	0	Lost	12–16
55	06/05/2011*	New Zealand	Skilled Park, Robina	Test	–	–	–	0	Won	20–10

Statistics

Notes on Venues:
Sydney Football Stadium was formerly known as Aussie Stadium, Sydney's Olympic Stadium at Homebush has been known as Stadium Australia, Telstra Stadium and ANZ Stadium Sydney; Melbourne's Docklands Stadium has been known as Telstra Dome and Etihad Stadium; Mt Smart Stadium was formerly known as Ericsson Stadium; DW Stadium Wigan was formerly known as JJB Stadium Wigan

Status key: Tri-N = Tri Nations; WC = World Cup; Four N = Four Nations

Position: Interchange (Anzac Test 1998 and first Tri-Nations Test 1999); Fullback 1998–2003; Five-eighth 2004–2011

Coaches: Bob Fulton 1998 (Anzac Test 1998 only); Wayne Bennett 1998, 2004–05; Chris Anderson 1999–2003; Ricky Stuart 2006–08; Tim Sheens 2009–11

Summary of matches: 55 Tests, 34 tries, 32 goals, two field goals, 200 points. Won 45, lost 8, drew 2.

Captaincy (matches denoted by asterisk): 34 games, 27 wins, 5 losses, 2 draws. Winning percentage: 79.4.

Awards: Harry Sunderland Medal 2008

Records:
Most Tests for Australia (55)
Most Test tries for Australia (34)
Most Tests for Australia as captain (34)

Statistics by: David Middleton, League Information Services (July 21, 2011)